Norse, Celtic Mythology & Runes:

Explore The Timeless Tales Of Norse & Celtic Folklore, The Myths, History, Sagas & Legends + The Magic, Spells & Meanings of Runes.

Sofia Visconti

By reading this document, the reader agrees that under no circumstances is the author responsible for any losses, direct or indirect, that are incurred as a result of the use of the information contained within this document, including, but not limited to, errors, omissions, or inaccuracies.

Click Here

Celtic Mythology:

Delve Into The Depths Of Ancient Celtic Folklore, The Myths, Legends & Tales of The Gods, Goddesses, Warriors, Maidens, Monsters & Magic

Table of Contents

References

Introduction

Since we were small children, we've learned of fairy stories, tales of great heroes, Gods, Goddesses, and mythical creatures such as unicorns or dragons. They capture the imagination, teach various life lessons, give hope, and encourage you, especially for most children who grow up in Brittany, Scotland, Cornwall, Wales, and Ireland. Children lucky enough to grow up in these societies get to live the tales as they passed from generation to generation. Some schools still teach mythology in these areas to keep the old traditions, beliefs, and ways alive.

To the rest of the world, however, mythology and related subjects can be quite confusing. Instead of getting lost in the romance, power, intrigue, and magic of mythology, you might often end up getting frustrated with the complexity of the way the story is written. I have published many books about runes, astrology, tarot, the Wiccan ways, and ancient mythology. My books are popular because they are well structured, engaging, entertaining, and written to take the reader on a journey through the topic.

Celtic Mythology: Delve Into The Depths Of Ancient Celtic Folklore, The Myths, Legends & Tales of The Gods, Goddesses, Warriors, Maidens, Monsters & Magic delves into the depth of Celtic mythology. By the end of this book, you will know who the Celts were, as well as their beliefs; you will also have a better knowledge of their Gods and Goddesses. If you were looking for a book about Celtic mythology to captivate your interest, this book is for you. You will learn about heroic adventures, mythical creatures, intriguing fairy tales, fair maidens, magic, folklore, and more.

Who Were the Celts?

The Celts were an extensive collection of tribes that originated in the central European Alps. They were a group of people from all walks of life, such as nobility, farmers, druids, commoners, noble knights, and warriors. The Celtic culture has been around since 1200 B.C. They were a nation that grew to occupy most of the European continent, expanding from Turkey in the east through to Ireland in the west. The Celts were the power in central Europe for many years before the Romans.

The Celtic people were bound by their customs, beliefs, and language; each tribe acted independently of the other. They had no formal governance or organization, although they valued their nobility, serving them with honor and pride. The Celts took war seriously and put a high emphasis on winning their battles. They also honored their Gods and Goddesses with significant monuments and festivals, which they celebrated through their astronomical calendar.

The Celtics would honor their dead by constructing tombs aligned with the stars. All of nature and her creatures were viewed as sacred to the Celts and treated with great respect. Celtic mythology has been around for as long as the Celtic people have, but it was never well documented except for bits and pieces put together by the earlier monks. It was the Romans that first recorded the Celtic beliefs, but they saw the Celts as barbarians and their enemies. Thus, many of the Roman accounts of the Celtic way of life were tainted. The Romans recorded the Celtic God's names with the Roman equivalent for them. It was mostly Christian missionaries in the eleventh century that transcribed the various pieces of scripts that had been written by the druids on bark or wands of aspen. The Celts were highly intelligent and excellent artisans and engineers; they wrote in a script called Ogham. But to them, their culture was of the utmost importance, and they preferred to pass down their stories, beliefs, knowledge, and skills verbally.

As you can imagine through the ages as stories passed from generation to generation, elements were added to them or exaggerated. Some stories were probably lost altogether, either forgotten or woven into another tale, leaving us with the ones we have today. Most of the myths, legends, and stories about Celtic mythology, as we know it in the modern world, come from the Welsh and the Irish. Legends that originated in Brittany, France, such as Isolde and Tristram, were retold by the Irish or Welsh. When the Romans started to be the dominating force in Europe, there were not many Celtic regions except for Britany, Spain, Scotland, Ireland, Cornwall, and Wales. Today the most abundant remaining Celtic culture can be found in Ireland, Scotland, and Wales.

Celtic Beliefs

The Celts had hundreds of tales, which would be sung in a lyrical form by the bards or by stories the village elders would tell. Each tribe of Celts had their own Gods that they worshiped to keep their village safe and prosperous. There are, however, a lot of commonalities between their Gods, stories, myths, creatures, and legends. Most of the Celtic mythology, as it is known today comes from the Irish.

Celtic Mythology has two main groups; each group shares a related language and beliefs. These groups are called Brythonic, for Cornish, Brittany, and Welsh, and Goidelic, for Irish, Scottish, and Manx.

Celtics Ways of Worship and Religious Sacrifice

The earliest Celts built significant monuments in their Gods' and Goddesses' honor, but Nemetons were the place they would gather or go to worship them. A nemeton is a large grove of trees which the Celts held as sacred. References to how sacred trees were to the Celts are in the tales of heroes or heroines named after trees.

The custom of building temples of worship came about during Roman times for the Celts. This was a tradition that they passed on to the tribes that displaced them, such as the Germanic tribes. The Romans like to paint the Celts as a bloody barbaric race that would participate in human sacrificial rituals as a standard practice.

Julius Caesar himself wrote, "In times of danger, the Celts believed that unless the life of a man is offered, the mind of the immortal gods will not favor them" (*Classic Authors Writing About the Ancient Celts*, n.d.). Up until quite recently, it was thought that a lot of what Julius Caesar and the Romans had written about the Celtic beliefs was hearsay. Archeologists have found that the Celtic druids may have practiced human sacrifice and maybe even cannibalism (Owen, 2009).

In ancient times tribes would go to any lengths to win if that meant taking the potions mixed by the druids or sacrificing prisoners or even their noblemen. As stated before, the Celts held victory in the highest regard and thus had some of the fiercest warriors.

Some of the Druids, such as the Druids of Erin, were considered to be sorcerers; they told fortunes, prophesied, made charms, and put a lot of faith in luck. Thus, they believed there were lucky and unlucky days and would look out for omens. As they mainly worshipped the sun and the moon, many of their festivals and rituals revolved around certain days of the year, such as November for Samhain (moon) and May for Bel-Taine (sun).

Chapter 1: Deities of the Celts

There are many different Gods and Goddesses throughout Celtic mythology, but there are a few common deities or variants of some of the more popular ones.

Popular Celtic Gods and Goddesses

The following deities are the more well known of the God and Goddesses in Celtic mythology. Some of the Celtics groups may have a different name or a variant of their name. As scholars of modern times that study Celtic mythology come to find, the Celts were not very good at keeping their pantheons in a neat row—contributing to the reason why one may see different versions of names of one deity.

The All-Powerful God

The Dagda (translates as the Good God), was the supreme God of the Celts. The Dagda is referred to as Sucellos in Gaul, where he is depicted with a hammer and cup.

Unlike in most other mythologies, the Supreme Celtic God was not the God of anything in particular, like the Supreme God Zeus in Greek mythology, who was the God of the Sky and Thunder.

In Irish mythology, The Dagda is always referred to as having immense power and holding a club. With one blow, The Dagda's club could kill nine men. The hilt of the club, however, could bring the dead back to life. The Dagda is usually standing near or next to a cauldron that was known as the Undry. This cauldron was one that could fill up everyone in the village and keep their bellies full, as it was a bottomless cauldron.

The Dagda was the protector of the various Celtic tribes. He watched over them like a father-figure and made sure the village was kept safe as well as prosperous. In Ireland, he was the king of the Tuatha de Danann. The Tuatha de Danann were the children of an earth Goddess named Danu. Danu has no surviving tales about her origins other than being the mother of the Tuatha de Danann. There is also a lot of debate about her name and the meaning thereof (*Danu (Irish Goddess)*. n.d.).

The Dagda rose to power by defeating Nuada. The laws in those days stated that for a person to become king, they had to be fit and their body whole. The Dagda wounded Nuada and took over his throne as the All-Father. He lived in a place called Brú na Bóinne, a known philanderer that had many lovers and lots of children.

The Dagda was said to be a giant of a man. Because of his size, his clothes were always too tight, and his stomach would stick out of his shirt. The same was true for his trousers, where the top of his buttocks stuck out. He was an offish God that wore a woolen cloak. His face was unshaven, leaving him with a long curly, unruly beard. Because of his incredible good looks, people barely noticed his attire. He may have been offish, philandering, and quite offensive, but he was also witty, wise beyond compare, and Wiley.

The Dagda's holy day is the 9th of August.

The Queen of Demons, or Phantom Queen

The Morrigan, sometimes spelled Morrigna, was the wife of The Dagda. Her name may sound familiar to those who love the Arthurian legends where she was known as Morgan le Fay or Morrigan the fairy. She was a fearsome deity as the Goddess of destiny and death.

As the Goddess of Fate, Morrigan was turned to before a battle offering favor to the heroes of the battlefields, both warriors and Gods alike. She was a triple Goddess comprising three of the most powerful Celtic Goddesses. She would appear on the battlefield as either a raven or crow to relish over the blood spilled. She would carry off the fallen in a conspiracy of ravens.

War and death are what Morrigan reigned over most of all, she was associated with ravens that would always be present somewhere on a battlefield. Before a battle, Morrigan would appear to either the kings and queens or warriors of the side she favored. For a price, she would offer up a prophecy or share their fate. As she could see everything in the future, including the end of the world, her prophecies were never wrong.

There are many stories where Morrigan appears as three Goddesses, there is a bit of inconsistency as the names of the trio. Although most tend to lean towards her sisters, Banba, Fódla, and Ériu, making up the triple Goddess.

Morrigan's title as the Queen of Demons, or Phantom Queen, stems from her link to the dead and the underworld. She was the daughter of a Mother-Goddess, Ernmas. Ernmas was the daughter of the king of the Tuatha Dé Danann, Nuada. Morrigan's father is not known. Along with her sisters mentioned above, there were another two, Macha and Badb.

Morrigan had five brothers, namely, Ollom, Glon, Gnim, Coscar, and Fiacha.

Master of Skills

Lug or Lugh reigned over kings, rulership, justice, and was the God of the kings. While he lived he was the first Tuatha Dé Danann chief Ollam. This was a testament to him being a judge, ruler, and poet. Upon Lug's death, the position of Ollam became ranked in most of the courts in Ireland. He carried a lightning spear that no mortal or God could withstand called the Assal.

Lug was both a trickster and master of all arts as well as a devious warrior who had no qualms stooping to tricks to get his way. Lug was celebrated on Lughnasa, August the 1st, which is the start of the harvest season. The first of the finest fruit and vegetable pickings for the season would be offered to Lug.

Lug's name has a few possible meanings, some of them include "to bind by oath," which would reference his role as a ruler of contracts and oaths. Another possible meaning would be "artful hands," which would reference his mastery of the arts. One other possible meaning would be "light," as he wields the lightning spear. The most popular name for Lug was "of the long arm" about the long spear of light.

Lug also had a mixed culture which made him a unique character in that he was born from a Fomorian mother, Ethliu. His mother's father was the dreaded Fomorian king Balor. His father was Cian of the Tuatha Dé Danann; Lug's paternal grandfather was a healer of the tribe named Cedh.

Lug grew up with foster parents, but who those foster parents were is a matter of great debate amongst scholars. Some of the potential candidates that pop up in scripts are the Queen of the Firbolg, Tailtiu. Another is the God of the smiths Gavida or Manannán, who was the Irish sea god.

There is no mention of siblings, but Lug did have many wives, namely Nás, Buach, and Buí. Some of Lug's more notable children were Cú Chulainn who he had with Deichtine, a mortal woman. Another would be the son born to him by Nás, the daughter of the king of Britain.

Lug was a highly-skilled character that served as the God of justice. His judging was swift, final, and given without mercy. He is also the inventor of entertainment such as fidchell, which was a game much like chess and horse-racing. He loved sports and many that are still played today he was attributed to.

Lug dwelled at Moytura in County Sligo, and he had another residence at Tara in County Meath.

Ruler of Winter

Caillech is the Veiled One, Goddess of the winds and cold, and controller of the winter weather. Still today there are some places in Ireland, Scotland, and the Isle of Man that believe in Caillech. She is known as a Divine hag that controlled not only how long the winter would be, but how grueling it would be. "Caillech" means hag or old woman, so many scholars think that she may have gone by another name.

Some depict her as Biróg, who saved Lug when he was a baby, or she could have been one of Lug's wives, Buí. There are quite a few regions in Scotland and Ireland that are named after her, such as the "Storm Hag" found in Scotland. "The Hag of Beara" in County Cork, Ireland, is another such place.

Cailleach appears in many different forms, depending on the mythology. In the Isle of Man, she is a shapeshifter that likes to take the form of a huge bird. In other areas, she could commit great feats like riding storms and jumping over tall mountains. Her skin was either blue or an eerie, deathly white, and she had red teeth. She liked to adorn herself in garments from which skulls hung.

Most of the tales about Cailleach don't make her out to be good or evil. She had a hammer that helped her to control the weather and shape much of the landscape. When it flooded it was said to be because of the magic well Cailleach controlled, which had overflowed. She could be a wild destructive force that blew through villages on the backs of raging storms. But she was also a lover of all kinds of animals, for which she was known to tend to throughout the icy winter months.

There were two faces to Caillech, an old hag through the winter and a young woman through the spring and summer. In Irish legends, Caillech was only able to regain her youth in the spring for seven periods. After the seventh period, she had to remain as the old crone she was through the winter months.

In Manx and Scotland's legends, Caillech would transform into the Goddess Brigid. Her transformation would take place at the fertility festival of Beltane on the 1st of May. It was a tradition for the Celt to dedicate the last of the harvested grain to her by using it to start the next crop.

Being the Goddess that forged all the landscape, none could rule over it without first getting her approval. Some of the most inaccessible and unforgiving landscapes throughout the Gaelic Celts is dedicated to Caillech.

The only known family of Caillech was Bodach. Bodach was a trickster spirit, well known in Scottish myths. Although she had quite a few children with Bodach, she also had many others with her many other husbands. Through Caillech's summer transformation back to her youth, she would once again become a maiden. Being an immortal, Caillech got to birth her children, their children, and so on, watch them age, and die. She outlived all of her family and is rumored to be an ancestor to nearly every Celtic tribe in Ireland, Scotland, and the Isle of Man.

Keeper of the Cauldron of Inspiration

Ceridwen originates from Welsh mythology and is a great sorceress, or white witch. There are many ways that her name can be spelled, including Cerrydwen or Kerrydwen. She is known as the Goddess of creation, and has a cauldron in which she brews powerful potions. These potions can change her looks, they can bring about beauty in people, as well as imbue them with knowledge. As a Goddess of creation, she is possibly the most powerful of all the witches of sorceresses in Celtic mythology.

Ceridwen has a magical throne from which she can lend her powers to others at her will. From her cauldron, she offers others the gift of awen, which is the power of insight and spiritual strength. Awen is a status used by the Druids, which is covered in another chapter in this book. Ceridwen's story was told long before the rise of Christianity; scholars deduce that she was written as a sorceress rather than a Goddess by Christian monks.

She is a white witch, meaning she only uses her powers for good and to help others, though her cauldron has both the power to imbue gifts and the power to harm. Once a potion from her cauldron is taken, that person can have the potion again. A few drops could do them fatal harm. On occasion she was known to get upset, but according to the myths she never did much harm.

Tacitus the Bald (Tegid Foel), is Ceridwen's husband and they lived at Bala Lake where he was a formidable ruler. They had a beautiful daughter named Creirwy; she was as fair as any maiden could be. Their son, however, was deformed and a bit demented. His name was Morfran Afaggdu, and it was written that his skin was burned. In Arthurian legend, Morfran is one of King Arthur's warriors.

Later in her life, Ceridwen gives birth to another son, Taliesin. Taliesin is often thought to be the origins of Merlin, the powerful wizard in the courts of king Arthur. Taliesin was a bard, but he was also gifted with his mother's powers. There is more about Taliesin in this book in a later chapter, as he was an important bard and advisor to many a king of Britain.

Ceridwen's cauldron of inspiration appears in many Celtic myths, and she shares some commonalities with other sorceresses in Slavic and Greek mythologies.

The Mother Goddess

Danu, an ancient Goddess, who was known as the mother of all the other Celtic Gods. She is also quite the mystery to Celtic mythology scholars, as there is not much written or known about her. Some theories link Danu to the Danube river which suggests she was a river Goddess with connections to the fairy mounds, dolmens, and fairies themselves.

Royalty would be blessed by Danu with wealth, power, and many other gifts. Danu was the Goddess who ensured that the Tuatha Dé Danann were highly skilled craftsmen and bore many exceptional talents. Even though most of her origins remain a mystery, the Irish depended on Danu to bless everything from good weather to health, and prosperity.

There is no reference to who Danu's husband was, but she was the mother or maternal grandparent to all of Tuatha Dé Danann's divine members.

God of the Wild Hunt

Herne was known as the God of the wild hunt and vegetation as well as the God of the commoners. Like a lot of the Celtic Gods, most of the story of Herne was lost due to poor transcription. He also mainly appears in British Celtic Folklore as he was known to haunt the forests of Windsor. In folklore, Herne was thought to have taken his own life; it was due to the shame of his death that he became a cruel, embittered figure.

He was a ghostly figure that would haunt the Herne Oak tree. People would know he was around when they heard the rattling of chains and eerie moans. All decay that was found in a forest or animal was associated with him. It was said that he could make a tree or creature wither and die by a mere touch. If he came near a farmer's cows he could produce blood instead of milk.

As the stories of Herne progressed he became depicted with antlers upon his head, he carried a horn and was accompanied by vicious hounds. A sighting of Herne was taken as a bad omen that would mean sure death or a disaster would ensue.

Wild God of the Forest

Cernunnos was a horned God that could tame any wild beast or creature. He was known as the mediator of both man and nature. An ancient God of the Gauls with a name meaning "horned one," he was also known as "God of the wild places."

Although he was primarily a God of the Gauls, there are many other Gods throughout Celtic myths that share his likeness and attributes. Some believe that Cernunnos was also a fertility God or God of life because of his love for, and way with, all-natural life.

He loved animals and would have gatherings in the woods where he would feast on wild berries, vegetables, and fruits. The animals that would gather together around him, and did so without preying on each other. Thus wolves, birds, snakes, deer, and so on would all come together in peace around him. Cernunnos could calm all creatures and make them live in peace side by side.

For the rural tribes, Cernunnos was the God that provided for their settlements and protected them against evil or raiders. Cernunnos was depicted with horns and a beard as the spirit of the wild hunt. Thus villagers looked to him for guidance to make their hunting prosperous.

Hearth Goddess of Ireland

Brighid, or Brigid, is the Goddess of life and fertility, she was also known as the Exalted One. Due to her association with life and fertility, she was also the Goddess of spring. She is celebrated on the holiday called Imbolc, which takes place on the 1st of February, mid-winter.

She is primarily an Irish Celtic Goddess, but as with the many other Celtic Goddesses she shares commonalities with other Celtic Goddesses. St. Brigid of Kildare, a Catholic saint, has a lot of similarities to this Irish Goddess. There are a lot of Irish waterways that are named for her and as such, she came to be the Goddess of the Wells.

As the Goddess of life, she was filled with all the contradictions that go with life. On one hand, she was kind, caring, gentle and healing, a nurturing mother figure. On the other side of her personality was a burning fire of passions that would rage against injustice. Her fire and passion were depicted in her image of flowing red locks and her cloak made of sunbeams.

Brighid was an inspirational Goddess which can be seen in the many poems, songs, and text written about her through the ages. Because of her affiliation with the sun, she was sometimes referred to as the Goddess of the sun. Most of the pictures of her show her wearing her cloak of sunbeams referenced earlier in this section. The Celts accredited her with always knowing what was needed, hence her ability to heal and insight. The Imbolc celebrates the breaking of winter's hold over the sun as it starts to return to the land.

Brighid was the daughter of the Dagda, and as such, she had many powerful gifts. Being his daughter lifted her to an exalted position as she was held in high esteem by the Celts. Bres, the High King of the Tuatha Dé Danann, was her husband. They had a son, Ruadán, who was known as the God of mystery or espionage. He was often used by his father to infiltrate their enemies' camps and spy on them to give their warriors an edge on the battlefield.

The God of Storms

Taranis is an important part of Celtic mythology. He is the God of thunder and was depicted by a Celtic symbol of the sacred wheel. Said to move in a flash across the sky, he would travel across the universe at high speed.

The God of storms and bringer of thunder was associated with bad weather. Because of his connection to the sacred Celtic wheel symbol, he was alternatively known as the Wheel God. In our time we at least have a basic understanding of the storms that rip across the skies. In ancient times they did not have the same understanding, so it was only natural the Celtic culture of old would be terrified of them.

It was that terror that drove the early Celts to deem Taranis worthy of whatever sacrifice it took to quiet a raging storm. According to the Romans, if the storm was too great the Celts would have no problem with sacrificing a human to please Taranis. He was the leader of all the other Gods, and as such also their protector. Humans wanted to keep in his good stead, as he wielded a lightning bolt and could move faster than a striking snake.

In Irish mythology, Taranis is known as Tuireann and Ambisagrus in Gaul.

The God of War

Neit died at the Second Battle of Moytura while fighting alongside the Tuatha dé Danann. He was the uncle of Dagda and husband to Badb and Nemain. Neit was the God of War in Irish mythology, a fierce master of the art of battle. The Fomorian Dot was his son and Balor, the king of the Fomorian was his grandson.

There is not a lot written about Neit, though he tends to have played a major role in fighting for the domination of Ireland. In Gaul, he is called Neto and bears a common likeness to Apollo from Roman myths and legends.

Chapter 2: Brittany Celtic Myths and Legends

Brittany is in the far northwest regions of France, with its capital being Rennes. It consists of beautiful small islands and idyllic coastal towns. Although still spoken in some parts of Brittany, Breton was once the dominant language. It is steeped in Gaulish history and takes pride in its Celtic heritage.

The Bretons were originally from Great Britain. They settled along the shores of north-west Gaul, or what we know today as France. They fled Britain when the Anglo-Saxons invaded and made Gaul their new home, as well as the place where their myths and legends were born. Brittany forms part of the Brythonic Celtic culture.

Popular Myths and Legends of Brittany

Like all the other Celtic tribes, the Bretons held their traditions in high esteem and took their beliefs seriously. This chapter tells the stories of some of the more popular myths and legends of the Bretons.

Ankou

There are not many graveyards in Brittany that do not have a stone statue of a hooded figure guardian at its gates. This stone figure is known as Ankou, a spirit that looks after the graveyard and ensures that the souls of the dead move on as they should. The Ankou is a hooded figure that carries a scythe that bears a resemblance to what we know to be the Grim Reaper. He is often mistaken as death. Often pictures of Ankou will have a wheelbarrow or cart near or with the hooded figure. This is the cart he collects the souls of the dead in.

The Ankou at each gravesite only gets to be the hooded spirit for a year. Each year a new Ankou takes over the role of the watcher of the dead. As legend has it, the last person to be buried at the end of each year takes over the role of Ankou.

The Midnight Washerwoman (Les Lavandières)

There are a few stories about the three women who appear in the dead of night at the water's edge to do the washing. Most accounts of them are of small women with webbed feet and ghostly pale skin. They wash the shrouds of those who are about to die.

These three women are incredibly strong, even though they are quite small in size. They do not like to be disturbed when they are doing their laundry and will curse any who dare do so. They may ask a stranger to help them, and if the stranger refuses they will drown or have a bone in their body broken.

In some stories, the three women are sinners that have been damned for all eternity to wash the shrouds of those about to die. They have been known to wash blood-stained clothes of people who are about to die in battle, and so on. Although they tend to shy away from the living or move them along if they are spotted, they are not to be trifled with. The best way to stay out of their grasp or get cursed is to not be out too late at night.

Mythical City of Ys

Like most myths, there are a few versions of the city of Ys which was fabled to have been engulfed by the sea. The legend has the city of Ys being built by the king of Cornouaille, Gradlon the Great (Gradlon Mawr). Cornouaille is in the Southern part of Brittany. Ys was rumored to be in Douarnenez Bay. It was one of the most beautiful cities around and was built below sea level. To keep the town from flooding, huge sea walls protected the city. When the tide was low the gates of the walls would be left open, but when the seas were high they would be locked tight to keep the water out.

There was only one key to the gate of the tidal walls which Gradlon wore around his neck at all times. Only he could lock or unlock the gates that protected the city. Gradlon fell in love with a beautiful woman who was half human and half fairy. Together they had a daughter, Princess Dahut. Because of his stormy relationship with the fairy he loved, he kept Dahut and raised her in the city of Ys. Dahut loved and worshipped the water and refused to give up her pagan ways, even when her father converted to Christianity.

Dahut was not a nice person and dreamt of only great riches and a place where she could be free to do and live as she wanted to. To fill the city with wealth, Dahut gifted a dragon to the people who live in the city. The dragon would help them capture merchant ships and fill the city with riches. Soon the city became the richest and most powerful in all of Brittany.

Dahut had a habit of killing her lovers, of which there were many. One day a knight, dressed in red and as handsome as any man she had seen before, arrived in Ys. She seduced the knight and the evening a storm broke out. The knight seemed intrigued by the waves pounded against the walls and gate, but Dahut was not worried. She told the knight that the gates and walls of the city could withstand any storm.

The knight got Dahut to steal the key from around her father's neck while he slept and give it to him. The knight opened the gates in the middle of the raging storm and the waters started to flood the town. It was then that the red knight revealed himself to be the devil and the town, now debauched in sin and fallen into ruin, sank into the sea. Gradlon climbed upon his magic horse, Marvarc'h, but as they started to leave the city, Gradlon was warned to leave the demon Dahut behind. So Gradlon pushed Dahut off his horse and got himself to safety.

Dahut, however, was pulled into the sea and turned into a mermaid (morgen). She became a water spirit that was doomed to swim the sea for eternity. In most myths, mermaids are believed to drown men.

Korrigans

The Korrigans are small fairy-like creatures, with the word Korrigan meaning small dwarf. They are small water sprite creatures that can be found near rivers and springs. Said to appear as beautiful golden-haired lusty maidens during dusk, they lure men into their beds–only their beds are watery graves for any man who is tempted by these small sirens.

If they were to be seen during the day, their appearance would be different and not at all alluring. During the day their eyes are red, the skin all wrinkled, and their hair scraggly and white, much like that of an old chrome. This is the reason why they are not seen during the day, as they hide away so people cannot see what they truly look like.

Much like sirens from dusk and well into the night during the moonlight, they can be seen brushing their long golden hair and singing. Their voice and beauty lure men in, making them fall deeply in love before the Korrigan drowns him.

They were also known to steal human children, especially babies, swapping them out for changelings.

Lady of the Lake

Viviane, or the legendary Lady of the Lake, was believed to have raised Lancelot and stolen the heart of the wizard Merlin. She was the Lady that gave Arthur Excalibur, that proved him to be the true king of Britain.

Viviane was a faerie who enchanted Merlin. Although Merlin could tell his own fate, he could not stop himself from falling in love with her. He built her a magical crystal palace in the waters that surround the Chateau de Comper in Brittany. This palace was a testament to his great love for her.

But Viviane did not return his love, instead, she used him to teach her some magic. Viviane tricked Merlin into meeting her at the fountain of youth, where she restored the magician's youthful features. Once he was young and virile again Viviane trapped him in a magical prison, where he died a slow death.

Merlin

Merlin is one of the most well-known wizards in the world today; even Disney movies have fashioned wizards after him. He was an advisor to Uther Pendragon, and some say he raised Arthur in secret until the day Arthur pulled Excalibur from the stone.

There is not a lot written about the origins of Merlin, but a lot is written about his personality as a joker and his love for wine. He was also a shapeshifter who became a wizard in Arthur's court. It was during his time serving Arthur that Merlin met and became enchanted with Viviane. He was, by then, a lot older than Viviane. She did not return his love; in fact, she was repulsed by him.

Merlin taught Viviane magic and she, in turn, used that magic against him. Paimpont Forest was once known as the legendary Broceliande and is where Viviane trapped Merlin after giving him back his youth at the fountain of youth. Legend has it that

Merlin's tomb is somewhere in the heart of the forest, quite close to the fountain of youth.

The Golden Tree

Everyone who knows about king Arthur will know who the legendary Morgan Le Fay is. She is sometimes shown as an evil vindictive sorceress, and other times as she came across as a strong woman. Men feared her with good cause, as she was said to trap and imprison her lovers in the Broceliande Forest—specifically in a golden Chestnut tree that stood in the center of the forest.

She was known as a shape-shifter that would go to any lengths for power and control. She is also a half-sister to King Arthur. In some stories, she takes Excalibur and gives it to Accolon, one of her many lovers. He takes the sword to use it against Arthur but his plot fails. Not wanting to admit defeat, Margan throws Excalibur's scabbard into the lake. The scabbard was what protected Arthur from harm.

Morbihan

The Gulf of Morbihan is said to have been formed from the tears shed by the fairies as they were driven from their home in the forest of Brocéliande. The Gulf of Morbihan lies just south of Brittany, where 368 islands can be found. These islands were believed to have formed from the pretty garlands the fairies either lost or threw in the sea. Houat and Hoedic Islands in the

Atlantic Ocean were formed when two of the garlands landed there. The Isle of Beauty in the Atlantic Ocean was formed from the crown of the Fairy Queen.

Megaliths

If you have ever read an Asterix and Obelix book, you would see that Oblix always seemed to be holding a huge boulder in his hands. In Brittany, there are many, many rock formations or standing boulders that have some connection to their myths and legends. Most of these rocks or stone formation can be associated with wizards, druids, and fairies. Some even have more sinister folklore connections.

There are different types of stones such as:

Menhirs

Menhirs are tall stones that are mostly shaped like tall round columns. There are many stories associated with such as worship for the druids and celebrations for the fairies. Because of the shape, they can resemble a human form. This brings about the story of two blasphemous priests that were turned into menhirs in Locarn.

Dolmens

Dolmens looked like large tombs that were made as a burial ground mark. They may also have been used as places of worship. Dolmens were built with four tall supporting stones on top of which was a large flattish capstone. They were all made to stand at an angle with the capstone tilting off to one side.

There is a lot of superstition surrounding these portal tombs, some of which say they were made with the help of or by the fairies.

Carnac Alignment Stones

The Carnac stones are large stones that were positioned across an axis each at a certain distance apart. These stones were mined from local granite by the people of Brittany, who erected over three-thousand of them.

There is a myth from Christian times that the stones are Pagan soldiers that were chasing down Pope Cornelius, who turned them into stone.

Much like the alignment stones at Stonehenge, these were thought to be in alignment with the direction of the sunsets. Some alignment stones were used to mark tombs or druid burial sites.

Steles

Stele were large monumental stones that would often have carvings on them. They were created to commemorate the fallen, as a monument to Celtic gods, or places of magic. For instance, a stele in Seven-Léhart was where sterile women would go on certain nights to rub their bellies on the stone's flat surface. It was believed to be a fertility stone that would allow the women to conceive and have a baby nine months later.

Tumuls

Tumula were dolmens that were not as high as most dolmens, and they were covered with earth. They were mainly used as tombs to house the bodies of the high born.

Chapter 3: Cornish Myths and Legends

Cornwall is one of the six Celtic nations and forms part of the Brythonic Celtic culture. Its history is different from that of the rest of England. Up until around the 16th century, Cornwall was closely linked to Ireland, Wales, and Brittany. During the Iron-Age the Cornovii and Dumnonii Celtic tribes inhabited what is known as Cornwall today.

During the Anglo-Saxon invasion, the Celtic tribes were known as Westwals in reference to West Welsh because of the Celtic heritage. The Cornish Celts stood steadfast in protecting their Celtic heritage and were often at war with the Anglo-Saxons. The River Tamar became a formal boundary between the Cornish Celts and the Anglo-Saxons. The Celts in this region of Cornwall never let go of the culture, even when there was no longer a boundary dividing the two nations. The Anglo-Saxons saw the Celtic nations as fiercely private people who kept to their own kind and closely guarded their customs.

Popular Cornish Myths and Legends

Like all the other Celtic nations, Cornwall's history is steeped in the dark mysteries, intrigues, and romance of myths and legends. This chapter looks at a few of the more popular myths, legends, and stories of the Cornwealas.

Tristram and Iseult

The tale of Tristram and Iseult, or Tristan and Isolde, is one of the most famous of the Cornish legends, as well as the most tragic. It is a tale of deep love, betrayal, and jealousy that ends in the death of the hero and heroine. It is a story about Tristram, the nephew of King Mark of Cornwall, and Iseult, who was the daughter of the king of Ireland.

Tristram's tale begins with tragedy, in that his father was killed in battle as his mother gave birth to him. While Tristram was born as a healthy baby boy, his mother did not recover. To protect the boy from his father's enemies, Tristram was spirited away by his father's trusted companion, Rual, who adopted him. Rual and his wife raised Tristram as their own and taught him in the manner that all royals were. He learned all the airs, graces, and skills that befit a prince.

Tristram was a fast learner and mastered many skills including swordsmanship, hunting, and music. He could play the harp as beautifully as the angels themselves. When Tristram was fourteen years old he was kidnapped by Norwegian merchants. But as luck would have it a terrible storm befell the Norwegian ship. As a superstitious culture, the Norwegian's were sure their ship was being pummelled because they had kidnapped Tristram.

The Norwegian merchants vowed that if the storm subsided and spared them as well as their ship they would set Tristram free. The storm died down and they set Tristram free at the next port, which happened to be Cornwall. From there Tristram made his way into the court of King Mark before the two knew they were related. King Mark was impressed by young Tristram's skills and valor. King Mark made Tristram his confidant, courtier, and companion.

While Tristram was setting himself up in the king's court, poor Rual was searching for his adopted son. He hunted down the Norwegian ship that had taken Tristram and was told that he had been set ashore in Cornwall. Rual made his way to Cornwall where he found Tristram, who instantly recognized Rual. Rual was brought in front of king Mark where he explained who Tristram was. king Mark was both amazed and happy to find out his nephew lived and proclaimed Tristram to be his heir. He also swore to protect Tristram's claim to the throne by never marrying. Tristram was soon thereafter knighted.

King Gurmun and his Queen Iseult (or Isolde) of Ireland used the giant Morold, the Queen's brother, to extract a tribute from both England and Cornwall. Each year the tribute to Ireland would grow and because it was Morold who would come to collect king Gurmun's due, none would challenge the giant. Morold's strength was legendary as was his skill with the sword.

Tristram, however, was tired of his country being oppressed by Ireland and having the threat of Morold hung over them. So he set out to challenge the giant to a duel on a small island in sight of Cornwall. Tristram and Morold each arrived on the small island in their own boats. Morold arrived first and soon thereafter Tristram arrived only to push his own boat back out into the sea.

When the giant asked Tristram why he had done that, Tristram replied that only one of them would be getting off the island alive. As it would be Tristram, he found the giant's boat more than adequate to take himself home.

Morold was fierce and skilled but he was also devious, for his blade was laced with poison. As the furious fight between Morold and Tristram ensued, Morold managed to stab Tristram in the leg drawing first blood. The giant gloated of what he had done to Tristram. He told Tristram that only Queen Iseult knew how to cure the poison that now ran through Tristram's veins. He tried to get Tristram to give up and accept defeat by offering to take Tristram to his sister, the Queen, to be cured. But Morold would only take him if he vowed to continue paying tribute to the king of Ireland.

Instead of relenting, Tristram charged the great giant and knocked him down. As Morold tried to get back up, Tristram managed to cut off the giant's arms with one blow. As the giant screamed out in pain, Tristram brought down another heavy blow that split Morold's skull. The blow to Morlod's head was so intense that a chip of the blade got wedged in the giant's head.

As Morold lay dying, Tristam leaned over his body and told the giant that he now needed his sister's to doctor him because he was the one now seriously wounded. Tristram raised his sword one more time and cut off Morold's head. Ignoring his own wounded leg, Tristram returned to the mainland of Cornwall where he was greeted with cheers for his victory.

Tristram was soon to find out that the giant had spoken the truth about the poison. The wound on Tristram's leg was not healing, but getting worse. He had to make a plan to get to the Queen Iseult. Tristram gathered up his most trustworthy men and set sail for Dublin. When they arrived near the shoreline, Tristram was put into a small boat with his harp and a few supplies.

Although Tristram's wound was dire, he was still able to play sweet tunes on his harp. As the small boat drifted onto the shore some passersby heard his music and went to investigate. They found Tristram and he told the strangers his ship had been set upon by pirates who had wounded him and set him adrift. Tristram managed to charm the strangers into taking him for an audience before the Queen to ask for help. He claimed that he had heard about the Queen's unparalleled healing skills from stories told of her.

When he met the Queen she was impressed with the stories the strangers had told her about his ability with the harp, even while being near death. She took pity on Tristram, thinking him to be a minstrel, and she agreed to help heal his wound. In return, however, she wanted him to teach her daughter, Princess Iseult (named after her mother), how to play the harp.

Tristram agreed to this deal. He told the Queen his name was Tantris and the Queen set about curing Tristram's poisoned wound. It was not long before the wound started to heal enough for Tristram to begin giving Princess Iseult harp lessons.

Tristram was immediately struck at Princess Iseult's beauty, of which he thought none other was near equal to. The Princess was not only a fair beauty but a keen and eager pupil who became nearly as adept at playing the harp as Tristram was under his tutelage. Trist was so taken with her magical voice that he compared it to that of a siren's voice that could tempt and lure a man to give up their heart.

Once Tristram was fully recovered from his leg wound and the princess well versed in playing the harp, Tristram knew he needed to leave Ireland. He also knew that the Queen would not let him leave without just cause. Knowing how sacred the Queen held holy wedlock, Tristram told the Queen that he had to leave because he was married and had a family back in Cornwall. He knew that the Queen would bid him his leave if he told her that his wife had to be his first loyalty. So the Queen bid him his leave to return to his country of Cornwall and to a wife he did not have.

King Mark was overjoyed when his nephew returned, fully recovered from the giant's near-fatal wound inflicted upon him. However, the king's followers were not happy with the fact that he had vowed not to wed and less happy that the king protected Tristram so fiercely. They did everything they could to make Tristram look bad or unworthy in the king's eyes, but nothing worked. The king remained true and loyal to his only nephew.

In his recounting of how he had tricked the Queen into healing him, Tristram had told King Mark of the princess. He had sung her praises and painted a picture of her unrivaled beauty to king Mark. Upon hearing of this, King Mark decided that Princess Iseult was to be his bride and no other would do. The princess would also ally Ireland to Cornwall, and Cornwall could use such a powerful country to back it up.

The problem was that Cornwall and Ireland were sworn enemies. There was no way the king of Ireland was going to let King Mark bid for his daughter's hand in marriage, and King Mark had no way of wooing the princess of Ireland.

Tristram thought up a cunning plan to help his uncle win the hand of Princess Iseult. Tristram had heard about a dragon that was plaguing the lands of Ireland. The word was that the king was so upset about this beast that he had offered the hand of his daughter to whoever could slay the wretched beast. Tristram offered to be his uncle's spokesperson to Ireland and king Mark agreed to Tristram's plan.

Tristram once again set sail for Ireland, and once there he hunted down the voracious fire-breathing beast until he found it. Armed with a shield, sword, and spear, Tristram attacked. It was by no means an easy battle, as the dragon was large, had sharp teeth, claws, and could breathe fire. But Tristram did not back down and stood his ground, finally defeating the beast. Tristram was exhausted and bore wounds from the attack of the dragon, but he knew he would have to get proof that he had slain the beast for the king.

Using the last vestiges of his strength, Tristam managed to pry open the great jaws of the dragon and cut out its tongue. He put the tongue in his pocket not realizing that it was a poison that would seep into his system. Exhausted, and sick from the poison, Tristram dropped himself into a shallow pool to keep himself alive.

At the court of the king of Ireland, another suitor was vying for Princess Iseult's hand. The king's chief steward wanted her badly, despite his ardor not being reciprocated. This steward happened to stumble upon the slain dragon, and having heard nothing of anyone claiming the kill, he claimed it for himself. This devious steward made sure friends and others witnessed him with the dragon. The steward cut off the dragon's head and took it to the king. Here the steward lay claim to the hand of the Princess for slaying the beast that was terrorizing the land.

This did not make the Princess Iseult happy, so she shared her grief and anguish with her mother. The Queen was a woman adept in a certain magic, and she had an inkling that what the steward claimed was not true. The Queen had a vision, and in that vision, she pictured a handsome man that had slain the dragon. She also saw that the man was wounded and had fallen into a shallow pond.

Together the Queen and the Princess hurried to where the Queen knew the handsome hero to be. There they found Tristram barely conscious, lying in a shallow pool of water. While the Queen was trying to revive him, she found the dragon's tongue in Tristram's pocket. The Princess recognized Tristram as the minstrel Tantris and told her mother as such.

The Queen asked a now semi-conscious Tristram if he was indeed the minstrel Tantris to which he replied he was. She asked him why he was back in Ireland to which Tristram told her he was seeking safe trade as a merchant from Ireland. That is why he had slain the dragon, in the hopes that the king would grant him favor and protection.

As Tristram had done Ireland a great favor by slaying the awful dragon, the Queen promised Tristram Ireland's protection. She had him taken back to the castle where she once again nursed him back to health. It was during this time that the now more mature Princess Iseult began to notice how handsome and manly Tantris was. While Tristram was recovering, he had heard that another had laid claim to his kill and the claim for the princess's hand. He knew too that the princess was not in favor of the steward laying the claim.

Tristram was nearly fully recovered when the princess found Tristram's sword and recognized the piece missing from it. The nick in the sword matched the mark in her uncle Morold's head. She immediately held the sword defensively at Tristram and got him to admit the truth.

The Queen found them and the Princess explained who Tristram was and that she was going to kill him. But the Queen forbade it, telling the Princess that they had already granted Tristram protection.

Tristram took the opportunity to offer the two ladies a deal. He would solve the princess's problem of disproving the stewards claim to her hand a lie. He would also offer a match for the princess to King Mark of Cornwall. Both the Queen and the Princess agreed to Tristram's proposal and so the deal was done.

When the the dragon's head was presented to the king by the steward, the steward promptly demanded his reward. This reward was the promise of the the pricesses princess's hand in marriage. Tristram was able to disprove the stewards' claim to killing the dragon as he had the dragon's tongue, proving the dragon had been killed by Tristram and not the steward who had found its lifeless body.

As King Mark had already agreed to the arrangement, it was not that hard for Tristram to get a contract between King Mark and Princess Iseult. Tristram was to escort Princess Iseult back to Cornwall for her marriage to King Mark. The Queen set about making a very potent potion, which she entrusted to the princess's confidant. The potion was to be given to both king Mark and Princess Iseult upon their wedding night. It was a potion that would ensure they had a marriage of blissful love. The potion was mixed with a bottle of wine.

During the voyage from Ireland to Cornwall, Tristram and Iseult did not get along and clashed when their paths crossed. The weather was also not in their favor during the voyage. Storms made the journey very choppy, and as a result nearly everyone on the ship became seasick. To give the crew and passengers a break, Tristram had the ship dock at the next seaport they came across so all those aboard could regain their land legs and well-being.

The only two who stayed aboard the ship were Tristram and Princess Iseult. While alone on the ship they had time to talk about trivial matters. They went to find something to drink and came across the bottle of wine Iseult's mother had given her companion. Thinking it only wine, they drank the contents of the bottle together.

Brangaene, the one who was entrusted with the love potion, then returned to the ship. She immediately recognized the bottle of wine that was being shared between Tristram and Iseult. Brangaene snatched the bottle and threw what was left into the sea warning the two that no good was going to come of this.

Not long after the wine was thrown into the sea did Iseult and Tristram began to realize that they no longer hated each other. Their hate, mistrust, and animosity had been replaced by the exact opposite emotions. They had fallen in love and could not bear to be parted for too long. By the time they returned to King Mark's court Iseult faced another problem, as she could no longer call herself a maiden. To make sure King Mark was not made aware of this, on the wedding night, Brangaene was who the king unknowingly took to his bed. As time passed, Tristram and Iseult's love, as well as their affair, only grew stronger.

King Mark grew more and more suspicious of his wife and nephew as time went on, until one day King Mark was forced to banish both Tristram and Iseult from his court. The two took refuge in the nearby forest and found a cave where they could stay. They were undisturbed for a long time, until one day the king's hunting party found them. But before they could peek in the cave where Tristram and Iseult were, the two hatched a plan. What the huntsmen saw when they looked in the cave was Tristram and Iseult sleeping on the crystal floor with a sword forming a barrier between them. The king took this as their loyalty and fidelity, and welcomed them back into his kingdom.

Thereafter it became harder and harder for Tristram and Iseult to be together so they decided to end their affair. Tristram left Cornwall to make his home elsewhere, before he left Iseult gave him a ring. The ring was a memento of the deep love they shared. Tristram left Cornwall on a ship bound for Normandy with a very heavy heart.

He made Arundel his home, a small island that sat between Brittany and England.

It was here that Tristram met Kaedin and his sister Iseult. Kaedin was a knight and Iseult was lovely and unwed. As Tristram was staying in Kaedin's castle, he and Iseult were often found in each other's company. It was only to be expected that Tristram would find himself thinking about her in a more desirable way. Tristram was confused over what he felt for Iseult, but over time he gave in and married her. On their wedding night, Tristram made up an excuse not to sleep close to his new wife. He told her that he had an old injury that was causing him pain.

Tristram could not bring himself to touch his new wife, and one day Kaedin found out. He confronted Tristram, who told his friend everything. Not long after that Tristram was injured in a battle with a poisoned spear, while in Kaedin's service. Tristram knew that only Queen Iseult, the love of his life, could save him as she now possessed her mother's healing abilities.

Kaedin set sail for England, as this is where Queen Iseult now resided, hoping to get her to agree to come back and help Tristram. Tristram told Kaedin that if she agreed to come back with him, he must fly both a black and white flag. If not, only a black one. He told Kaedin that this would help him know what was to come of him before Kaedin reached land.

What Kaedin and Tristram did not know was that Tristram's wife had overheard the entire conversation. She knew what the plan was, and her jealousy rose into hatred. When the ship returned Tristram asked his wife if she could see the ship's flag, and if so what color were they. Tristram's wife went to look and came back to tell him that the flag was black and only black.

Tristram knew that it was not only his wound that was sealing his fate but his broken heart and spirit. He repeated "Dearest Iseult" four times as his heart broke and he closed his eyes for the last time. But Tristram's wife had lied out of spite and jealousy, as the ship had both black and white flags. Iseult had indeed come to help her love, but upon embarking, they were told that Tristram had died.

Iseult the Fair ran to where Tristram lay dead, she laid her head upon his chest proclaiming that he had given up his life for her and so she would give up hers for him. Those were the last words she spoke, as she, too, died on the spot in her lover's arms.

Tristram and Iseult were buried next to each and a rose vine grew from each of their graves. As the rose bushes grew their branches met and intertwined joining the two lovers forever and proving that love conquers all.

Chapter 4: Welsh Celtic Myths and Legends

Wales occupies the western part of the United Kingdom. It is nestled between the Bristol Channel in the south and England to the east, with the Iris Sea surrounding it on the north and west. Due to the location of Wales, not many invaders conquered Wales, nor did they mix with the inhabitants of that part of the British Isles.

Still today the Welsh maintain their proud Celtic heritage with their own language and culture. The craggy shores and diverse lands of Wales add to the colorful Celtic myths and legends with their renditions and unique stories. The Welsh form part of the Brythonic Celtic culture.

Popular Welsh Myths and Legends

Wales was inhabited by neanderthals, and later homo sapiens, that came to the land over 30,000 years ago. As man developed through the ages, so did their many myths and legends about the world and the beings in it. This chapter looks at a few of the more popular myths, legends, and stories of the Welsh.

Lludd and Llefelys

This is the story of dragons, demons, a thieving wizard, and two kingly brothers. In the early years of Wales and Britain, a wise king named Llefelys ruled France while his brother Lludd ruled Britain. It was ancient times where demons, dragons, and magic prevailed throughout the kingdoms of both Britain and France.

Britain, however, became overrun by a demonic trice that was called the Coraniaid. This was not King Lludd's only problem; the people of Britain were also being terrified by the most awful, mysterious screams. The screams were so bad they were said to make women miscarry and leave animals barren. The screams were also making crops not produce. On top of all these problems plaguing King Lludd's kingdom, provisions kept vanishing from the court.

King Lludd called upon his brother king Llefelys of France for help. King Llefelys helped his brother by telling him about a potion consisting of water and crushed insects. The potion would destroy the Coraniaid. They devised a trap that caught the wizard stealing supplies and made him subservient to king Lludd.

After investigation, it was found that the awful screams were coming from two fighting dragons. King Llefelys told King Ludd that he needed to dig a hole in the middle of Britain. The hole or pit needed to be filled with mead and then covered with a cloth. The two dragons got trapped in the cloth and were buried far underground in North West Wales, at Dinas Emrys.

Dinas Emrys

There is a legend that surrounds Dinas Emrys that also involves two dragons. King Vortigern tried to build a castle on top of Dinas Emrys, but was unsuccessful. The King could not understand why the walls that had been built during the day would be destroyed each night.

King Vortigern sought the help of Myrddin Emrys (Merlin the wizard). Myrddin told the King that there were dragons that were trapped in Dinas Emrys. Each night they would fly around in the mound, fighting.

The king got his men to dig up the mound and release the dragons. There was a white dragon and a red dragon. When they were released they brutally attacked each other and the red dragon killed the white dragon. The red dragon returned to his lair and king Vortigern was able to build his castle upon Dinas Emrys.

The castle was called Dinas Emrys in honor of Myrddin and the red dragon became a celebrated figure in Wales.

The Devil's Bridge

There is a tale of the Devil that visited Wales in the 11th century. He appeared in the form of a human. There he came upon an old woman staring across a river. She seemed very upset and so the Devil approached her asking her what was wrong.

She told the devil that her cow had crossed the river and she had no way to get it back. The Devil saw this as a great opportunity to get a soul, so he made a deal with the old lady.

The Devil promised the old lady that he would build her a bridge, and in return he got to keep the first living thing that crossed the bridge. The old lady made the deal and went home on the promise the bridge would be built for her the next day.

That night, upon reflection, the old lady wondered about the stranger and his offer. Although it was a very tempting one, the old lady thought, if she was the first living thing across the bridge she would not get her cow back.

The next day the old lady set off to the bridge only this time she took her old farm dog with her. When she got to the river, to her surprise was the most beautiful bridge she had ever seen. The Devil saw the old lady and told her that he had lived up to her end of the deal now it was her turn to do so.

The old lady walked to the edge of the bridge, stopped, drew out a piece of bread which she threw onto the other side. The huge dog took off after the bread. The Devil looked on in disbelief and screamed at the old lady that he could not use a dog. The Devil disappeared in a cloud of anger and the old lady was able to cross the bridge to get her cow.

The Devil was never again seen in Wales.

Gelert

Another well-known legend in Wales is the story of a dog named Gelert. In Wales there is a village called Beddgelert, it thought the town was named after this dog as the town was built around his grave.

Gelert was the favored dog of Prince Llywely of Gwynedd. Gelert was a fearless hunting dog and a gift from King John of England. Gelert was also the Prince's loyal companion. One day the Prince and his Princess set off to go hunting and left their baby son with his nurse and one other servant in their hunting lodge.

The nurse and the servant left the baby prince asleep and unguarded in his crib when they went for a walk in the woods.

While out hunting, the Prince noticed that Gelert was missing. Worried about his dog, the Prince turned the hunting party around to go find him. One of the first places the Prince looked at was at the hunting lodge.

As they approached the Prince saw Gelert run out of the lodge. When he dismounted and upon closer look, he found that Gelert was covered in blood. Panicked and afraid the Prince rushed into the lodge. There he found his son's cradle overturned and blood everywhere. There was no sign of his son.

Enraged and grief-stricken, the Prince drew his sword and ran it through Gelert. Gelert whimpered and died as the cries of the Prince's son could be heard. Shocked, the Prince rushed back into the lodge and behind the crib was his son unharmed. That is when the Price saw the large wolf lying dead and bloodied on the floor near the crib.

Gelert had sensed the baby was in trouble and taken off to go and save it. The dog had killed the wolf and saved the young Prince. Stricken with remorse at what he had done to his dog, especially after such a heroic act, Llywelyn never spoke again.

Llywelyn buried Gelert in a meadow nearby, marking the dog's grave with a cairn of stones. For the rest of his life, it was said that Llywelyn was haunted by the dying sounds of his faithful hound.

Cadair Idris

Standing approximately 893 meters high, Cadair is one of Wale's most well-known mountains. It overlooks the Welsh town Dolgellau in Gwynedd, in northwest Wales. Historically it was the county town of Merionethshire that ran along the River Wnion. The mountain stands at the foot of what is known as the southern gate of Snowdonia.

This mountain is said to be the throne of the giant Idris that sat upon it. The mountain has three peaks: Pen y Gadair, which means head of the chair; Cyfrwy, which means the saddle; and Mynydd Moe, which means the bare mountain.

The mountain is said to have been built as Idris' chair so he could sit in it and stare up at the heavens. At the bottom of the mountain is a bottomless lake called Llyn Cau. At the foot of the mountain are three large stones. These stones were said to have been cast there as pieces of grit that Ibris found in his shoe while sitting upon his throne one day.

There are few of these large stones that can be found in some of the villages around the mountain. Each one said to have been thrown there by Idris, well the larger ones, the smaller being put down by his wife.

The Oldest Tree in Wales

One of the oldest trees in the world is a Yew tree that was planted in a small graveyard around 4,000 years ago. This tree can be found in a village in north Wales—Llangernyw, Conwy. This particular Yew tree comes with a frightening legend. To this tree comes a spirit that appears twice a year to announce the names of the parish members that were going to die that year.

Twice a year the parish members gathered together and listened from beneath the east window of the church to the names the spirit would say out loud. These names were said to be the angel's list. The dates upon which this spirit appears each year are October 31st and July 31st.

The spirit is said to live in the Yew tree and the land upon which the church now stands has always been sacred land.

King March Ap Meirchion

King March Ap Meirchion, or king March for short, is a tale about deformity and the lesson to not to judge a book by its cover.

King March was a king that had everything: riches beyond compare, possessions of every kind, and a rich prosperous kingdom. His subjects loved him, as he was a fair, kind, generous, and just king. His people were happy with their lot in life; they worked hard and lived good lives.

Although he had everything and people saw him as a happy king, he was not. For he bore what he thought was a terrible secret: he was born with the ears of a horse. No one, except for his barber, Bifan, and his long passed parents knew his secret. The king grew his hair long to cover his ears and had a special crown made which covered them up.

Bifan was sworn to secrecy with the threat of losing his head if ever the king's secret were to come out. Keeping the secret weighed heavily on Bifan, and for years he kept his word to the king and the secret was never revealed. Through the years the burden of the king's secret felt heavier and heavier to Bifan until he stopped eating, he became depressed, and fell ill.

A wise and experienced physician was sent to tend to Bifan. The physician examined Bifan and asked him many questions. When he was done he told Bifan that the problem was physically but it was some burden or secret that was causing Bifan distress. Bifan told the physician that he did have a secret one he had sworn a sacred oath to keep. If he did not keep this secret he would lose his life. He did not tell the man what the secret was, only that he had one he could not share.

The physician warned Bifan that if he did not tell the secret he would die of depression. After the physician had left Bifan pondered upon his problem and a solution came to him. The next day he set out into the wilds where there was no one around for miles and miles; it was just him and nature. He found a river that was dense with reeds. He sought a dry spot near the banks where he could lay. As he lay with his belly in the sand and his face near the earth, he told his secret to the ground, the river, and the reeds.

When he was done, Bifan started to feel better. The weight had been lifted from his shoulders and he even felt hungry again. He went back to the town where he had a good dinner and after a few days started to recover.

Back at the court of King March, the king wanted to have a huge feast complete with pipers at the Great Hall of Castlemarch. King March summoned the best piper in all of Wales to play at the feast.

The piper was on his way to Castlemarch when he came across some fine reeds growing at the river banks in a wild spot. He thought that they would make sweet music to play at King March's feast, so he cut some of the reeds. The piper was unaware that the spot where he cut the reeds from was the spot where Bifan had confessed the secret he had been keeping.

It was a merry day at Castlemarch; the feast was well underway. When the guests had eaten their fill, the king decided it was time for the piper to play for them. Having made his new pipe, the piper stepped up and started to play. But what he played did not come out of the pipes; instead, the only sound to come out of them was "King March had horse ears!"

The piper was confused and mortified, he tried to play again but again the pipes repeated the sound about King March's ears. The pipes repeated this statement again and again. The guests were shocked and King March was utterly humiliated; he immediately went to cut off the piper's head. But the piper dropped to his knees in front of the king beginning his merch and explaining it was not him. It was a new pipe he had made from these reeds he had cut on the way to the castle.

Realizing that the reeds must have been the same reeds where he had confessed the King's secret, Bifan came forward. He told the king about his illness and what the physician had said to him. Bifan told the king that he did not want to betray him so he had told the earth in the most remote spot he could find. But the reeds had absorbed this secret and it was not the piper's fault.

King March was hurt and enraged, although it was more his humiliation that influenced his actions, and so he drew his sword on Bifan. But as he was about to cut off the barber's head, he turned to his guests; they stared at him, but not with pity. Something inside the king no longer felt hollow, it felt warm and filled. The king dropped his sword and burst out laughing as he pulled off his crown to reveal his ears.

His guests looked upon their king with admiration and cheered him for his courage. The king forgave both the piper and Bifan, assuring them that no harm would come to them. For the first time in his life, the king felt happy and unashamed. The king learned that day that his people loved him for who he was, and that people will judge you on your deeds–not your looks.

This tale has many lessons in it, it shows acceptance, forgiveness, and human weakness. It is a story that encourages people to be themselves and not be ashamed of who you are.

Chapter 5: Irish Celtic Myths and Legends

The word folklore immediately makes Ireland spring to mind: a country that is steeped in rich traditions, mythical creatures, superstitions, and eerily beautiful landscapes with heartbreaking tales. As with all the other Celtic nations, Ireland consisted of many tribes each with their own chieftain overseeing the village. Although each village had its own chieftain and worshipped their own gods, they did all share a common law system: Brehon law.

The Irish form part of the Goidelic Celtic culture. This chapter looks at some of the more popular Irish myths and legends.

Popular Irish Myths and Legends

Irish history has through the ages inspired poets, authors, and songwriters alike with its ancient heritage of sagas, myths, legends, and battles. It is thanks to the Irish that most of the popular Celtic myths and legends we know about today survived the ages.

Dagda's Harp

The Dagda had a golden harp; it was a magical harp that only he could play. The harp would play the music that could tame a beast, incite his men for war, bring joy, sorrow, or cures for what ailed his battle-weary men.

After the Battle of Moytuirné, which fought between the Tuatha de Danann and the Fomorians, the Tuatha returned home victorious. That night they celebrated their defeat of the Fomorians with a huge feast. The soldiers ate their fill from Dagda's bottomless cauldron that the Dagda took out the sword of the Tethra. The Tethra was a great sword in which a spirit lived. The Dagda ordered the spirit inside of the sword to regale his men with the tale of how the sword came to be.

As the men listened intently, they were unaware that some Fomorians had broken into their camp and stoled Dagda's magical harp.

It was not until the soldiers asked Dagda to grace them with the sounds of his magical harp that he found his sweet-tongued harp was missing. He was enraged and worried as the harp not only played magical music but it helped to control the weather. Without the harp, the farmers and hunters would suffer.

The Dagda asked of his men who would go with him to rescue his harp. The taking of the harp was also of great insult to the Dagda. Lugh Longarm and Ogma the Artificer rose and united with Dagda to embark on the mission to rescue the harp.

The Fomorians and the Tuatha de Danann were two very different people. Where the Tuatha were light and fair, the Fomorians were dark. To reach the Fomorians Dagda, Lugh, and Ogma had to travel through nine valleys, nine mountains, and nine rivers. When they came upon the camp of the Fomorians it was dark, dank, and cold. The camp bore witness to the Fomorians' recent defeat, leaving the people with very little food.

At the edge of the camp, the three men saw that many soldiers protected the harp and they needed a plan to get to it. Dagda was not worried; instead, he stretched out his arm and called for his magic harp. Hearing its true master's voice, the harp sprung from where it had been hung on the wall. The harp flew to Dagda, and the men that got in its way were cut down.

Noticing what was happening, the camp sprang into action, but the harp had found its way back to Dagda. The Fomorians started to advance on Dagda, Lugh, and Ogma when Lugh told Dagda he needed to play his harp.

Dagda swept his fingers across the strings of the harp, and a beautiful melody started to play. It was the music of grief that had the Fomorians stop and bow their head as they sobbed. Even the soldiers sobbed, but they drew their mantles so none could see the tears flowing from their eyes.

The music stopped and again the Fomorians started to charge the three men. Dagda once again drew his fingers across the strings of the harp and this time the music of mirth filled the air. The Fomorians fell into fits of laughter, and once again tears rolled down their eyes as their bellies ached from the laughter. The music stopped and once again the soldiers charged the three men.

Once again, Dagda drew his fingers across the strings of the harp, and this time the music was gentle and soothing. It lulled all in the camp into a deep sleep.

Dagda, Lugh, and Ogma rode away back to their home with the harp back where it belonged. The harp was never stolen again or touched by anyone other than Dagda.

Macha the Goddess of Horses and War

Crunden was a farmer who lived in Ulster and tragically lost his wife. She left him to look after three young children. As he had to work during the day, he had no option but to leave his kids to run amok in the house. The house had fallen into disarray and each day his guilt sliced through him about having to raise his children this way.

One day Crunden came home from working in the fields feeling exhausted and dreading the mess he would find. As he stepped into the house, he could not believe he was in the right place. The kids were sitting all quiet, clean, fed, and happy. The house too was the clean and fine smell of cooking met his nostrils.

As he wandered to the kitchen a beautiful woman stood dishing up a plate of food for him. Macha introduced herself to Crunden and told him that she had come to be his wife and help him. Crunden, a kind and good man, could not believe his luck. He settled into married life with Macha. He did, however, realize that she was not from this world but the otherworld. She did not walk like a normal person, but instead she seemed to glide. Macha, he noticed, could run faster than the wind. They settled into married life together and were quite happy, as were Crunden's children.

One day the king received some new horses that were as fast as any their kingdom had ever seen. The king wanted all his people to celebrate his new purchase, and thus threw a feast. Crunden was invited to go, but before he did Macha made him promise not to say a word to anyone about her. Crunden, not waiting to ruin their life together, promised he would not say a word about her.

At the feast, Crunden had a fair share of wine to drink. While all the other men boasted of how beautiful their wives were or what good cooks they were, Crunden kept quiet and said nothing. This continued until the king stood up and boasted at how fast his horses were. No longer able to hold his tongue, Crunden boasted that his wife was so fast she could outrun any horse.

The king was taken aback and highly offended. He immediately sent his men to get Macha. When his men got to Crundens house they found Macha to be very pregnant. They brought her before the king, who insisted that she race against his horses or her husband would lose his life. Macha agreed, but pleaded with the king to wait until after she had given birth. But the king refused. Macha turned to the king's soldiers and implored them to help her. She knew that a lot of them had families and must know the risks of her running a race so far pregnant.

However, not one warrior stood up for her or came to her aid, nor did any of the other guests. They had all been drinking and feasting, and they thought that this would be excellent entertainment. There was something about Macha that made the king hesitant, and he insisted his chariot not be weighed down with unnecessary objects. He wore no armor and made his charioteer step down.

Macha implored the king one last time to reconsider and wait until she had given birth, but he refused. The race began, and Macha of course proved she was as fast as the wind and won the race. At the end of the race she collapsed onto the grass, writhing in pain as her contractions started. She gave birth to twins on the field–but they were stillborn. In her grief and anger, Macha gathered her lifeless children in her arms. She stood staring at the soldiers. She cursed them for not using their strength and courage to stand up for her.

Because they did not defend her, Macha cursed them for nine generations to come. The curse would render every soldier or warrior in the court's strength to fade when they needed it the most. They would feel the pangs of childbirth for nine days and nights. This curse would go through the next generation starting when a boy child was old enough to grow facial hair.

Macha took her dead twins and left the field; she was never heard of or seen again. But her curse remained true and for the next nine generations before each battle, the men would endure the pains of childbirth for nine nights and night days. Thereafter for nine generations the soldiers of the court of king Ulster suffered the pains of childbirth before each battle.

The Headless Horseman — The Dullahan

Dullahans have inspired many a tale and movie in the modern-day. They are terrifying spectacles that race across the countryside on a demon horse with glowing red eyes. One would think a wild black demonic horse would be enough to scare the wits out of a person, but the demonic horse rider has no head upon his shoulders. Instead, it carries its head mounted on its saddle, beneath its arm, or raised high in one of its hands. The Dullahans head looks like it is pasty and rancid, like dough left to rot and sour. Its black eyes rattled around like they were darting all around the sockets. On his face he wears a smile that looks like it has been carved from ear to ear, and his head glows.

It is said that wherever the Dullan stops, there is going to be a death nearby. This creature can see for miles ahead of him, so he can spot one who is dying from wherever he is. People fear to look upon him for he will poke out an eye or hurl blood in their face. The Dullahan thunders over the countryside on his demonic horse using a human spine as a whip.

Each journey the head can only talk once and when it does it is to call out the name of the one that will die. The Dullahan is mostly seen on the nights of Irish feast days. The Dullahan does not seek out souls but rather responds to cries of a dying soul. He is thought to be the ancient god Crom Dubh. He was a god of fertility, and to give life he demanded human sacrifice each year. The human sacrifice was to be beheaded in his honor.

When sacrificial religions in Ireland were done away with, Chrom Dubh was not happy, so he took on physical form to hunt down souls. It is said there is nothing you can do to ward off the Dullahan, as he is the herald of death. But, he has a fear of gold; wearing an object made of gold may scare him off.

Butterflies and The Wooing of Étaín

In Irish legends, butterflies are the souls of the dead making their way to the Otherworld. One of the most beloved stories about this is the Wooing of Étaín. Étaín was the daughter of King Ailill of Ulaid. Étaín is often depicted much like how Snow White is; her skin was as white as snow, her lips a ruby red, her cheeks flushed, and her eyes an unnatural blue.

Étaín caught the eye of the fair-haired Tuatha de Danann warrior, Midir. Midir lived in the mounds of the earth with the fairy race and was first married to Fúamnach. When Midir came upon Étaín he was smitten and had to have her for his second wife. With the help of his step-son, Oengus, Midir was able to get Étaín's father's approval to marry her.

Midir was so taken with Étaín, that Fúamnach was all but forgotten. Fúamnach became embittered and jealous of Étaín, and devised a way to get rid of her. Fúamnach used magic and turned Étaín in a pool of water, then a worm, and then finally a butterfly. Afterward, Étaín found Midir as a butterfly and stayed close to him. Midir was unaware that the butterfly was Étaín, but got a strong attachment to it anyway. He took it wherever he went. Over time, he lost interest in human women and only cared for the butterfly.

Fúamnach became more enraged, and conjured a wind that blew Étaín seven years into the future. However, Étaín landed with Midir's step-son Oengus. Oengus knew that the butterfly was Étaín, so he created a sweet little glass chamber for her and he too carried her with him.

Once again Fúamnach found out that Étaín had returned to her circle, so she conjured yet another wind to blow Étaín even further into the future. Each time Étaín returned, Fúamnach blew her further into the future until Étaín landed in the wine goblet of the Chieftain Etar's wife. His wife drank the wine, unknowingly swallowing Étaín and soon thereafter became pregnant. Étaín was born again with no recollection of her past.

When she grew up, Étaín married the High King of Ireland, Eochaid. Midir found her again and tried to get her to remember her past. He attempted to trick her into his bed, hoping that if she slept with him it would bring back her memories. But, she evaded his tricks numerous times.

Desperate to win her back, Midir approached Eochaid and tried to trick him into giving Étaín back to him. After being given a series of tasks and challenges by Eochaid, who knew Midir was trying to steal his wife, Midir completed them all successfully. Midir demanded a kiss from Étaín as his prize. Ecochaid agreed and Midir embraced Étaín, kissing her with such a passion that it sparked the memories of Étaín's previous life with him.

Étaín allowed Midir to whisk her way, and they retreated to Midir mound while Eochaid, distressed and mourning his wife, spent the rest of his days digging up every fairy mound looking for her.

Chapter 6: Scottish and Isle of Man (Manx) Celtic Myths and Legends

Like Scotland, the shores of the Isle of Man have been raided by various other nations many times throughout history. This island lies in the middle of the Irish Sea and is an equidistant between Scotland, Ireland, England, and Wales. It is also said to be where the Manx cat, a tailless domesticated breed of cat, originated from.

The King of Norway sold his suzerainty to Scotland in 1266. Like the Scottish, the Manx are superstitious and fiercely proud of the heritage. Their culture is filled with folklore, mythology, and the ever-popular ghost stories.

The chapter looks at some of the myths of Scotland and the Isle of Man.

Popular Scottish Myths and Legends

Misty rolling hills, lochs, rugged mountains, and mysterious creatures form the grounds for Scottish myths and legends. This proud nation has many tales that inspired, intrigued, and warned the Celtic people who once lived there. The Scottish form part of the Goidelic Celtic culture.

Stories of the Loch Ness monster, ghosts that wander the hills, and great heroes echo through the beautiful land that makes up

Scotland. This chapter takes a look at some of the more popular myths and legends of Scotland.

Sawney Bean

This story is about one of Scotland's most famous cannibals, Sawney Bean. Born in East Lothian, Sawney moved to Ayrshire where he married and had a home near Ballantrae in Bennane Cave. His home was a mass of tunnels that ran inside solid rock, into which they excavated a few rooms as their family grew. When he and his wife were first wed, he found himself unemployed and having to find another means by which to support his wife.

Sawney took to robbing stagecoaches or lonely travelers traveling along small narrow roads. These types of roads made it easier for Sawney to ambush his prey and rob them. He worried that his victims might identify him, so to keep his crimes from being discovered he murdered his victims. Butchering them to destroy any evidence would allow him to dispose of the bodies, and from there he could feed his family.

Soon the Beans had fourteen children with a lust for human flesh. As the children grew so did the list of missing persons in the area. Although the local authorities looked for the missing, no one thought to check the caves.

The Bean family grew and the children became adept at finding their prey. One night, however, a man and his wife were riding home from a fair when the Bean family attacked them. They managed to get the wife off her horse, but the man fought them back. They were not prepared for the fight that ensued, nor to be discovered as a troop of other people returning from the fair came upon the man fighting off the savages.

It was not long after that that the search for the Bean family began, and they were found in the caves. What the authorities found was beyond horrific. Human body parts had been pickled and hung from hooks, much like a leg of mutton in a butcher shop. There were piles of human bones, clothes, and other evidence for their crimes.

All of the Bean family was arrested and taken to prison in Edinburgh. Their crimes were considered so heinous that the courts thought conventional law did not apply. Thus, the Bean men had their arms and legs cut off and were left to slowly die as they bled out. Meanwhile, the Bean women were burned alive in huge bonfires.

Strike Martin

On the northern outskirts of Dundee, Scotland is Strathmartine. It was named after a brave young man named Martin. The legend tells of a farm called Pitempton, on which lived a humble farmer and his nine daughters. One night he asked his eldest daughter to go down to the well and fetch some water. When his daughter did not return, he sent his next eldest to go look for her sister. His second eldest daughter did not return either, so he kept sending his daughters until they were all gone.

Worried, he himself went looking for them, only to come across their bloodied bodies laid out in a row. Eating off their flesh was a creature resembling a dragon that looked like it was mixed with a serpent. Frightened, the farmer ran off to seek the help of his neighbors. They all banded together and allowed the farmer to lead them to the well where they found the creature still feasting upon its recent kills.

Outnumbered, the creature tried to make its escape, but a young man named Martin struck the beast down with his club. The crowd cheered as the beast fell and died, and Martin became known as Strike-Martin. The spot where he had slain the dragon became known as Strike-Martin as well, and later it was named Strathmartine. Near the village of Bridgefoot, there is a lone stone that stands in a field known as Martin's stone.

The Ghost Piper

Scotland is full of ghosts and ghost stories that make a person's hair stand on end. One such story was the story of the ghost piper of Clanyard Bay. Scotland is notorious for the wailing soulful sound of bagpipes. Scotland is awash with mountains and hillsides that extend as far as the eye can see. Within these hillsides are often a series of caves or mysterious tunnels that network different villages together.

There is said to be a network of tunnels that start at the Cove of Grennan and extend to the craggy cliffs of Clanyard Bay. In times gone by, the locals believed these tunnels to be where the fairies lived, and none dared to disturb them by going in. One young piper, however, decided to find out for himself if the fairies really did live there.

Armed with his bagpipes and his dog, he entered the caves. He blew loudly on his bagpipes as he walked deeper and deeper into the depth of the tunnels. His bagpipes got softer and softer until they could be heard no more. After a lengthy silence, his dog rushed out of the tunnels whimpering. All the dog's hair was gone, and so was the young piper.

It is said that some nights or at certain times of the day you can hear him play his bagpipes. The sound wails from beneath the ground as he plays.

Brownies and Giants

In Scotland there were tiny little people known as Brownies that were like little elves, only they did good deeds for people. It was said that late at night when the people slept those in need would get a visit from the Brownie people. They would come into the house and do what needed to be done. They were shy and would run away before they were discovered by humans. Many tales incorporate these little people; even the Romans believed in small people who helped out, though they called them Lares.

From tiny people to giants, nearly all mythology has something written about giants. Scotland is no exception. One particularly well known legendary giant is Cailleach, a female giant. In the Forest of Mar in Aberdeenshire is a large formation of rocks that looks like a collapsed house. This is said to be the remains of Cailleach's house and the Alisa Craig island was formed by her when a large pebble fell out of the apron she always wore.

Isle of Man (Manx) Celtic Myths and Legends

The Isle of Man is a small island perched between Ireland and Britain in the Irish Sea. Like Wales, the Island was not of any interest to the invaders of Britain at the time the Celts occupied the land. The Vikings invaded the island in the 8th century and brought with them significant change. The Tynwald is the Isle of Man's parliament and has been around for a thousand or so years.

This small island has been around since about 8,000 years BC, and has its myths developed through many significant ages of man. The Isle of Man forms part of the Goidelic Celtic culture.

The Isle of Man was populated for centuries before the Celts came along, during the Iron Age. Through the different periods of the Island's development many dark, mysterious, and entertaining stories were woven to a captive audience that looked to the bards, druids, and Gods for explanations for things we take for granted today. The event of dying crops was most likely something to do with an unhappy God, a child taken early was some demon's doing, and so on.

Ancient accounts of the weather, death, and natural disasters built up a collection of stories that we read today as myths and legends. This chapter looks at a few of the more popular myths, legends, and stories of the Manx.

The Old Caillagh

Caillagh ny Groamagh was known as the sullen or gloomy old woman. She was thought to have been a witch that was cast out Ireland and into the sea where she would be drowned, only she kept herself afloat and landed on the shores of the Isle of Man on the 1st of February, St. Bridget's Day. To dry herself off, she went about gathering up as many sticks as she could find to light a fire.

The following spring was a very wet one, and the entire spring had only bad weather. The legend that followed was that every ditch on the Isle of Man had to be covered with snow on St. Brigid's Day. This was so that the Caillagh could not find sticks to gather up to dry herself with.

If Caillagh found enough sticks and got dry on the 1st of February, spring on the Isle of Man would have bad weather. If Caillagh could not find sticks to gather and remained wet, spring would have nice weather.

Fairy Bridge and Mooinjer Veggey

On the Isle of man, the little people are called Mooinjer Veggey and never referred to as fairies. This is especially true when crossing the fairy bridge on the south-east of the Isle of Man. The bridge lies between Castletown and Douglas.

When crossing the bridge you have to greet the fairies and if you do not bad luck will befall you. You have to say either:

- Moghrey mie Mooinjer Veggey — Good morning Mooinjer Veggey.
- Fastyr mie Mooinjer Veggey — Good afternoon or evening Mooinjer Veggey.
- Laa mie Mooinjer Veggey — Good day Mooinjer Veggey.

Arkan Sonney

The Arkan Sonney are little magical fairies that look like a pig crossed with a hedgehog. To catch an Arkan Sonney is meant to bring good luck and fortune to the one who catches it. It is a little white pig with hedgehog type quills, and those that cross its path will find a silver coin in their pocket.

The Little Shoe

One day, Mr. Coote saw Molly walking along the side of the road. He saw she was not looking very happy on this day. Mr. Coote loved telling stories of the little folk and fairies that roamed the Isles. He had just the story for sweet little Molly to put a smile back on her cheeks.

He called her, and she stopped to greet him. He asked her why she was so blue and she shrugged; she was not too happy on this day. He asked Molly if she had ever heard of the Cluricaune. As he suspected, she had, as her father told her stories of these little people much like the Irish Leprechaun.

Mr. Coote asked Molly if she had ever seen one, to which she replied she had not. She asked Mr. Coote if he had seen one, but he had not either, though, his grandfather had way back when he was a much younger man. His grandfather had suspected there may be Cluricaune living in the barn, as he had heard scuffling and whistling late at night.

One night his grandfather had gone out to the barn to feed the old mare that was ailing. As he got to the door, he heard hammering like the sound a shoemaker makes. His grandfather was curious, and he slowly stepped into the barn. That is when he saw the little man hammering away at a tiny shoe while singing the sweetest song.

His grandfather looked all over the barn to see if he could find the little creature, and found him hidden in the mare's stable between some bales of hay. The little man was whistling and singing so loudly he did not hear Mr. Coote's grandfather sneaking up on him. Before the Cluricaune could react, his grandfather had captured him in his hand.

Mr. Coote's grandfather laughed in glee, as he had captured a Cluricaune. It is said that if you can get a Cluricaune's purse, you will have endless riches. But the Cluricaune was not about to give up his purse. Mr. Coote's grandfather would not set the little creature to go until the Cluricaunned told Mr. Coote's grandfather that he would need to get it back at his house. So like an old fool, his grandfather opened his hand, allowing the Cluricaunne to escape. He was so excited to be getting the little creature's purse that he did not realize it had tricked him.

The Cluricaunne had, however, left behind his little shoe he had been working on. So Mr. Coote's grandfather took the shoe, and that year his farm gave good crops and his cows had an abundance of milk. To the end of his days, Mr. Coote's grandfather was convinced it was because he had kept the little creature's shoe that such good luck had come to them.

Molly asked Mr. Coote if he had seen the shoe, but he said he had not. But his mother had. They had lost it long before Mr. Coote was born. But every night he still leaves a little of food and water out in his grandfather's old barn just in case the little man comes back.

Molly had loved the story and thanked Mr. Coote for the tale. As she skipped off home and neared the barn of their farmhouse, she heard hammering. Slowly Molly walked into the barn, but there was nothing there except a tiny little shoe. Molly smiled as she picked it up. It was beautiful. She thought about the story Mr. Coote had told her, then carefully put the shoe back.

As she went to get her dinner, Molly was no longer feeling blue.

Chapter 7: An Overview of Popular Celtic Fairy Tales

Not only did the Celtic nation have some of the greatest myths and legends, but they were also excellent storytellers. Each story would be one of either inspiration, encouragement, love, strength, forgiveness, or instead be a lesson or warning.

Some of their fairy tales would be entwined with one of their Gods/Goddesses, heroes/heroines, royalty, or beasts. Others would be of normal everyday people that things would happen to.

This chapter takes a look at some of the Celtic fairy stories from the Celtic nations.

Many of the fairy stories of today have been taken from the fairy stories of old Celtic tales. Here are a few popular Celtic fairy tales that you may find you have heard a different version of.

A lot of fairy stories as we know did originate for Celtic folklore such as:

- The Goose Girl
- Frau Holle
- Clever Hans
- The Girl Without Hands
- Goldilocks and the Three Bears
- The Frog King
- The Pied Piper

There are hundreds of old stories to choose from, below are some of the older Celtic fairy tales for you to enjoy. They have been written as the old story, but in a more modern-day English language.

Jack and His Comrade

Jack lived with his widowed mother, and they were very poor. They grew potatoes and would live from meal to meal, waiting on the potatoes to be fit for eating. One summer, however, the potatoes were very scarce. So Jack decided it was time for him to take charge and seek his fortune.

Jack told his mother that he was going to go out and do what he could to find his fortune. As soon as he found it, he would be back to share it with his poor mother. He asked her to bake him a cake and kill his hen. Jack's mother did as he asked and he set off at sunrise the next day.

Jack's mother walked him to the gate and at the gate, she asked him if he would take only half the chicken and half the cake, or take the whole lot and her curse. Jack looked at his mother and laughed that he would never want her curse. Happy with her son's answer, she gave Jack the full cake and all the chicken for his journey.

Jack walked and walked until he could walk no more, as fatigue caught up with him. He saw a farmer's house and thought to ask for a bed in the barn for the night. As he turned onto the road he found an ass that was stuck in the bog that ran alongside the road. The ass had tried to get to the sweet grass on the other side of the bog when he got stuck.

The ass called out to Jack to help him out of the bog or he would surely drown. Jack, always willing to help, found stones which he threw into the bog until the ass was able to climb out.

When the ass was safely on solid ground, he thanked Jack and promised to pay him back for his good deed one day. He then asked Jack where he was going. Jack told the ass (Neddy was his name) that he was on his way to find his fortune.

Neddy asked Jack if he could come along as he too may find some good fortune. Jack was happy for Neddy to come along on the journey, so they headed off to find shelter for the night. As they passed through a small village they saw a dog with a tin tied to his tail and a troop of gossoons (small boys) chasing it with sticks.

The dog saw Jack and Neddy and ran to them for protection. Neddy was mortified at the treatment of the poor dog so he let out the mightiest of roars, scaring the gossoons. As they ran off, the dog thanked Jack and Neddy then asked them where they were headed. Once again Jack told the dog they were going to find their fortune.

The dog asked if he could join Jack and Neddy as he too could do with a change of scene and be rid of the boys chasing him. The dog's name was Coely. The three of them set out to find shelter for the night and came upon an old wall. They sat down below it, Jack pulled out the provisions his mother had made him, and gladly shared it with his friends.

Neddy decided he would prefer the thistles he found on the side of the road while Coely shared with Jack.

While they ate and chatted, a half-starved cat came over to them, his meow was as pitiful as can be. Jack and his new companions felt sorry for the cat and Jack offered it some food.

The cat's name was Tom and he thanked Jack by blessing him with hopes that one day Jack's children never knew a hungry belly.

The cat asked where they were going, so Jack told Tom and asked if he would like to join them. Tom was delighted by their offer, and when their bellies were full and their feet rested the four of them set off. As they walked and the night shadows grew longer, they heard a great crackling coming from the bushes alongside the road.

As they neared the noise a fox jumped out of a ditch; in his mouth was a large black rooster. Neddy once again roared like thunder, scaring the fox. Jack sent Coely after it. The fox, Rynard was his name, dropped the rooster, and ran off into the night. The rooster was a bit battered and bruised, but he thanked Jack and his friends for saving him. The rooster then asked where they were all heading, so Jack told the rooster they were going to seek their fortune. Jack offered for the rooster to join them, which the rooster gladly accepted.

So they set off down the road again as the night grew later there was no farm or barn in sight. As it was summer night Jack decided they could go into the wood and make a camp there in the long grass. So off they went once again to make a camp in the woods.

Jack stretched out in the long grass, Neddy lay next to him, Coely on the other side, the rooster took a tree and Tom cuddled down in Neddy's lap. They had all drifted into a deep sleep when the rooster decided it was time to crow. Neddy got such a fright he yelled at the rooster for disturbing him from his sleep.

The rooster yelled back that it was daybreak and couldn't he see the sun starting to shine?

But it was not the sun, it was candle light that glowed in the distant dark. The five of them set off to go explore. They found a cabin and from inside they could hear the sound of merriment. Being very quiet, they tiptoed to the window to see inside. There was a band of thieves eating, drinking, and bragging about the theft of Lord Dunlavin's gold and silver. They toasted to the porter at the Lord's house that had helped them steal all the gold and silver.

Jack and his friends decided to scare off the robbers so they could return Lord Dunlavin's gold and silver to him. So Neddy put his hooves upon the windowsill, and Coely jumped onto Neddy's back. Tom climbed up on Coely's back, and the rooster on top of Tom's head.

They started to make a big noise of barking, hissing, and roarings, and Jack shouted at the window for the thieves to surrender as they had the house surrounded. The thieves were deeply frightened and ran off into the woods, leaving their weapons, food, and loot behind. Jack and his friends ran into the cabin, closed the shutters, locked the doors, and finished what was left of the robbers' feast.

Later that night the captain of the robbers decided to double back and go check back at the cabin, but when he got inside the cabin was dark. He quietly snuck towards the fire. When he got there the cat flew at him and landed in the captain's face, scratching at him with his sharp claws. The captain screamed and tried to make it to the door, but he stood on the dog's tail while doing so. As a result, the dog bit him on the arm and legs. Swearing, the captain ran for the door only to have the rooster drop down on his head clawing and pecking at him.

The captain dashed out of the cabin and headed straight for the woods, where he told the rest of his band of thieves how he had been brutally attacked. All the thieves decided it was best not to attempt to go back there.

When the morning came, Jack and his friends had a good hearty breakfast. They collected Lord Dunlavin's loot and set it on Neddy's back. The five friends then set off, headed for Lord Dunlavin's castle. When they arrived at Lord Dunlavin's court, they were greeted at the door by the thieving porter.

The porter asked them what they were doing there, to which Jack replied he had business with Lord Dunlavin. The Porter was shirty with him and told him the Lord did not have a place for the likes of them. But the rooster was not having this thief stop them from their quest, so he challenged the porter about the robbery, making the porter's cheeks go red. It was then that the Lord and his daughter made their presence known. They had been listening to the entire time at the window.

The porter tried to discredit the five friends saying he did not open the door to let the six thieves in. To which Jack replied, "How did you know there were six if you did not let them in the door?"

Jack handed the lord the bags of silver and gold they had brought back and asked for nothing more than a bed and food for the five of them. But the Lord was not having any of that. He told Jack and his friend that they would never be poor again, for what they had done was a truly noble deed.

So the rooster, dog, and the ass got a prime spot in the Lord's farmyard, while the cat got a nice warm kitchen. The Lord took Jack under his wing and decked him as any fine gentleman should be. Jack was made the Lord's steward.

Jack went and fetched his mother, settling her into a nice cozy house with everything she could need. Jack and his mother never wanted for anything ever again.

The Three Crowns

Once upon a time, there lived a king who had three daughters. While his youngest was as good as gold, his two eldest were bossy and quarrelsome. Three princes visited the king's castle, all brothers, and the king found that two of the brothers were just as troublesome as his eldest daughters. One of the brothers, however, was just as good and easy as his youngest daughter.

The king, his three daughters, and their suitors all went for a walk around the lake one day. There they met a beggar. The King would not give the beggar anything, neither would the eldest two of the princesses or princes. But the two youngest out of the brothers and sisters gave the beggar food and treated him with kindness.

As they walked further along the lake, they came across one of the most beautiful boats they had ever seen. The four eldest of the brothers and sisters all said they would take a sail in the boat. The two youngest of the siblings both said they would not like to take a sail in the boat. The youngest did not want to get onto the boat, for she feared that the boat was an enchanted one.

The youngest princess's father finally got her to get on the boat. The princesses climbed aboard first. But when the king and princes wanted to follow, a small man no bigger than seven inches tall sprang in front of them. The princes went for their swords, only to find they could not draw them. The tiny man laughed and told the men to say goodbye to their princesses for they would not be seeing them for a while.

As the little man started to sail away, he said to the youngest of the brothers, fear not, for you will see your princess again. The little man also told the youngest man that he and the youngest princess would live a very happy and loving life. The little man left the men with a final word: "Bad people if they were rolling stark naked in gold, would not be rich." With that, he bade the four men good-bye and sailed away with the princesses.

Although the princesses tried to speak they found that they could not; they had no voices. Once the boat was out of sight the princes and king could move again. They rushed after the ship, but it was gone. But there was a well from which hung a rope, the same rope that had tied the boat to the lake's edge.

When they pulled the rope up, there was a basket at the end of it. The eldest prince was the first to climb inside the basket to go find the princesses. After a day, he did not return. The second eldest prince went down the well to find the princesses. Then on the third day, the youngest prince went down the well while their men stood guard of it.

When he got out at the other end, there was a beautiful garden with a castle in the middle. The prince walked into the castle looking from room to room but could not find a single soul. Eventually, he came across the dining room where a feast was laid out. The prince was very hungry, but thought it was rude to eat other food without invitation. The prince made himself comfortable by the fire and waited.

It was not too long when the seven-inch man came into the room with the youngest princess. The prince and princess rushed to each other, and the man asked the prince why he had not eaten; the prince told him he thought it would be rude.

Seven-inches laughed and told him that his brothers had not felt that way. That is when he saw that his two brothers had been turned to marble statues. The man told the young prince that he would have to rescue the other two princesses from the giants they were imprisoned with.

The next day, the prince set about rescuing the other two princesses from the two giants. The man turned the older princes back to flesh and let them all leave together. But before they could go, the man gave each of the princesses a set of three crowns and told them that they had to wear them on their wedding. They had to all be married together, or ill fate would befall them.

The oldest brothers were not very happy with their youngest brother, and were plotting something against him. The youngest princess heard this, turned to her prince, gave him her crowns, and told him to put a stone in the basket if the eldest two made him go last. When the princesses were safely above, the two eldest brothers made the youngest wait to go last.

When the basket came down for the young prince he put a stone in it. As it was pulled to the top the rope was cut, and the basket with the boulder in it came crashing down. The prince was beside himself, but he had nothing more to do than go back to the seven-inch man's castle. There he was treated to the heartiest of meals and finest of wine, as well as given a comfortable bed. After a week had gone by, the young prince was lonely and missing his true love.

To appease him, the seven-inch man gave the young prince a beautiful snuff box. The snuff box would call the man if ever the prince needed him, as it was time for the prince to leave the castle. He pointed the young prince in the direction of walking, and as he did he felt so tired that he bowed his head and did not pay attention to where he walked.

It was not until he heard a hammering that he raised his head and realized he was no longer at the seven-inch man's castle. His attire was not that of prince's any longer, but of a commoner. He walked past a smith's shop, where the smith called to him and asked him if he was any good with a hammer. The young prince said that indeed he was, and went to work with the smith.

The prince and the smith were turning horseshoes when in walked the tailor with news of the royal wedding of the two older princesses. They were all finely dressed with their beautiful crowns upon their heads, but as the grooms walked down the aisle, the floorboard opened and down they fell. The king then decided to put off the wedding until the youngest had her crowns and her groom. The king offered the princess's hand to whoever could make the crowns. The king was also willing to put up the gold, silver, and copper to make the crowns with.

The young prince knew that he could get the crowns down, for he had them hidden beneath his tattered old clock. He sent the smith to go fetch the metal from the king, and promised that he would forge the crowns for him. The smith did as the young prince asked and brought him back the metal.

The prince told the smith to leave and then sealed up the forge tight. That night the villagers heard the hammering and cursing of the young man they thought to be the smith's apprentice. In the morning the young prince handed the smith the crowns. The smith told the young prince to come to the castle with him, but the young prince refused.

When the smith showed the king the crowns he was overjoyed, and offered the smith the young princess's hand in marriage. But the smith could not lie and he told the king it was not he who had made the crowns, but a young man he had taken in the previous day. The king asked his daughter if she would take that young man as her husband but she wanted to see the crowns first.

The young princess recognized her crowns instantly and knew they were from her true love. So the princess agreed to marry the young man who had sent the crowns to the castle. The king told the eldest prince to go and fetch the young man in the king's carriage. They then lived a full and happy life, always together.

Golden-tree and Silver-tree

Once upon a time, there was a great king with a beautiful wife whose name was Silver-tree. They had a daughter whose name was Golden-tree, and she was even more beautiful than her mother.

Silver-tree was a very vain person, as well as a jealous one. She wanted to be the fairest in all the land, so each year she would go down to the glen where there was well with a magic trout. In this one year she went down to the well, called upon the trout, and asked the fish if she was not the beautiful queen in all of the land.

The trout said she was beautiful Golden-tree was more beautiful than her. Enraged, the queen went home and lay down on her bed. She vowed she would not be well again until she had the heart of her daughter Golden-tree. The king was given word that the queen was ill; he went to see what was wrong. The queen told him that she needed the heart of Golden-tree if she would never be well again.

The king loved his wife dearly, but he loved his daughter too, so he sent his daughter away to be wed to a prince in a far off land. He told one of his huntsmen to find a goat, cut out its heart, and bring it to him. The huntsmen did as he was told, and the king presented the queen with the heart of the goat in the pretense that it was the heart of Golden-tree.

Meanwhile, Golden-tree and the prince were truly in love with each other and started their own happy life far away from her mother, the evil queen.

The following year, Silver-tree once again approached the trout in the magic well and asked if she was not the most beautiful queen there was. Once again, the trout told her that it was the Golden-tree that was the most beautiful queen.

The queen was now even more enraged, having found out that her daughter was still alive and she had been deceived.

The queen then commandeered her husband's boat and took off to the far off land, where her daughter was now wed to the prince. But Golden-tree had gotten word of her mother's arrival, and told her husband of her fears of her mother wanting to murder her.

The prince locked Golden-tree in a tower so her mother would not be able to get to her. Upon the queen's arrival, she called for her daughter but was told she was locked in a tower and could see the queen. The queen found her way to the tower and called her daughter to come and see her mother.

But Golden-tree said that she could not. The queen told Golden-tree to put her finger through the hold in the tower door so she may bestow her daughter with a kiss. Golden-tree thought no harm could come of this, so she did as her mother asked.

Triumphant, the queen pierced Golden-tree's finger with a poison dart, and Golden-tree fell dead to the floor. When the prince found his princess he was devastated, so he placed Golden-tree in a beautiful glass box in the tower. He locked the door and let no one near it.

Time passed, and one day one of the princess's companions made their way to the tower. There she found her princess laying so pale and lifeless. On closer inspection, the women found there was a poison dart in the princess's finger. The women pulled out the dart, and Golden-tree awoke.

The prince was overjoyed to see his beautiful wife alive and they one again resumed their happy life.

Another year had passed, and Silver-tree once again went to the well to ask the trout if she was the most beautiful queen of all. Once again, the trout responded that Golden-tree was still the most beautiful of all.

The queen was even more outraged than ever, finding out her plan to poison her daughter had failed. The queen set off for the far off land, and this time, she took a bottle of poison wine.

When she arrived, the princess and her companion approached the queen as she came off her ship. The queen feigned joy in seeing her daughter alive and offered her a drink of wine to celebrate. But the princess's companion told the queen that in their land it was custom for the guest to take the first sip.

The queen lifted the glass to her lips, but the companion pushed the glass as she put it to her mouth, and wine went down the queen's throat. The queen gasped as the poison flowed through her, and she dropped dead where she stood.

They buried the evil queen far from the kingdom and celebrated Golden-tree's freedom from her mother, the evil queen.

The Sprightly Tailor

The Laird MacDonald of castle Saddell employed a sprightly tailor to make him a pair of trews. As the tailor set about taking the Laird's measurements, they got to talking about the old ruined, haunted church. It was said that weird things happened in the ruined church by the light of the moon.

The Laird challenged the sprightly tailor to make the trews by night in the haunted church. If the tailor could make these garments there for the Laird, the tailor would be handsomely rewarded.

The tailor, wanting the reward and thinking himself to be a sprightly fellow, agreed to the challenge. That night he set off to go and make the Lairds trews in the ruined church. He found a gravestone upon which to sit and lit candles all around him so he could see to sew the trews.

The tailor was well into sewing the garments without incident, thinking to himself that the Laird was going to have to pay when he won the challenge, when the ground shook. The tailor kept his fingers busy sewing as he looked around for the source of the disruption. From a stone in the ruined church, he saw a great head rise.

The head asked the tailor if he saw him, to which the tailor replied that indeed he did but he had a garment to sew so he could not stop stitching. The head rose a bit higher out of the ground until its neck was visible and again it asked the tailor if he now saw his neck.

The tailor replied that he did, but he still needed to keep stitching as he had a garment to finish. This continued as each time the other part of the spirit's body would rise a bit higher from the ground. Each time it would ask the tailor if he saw, and each time the tailor responded that he did, but he had to keep sewing.

The tailor continued to sew until the giant of a creature pulled out his first leg and stamped on the ground. The tailor knew he would have to hurry with the garment, so he took to doing a long stitch. By the time the creature had extracted his last leg the tailor was finished with his stitching, and took off out of the churchyard the newly made trews under his arm.

The giant raced after the tailor, hollering for him to stop, but the tailor did not. The tailor ran until he came upon the safety of Saddell castle, and shut the giant out. Angry, the giant took a swing, leaving his fingerprints embedded in the wall. But the tailor had won his bet, and the Laird paid him handsomely for his trews.

Each time the Laird wore his trews, he had the greatest tale to tell about a brave tailor who spotted the creature that lived beneath the stones at the ruined church. The tailor had not only lived to tell the tale, but had sewn the finest trews–though if the Laird had looked closer, he would have seen the long stitch.

Chapter 8: Celtic Mythical Creatures and Beasts

In the ages of myths and legends, there were reportedly all sorts of fantastic creatures and beasts running around, from mermaids to fairies, leprechauns, dragons, and magical horses. These creatures were either fierce and frightening, or simply magical beings. This chapter delves into some of these Celtic mythical creatures.

Black Dog (Faerie Hound)

Dogs, especially black dogs, have been considered as the guardians of the gates of hell throughout Europe for centuries. The Cu Sidhe, which means faerie hound, in Celtic myths are either green or black large dogs with glowing red eyes. Some of them are as big as a small horse.

They do the bidding of their fairy master, whether it is to abduct a human woman to nurse a fairy baby or guide a soul through the gates to the underworld. They say that this large dog is silent and can sneak up on a person more silently than a cat. Sometimes they will howl three times as they appear, and the sound can echo over a far distance. When men heard this sound they would lock up their womenfolk in fear of them being taken to the faerie realm. The black dog is a prominent figure in Scottish and Irish Celtic myths.

Bugul Noz

The Bugul Noz is a type of faerie creature found in Bretton that is so ugly that some say if you see him you will die. The Bugul Noz is not at all an evil creature; he is a kind and gentle soul, only he is so ugly that he hates for people to see him. He will try and frighten people or creatures away so they will not look at him. He even tries to keep the creature safe in the woods late at night, as this is the time he goes out. In the dark of the night, no one can see how hideous he is.

Dearg Due

Dearg Due never started out as a bloodsucking vampire; she was just a young woman of incredible beauty who wanted nothing more than to settle down with the man she loved. However, her father was a cruel and selfish man who thought of nothing but wealth and owning large amounts of land.

The young woman's father refused to let her marry her true love, a humble father, and instead sold her for wealth and land to their clan's chieftain. The chieftain was as cruel as any man could be, and treated her like she was a possession that he alone could see. He locked her up so no other could see her or go near her.

The young woman was so unhappy that she withered away to nothing and died. Her husband had already married another by the time they had buried her. Her true love was the only one who bothered to visit her grave and each day asked for her miraculous return.

On the eve of the first anniversary of her death, the young woman clawed her way from her grave, rage burning through her breast. Her one purpose for coming back to life on the eve was to seek revenge on those that had mistreated her so.

The first she called upon was her cruel and selfish father. While he slept, she placed her lips on his and sucked out his life force. Her next victim was her even crueler husband, whom she found in the middle of a group of lustful women. The woman ran out screaming when they saw her. She captured her husband, and instead of sucking the life out of him, she drank every drop of his life's blood.

The blood energized her and gave her great power; she felt stronger, faster, and had become immortal. From that day forward on the eve of the anniversary of her death, she arose, luring men in with her incredible beauty and feasting on their blood.

Groac'h

The Groac'h are water faeries of Bretton. They are known to be quite ugly and old; some have even been reported to have long walrus teeth. They mainly come out at night and can change their form; in some tales, they lure men in and turn them into fish. They then serve the fish up for dinner.

They have also been known to overwhelm humans with the gifts of their desires, and have the human beholden to them for the rest of their lives as a result. They live wherever there is water and can be found beneath the sand on the beach, caverns, and beneath the sea. Some of the Groac'h can control the forces of nature.

Morgens

Morgens are water sprites from Bretton mythology. They are a lot like sirens, whereby they sit upon the rocks brushing their hair seductively to lure sailors to their doom. There are quite a few stories about Morgens; there are a few variations of this mermaid type water-sprite. Just off the coast of Brittany, there are legendary little mermaid type people who are said to be quite beautiful to look upon. They kidnap people and take them to their crystal dwelling beneath the sea to be married. These little people are known as "morganezed" for the females, and "morganed" for the males.

In one story there was a beautiful human girl that was kidnapped by an old ugly morganezed; he took her to his dwelling at the bottom of the sea to become his bride. But his handsome son found her, and the two of them fell in love. The young morganezed rescued the young woman from his father and spirited her away.

Morvarc'h

Morvarc'h is a magical seahorse that has been known to be able to walk or gallop on the waves. It is a horse that pops up in quite a few Bretton legends, including the story of the Ys. The horse is said to be large with a shiny black coat and flowing mane. It can breathe fire and is fiercely loyal to its master.

Yan-gant-y-tan

Yan-gant-y-tan is a troll-like figure that roams the night and makes a nuisance of himself. The only way to tell him apart from other trolls is by the five candles he holds in his one hand, spinning them around. If you want him to leave you alone, you need to appease him with gold. He also does not like to turn around too fast, as he does not like to have his five candles go out.

Faeries

Celtic myths and legends are filled to the brim with tales of faeries. There are many different types of faeries, and they come in all shapes and sizes. Although each Celtic nation may have different names for each type of faery, they all share a few commonalities. A lot of the myths and legends do not paint faeries as very nice, as we are taught to think of them as young children. Some types of faeries can be quite malevolent; for example, some love to snatch human children and leave changelings in their place.

Leprechaun

The little green man with his hat, shamrock, and pot of gold is synonymous with the Irish. They believe they are lucky, while others believe they are a small nuisance that loves to play pranks and steal ale. They also like to make shoes for some reason, and every coin gold they find they store in a pot and hide it at the end of a rainbow. If a person is lucky enough to catch one, they are said to grant you three wishes if you let them go. But just like a genie, you have to be careful what you wish for, as everything has a price.

The leprechaun myth goes back for centuries and originates from the word "luchorpan," which translates to "little body." Luchorpan were water spirits that bonded with garden faeries to produce the leprechaun that developed a healthy taste for alcohol and would raid cellars.

Pooka

The Pooka, also spelled Puca, is a shapeshifting creature that likes to take the form of either a dog, a horse, a goblin, a rabbit, or goat. The earlier accounts of the pooka were always that of a pitch-black horse with a very long flowing mane and tail. The Pooka is known to have either gold or red glowing eyes.

Pooka can communicate with any creature they come in contact with; they love to twist a story. Small dark pools and bottomless lakes that look black are often called Pooka pools.

There are many interesting and varied stories about the pooka, but none where the creature actually harms or has any intent on harming anyone. They do love to chat with humans and have been known at times to give good advice.

Loch Ness Monster

The Loch Ness monster, or Nessy as she is referred to in modern times, was first sighted around 560 AD. Nessy came up out of the water and snatched a servant from the water's edge. In the age of monsters and dragons, the rumors of the monster in Loch Ness spread far and wide. After the first sighting, other strange happenings and sightings around Loch Ness have occurred which all refer to the giant sea monster or kelpie in Loch Ness.

Dragon

As with faeries, much folklore, myths, and legends have to include the huge fire-breathing dragons that once plagued the lands of Europe. There were all sorts of dragons and they took on various shapes, such as the large flying dragon with a huge wingspan and scaly body resembling a lion. Then there are the serpent shape dragons with long twisting bodies that look a bit like a snake with legs walking on tippy toes. There are many different types of dragons in all shapes and forms, even colors like the red dragon of Wales.

Some breathe fire, others breathe ice, they have tails like thick sharp arrows points at the end. Their tails are also usually powerful and their hands have talons that extend from their fingertips. They usually all have wings.

The Wulver of Shetland

The Wulver is a legend from the Shetland Islands and is a lot like the myth of the werewolf. The Wulver stands up like a human, complete with arms and legs. But instead of fingers or toes, it has claws. Its body is covered in hair and its head is that of a wolf. It has never been a human and it has never been a complete wolf. The Wulver is also not a shapeshifter; he stays in the form all the time.

The Wulver lives all alone in a cave on the Shetland Island, and lives in peace with the inhabitants there. He does not attack humans as long as they do not attack him. He is also not vicious or fearful, but instead has a kind and generous heart.

He loves to fish, and most have spotted him fishing off the rocks or around rocky pools. If he does come near humans it is to help those that have lost their way or are in danger. He has even been said to leave fish on the windowsill of those that are poor and hungry.

Kelpies

Kelpies are shape-shifting spirits that like to haunt the rivers and lakes in Scotland. Their preferred form is that of a horse. They like to pose as a docile beautiful pony standing grazing beside the edge of a lake or river, but that is just to lure people to them as they are malevolent spirits. They particularly love children; some say the one reason they take the shape of a pony is that most children are drawn to horses.

The thing about a Kelpie when they appear as a horse is that they encourage a person to climb upon their back or touch them. But they have a sticky hide, and once a person touches it, they are stuck to the Kelpie that will run into the nearest body of water and eat them.

Kelpies have also been known to appear in human form, as beautiful young women. Like the mermaids, they try to lure young men in so they can drown them. Some Kelpies like to take the form of a hairy, bone-crushing ogre-type creature that will lie in wait beneath the surface of the water. When someone gets near, they jump out and grab hold of the person, crushing them to death.

Another power a Kelpie has is that of summoning storms and flooding rivers. It is said that if you hear a loud wailing that is coming from a water's edge, it is a Kelpie warning of an imminent storm. The only way to catch a Kelpie is in its horse form as its bridle is its weak spot, but a caught Kelpie is very dangerous and has the strength of ten men.

Changelings

Changelings were said to be human babies that were swapped out by faeries or demons. The human babies are either given to the devil or taken to the fairy realm, where they would be used to strengthen the fairies' stock.

Many a deformed infant or imbecilic child would be thought to be a changeling. The only way to get rid of a changeling was to beat it, pinch it, or put a red hot poker on it. It was believed that abusing the changeling would send it back to where it came from, and the human baby would then be returned.

Naturally, this myth was responsible for a lot of child abuse during the times of the changeling belief. It was believed in olden times that infants were the most susceptible to demonic possession and easier to abduct by the fairies or demons.

Banshee

The Banshee is another type of faery in Irish mythology and legends. The Irish call her "scream caoine," which translates to keening, and her wail is believed to be the call of death. Those that hear her are being warned that there will soon be a death in the family.

It is believed that there is a Banshee for each family, and that they can be killed or deterred by a weapon made of pure gold. But even if she is killed, it will not stop the death of the family member. Legend says that even those who have tried to leave the area or country were never rid of the Banshee, as she would follow wherever they went.

The Blue Men of Minch

Not far off the coast of the Isle of Lewis lives a race of sea creatures. They are both male and female creatures that are much like mermaids and mermen. Their skin is said to be like the skin of a dolphin, and their legs resemble the dolphin's tail. They will use whatever wiles they can to lure sailors to a watery grave.

They live in caves along the craggy coastline between the Shiant islands and Pabail Uarach peninsular. They are thought to be the ancestors of Pasiphaê and Minos, who was the king of Crete. They were thought to have fled to the Mediterranean sea with the destruction of Crete and made their home in the Scottish Hebrides.

Finfolk

The Orkney islands sit off the north coast of Scotland in the cold, unforgiving North Sea. The Finfolk are creatures that would live deep beneath the waves of the North Sea during the winter months. The area in the North Sea where they live is called Finfolkaheem, and it can be found in the sea's deepest darkest depth.

During the winter months, the Finfolk do not cause much threat to humans, but when the summer months come they swim ashore and make Hildaland their home. They are cunning, shape-shifting monsters that abduct humans to take them to live in Finfolkaheem. Once there, they start to lose their human selves and gradually become the same as the Finfolk.

They come ashore during the summer months to find humans to abduct to keep their race alive. Finfolk were how some people, in those days, would explain mysterious happenings. They could also explain or justify the disappearance of people, especially the disappearance of young women.

Chapter 9: Celtic Bards, Druids, Holidays, and Festivals

The Celts believed in magic, gods, and wizards, and Druids held a high status in the tribe. Bards were also held in high regard, as they were the people who sang the Celts' history, triumphs, tragedies, and more.

The Bards of the Ancient Celts

Bards were the poets, musicians, and singers of the Celtic era. They would regale their audiences with the music and songs of great heroes, royalty, beasts, and so on. Bards were regarded as storytellers, to praise whoever employed them, and commemorate certain dates or victories.

There were not many kings who did not have a bard in their court to take note of the king's lineage, his stories, and triumph. They also employed them to sing of these accomplishments at great feasts.

Bards did not just get up one day and think, "I have a harp, so I am going to be a bard." They needed to be trained, and some even had apprenticeships with other bards before they could become one themselves.

Bards needed to be able to add to their songs and create ones practically on the fly without writing anything down. They were the custodians of the Celtic myths, legends, and folklore.

Taliesin, Chief of the Bards

Taliesin was the chief of the Bards and served in many of the kings throughout Britain. In the Arthurian legends, Taliesin served in the courts of King Arthur. He was as beautiful as he was talented, and he had the gift of prophecy to add to his lure.

Taliesin's name means "radiant bow," and was a Bard of great renown that charmed with his wit as well as his talent.

Mongán

There are many tales about Mongán, a bard and the son of the sea god, Manannan Mac Lir. Mongán's mother was Caíntigern, the Queen of Dál nAraide which made her the wife of King Fiachna Mac Báetáin. The kingdom over which Mongán's mother reigned was not a very nice kingdom. It was no surprise that the kingdom ran into problems for which they needed Manannan's help. Manannan said he would help, but only if Fiachna let him lay with his wife Caíntigern. With that union, Caíntigern fell pregnant with Mongán.

Manannan raised Mongán, and when he was a boy Mongán told his father that he had had a vision of his own death. He told his father that he would be killed with a stone his mother had picked up when they had gone for a walk together.

Caíntigern heard about this and was mortified that the beautiful stone she had taken from the beach would kill him. Caíntigern tried to throw the stone into the sea but the next day the stone was back on the sand.

Mongán eventually became the leader of the Dál nAraide and a poet.

Aengus

Aengus was the God of love and poetry, as well as the chief Bard to the Tuatha De Danann. Dagda was his father, so he inherited a few gifts for the great man. One of them was Dagda's love of music and poetry.

Aengus was charming, crafty, and could inspire the masses with his poetry. Unlike most other bards, Aengus had power over the dead and could resurrect them. He resurrected those he wished to with his power, which was the breath of life.

He was a young and beautiful man that could also shapeshift. His powers allowed him to woo both the young and the old.

The Druids of the Ancient Celts

The Druids are from the ancient Celts and were of a learned class. They practiced as advisors, teachers, judges, and priests to the Celtic people. Most of what is known about these mysterious people was told by Julius Caesar, and later by Christin Monks. Some scholars believe that a lot of what was recounted about the Druids was speculation. For Julius Caesar, the Celts were his sworn enemies and for the Christians, they were Pagans and heathens.

The Druids knew of the art of healing through various herbs, which they would brew up or use as a poultice. They were also known as the wise men of the village, and drawings usually depict them as cloaked older men. They would have long white beards, wear cloaks, and carry a long crook-type staff.

They were always called upon to be the judge of a dispute or any other type of accusation. There were usually some sort of tests if the Druid was unsure. The Druids would also be the ones to decree the punishment for any crimes committed or to settle arguments.

The chieftains and kings would rely upon the Druids for prophecy and to advise them. They were also in charge of the sacrifices and worship of the Celtic Gods. Within the sector of the Druids was also a hierarchy. One Druid was appointed the chief of Druids and would remain so until his death, when another would be appointed to the position.

Druids were never expected to join in any battle, rather they would stay away from the fight and ensure the Gods were appeased. This privilege drew a lot of people to want to join the order of the Druids. It was an honor to be accepted by the order, whereupon the student would be taught many studies such as astronomy, philosophy, verse, and about various herbs, potions, and healing arts.

Many feared the Druids as they had incredible power, not just mythical but within the Celtic societies. They had the power to get between warring nations and stop or prevent war. Through the supposedly prophetic visions and gifts of being able to see well into the future, kings and chieftains would turn to them for advice on many matters, including invasions and war.

There is a lot of speculation about the Druids' sacrificial practices. According to Julius Caesar, he believed that the Druids had no problem sacrificing prisoners of war or their own men to ensure that they were victorious over the enemies.

A lot of the megaliths that are found around ancient Celtic ruins, or where it was thought there was a Celtic burial or scarce ground, have megaliths associated with the Druids. These megaliths, such as the likes at Stonehenge, seem to be strategically placed to align with the stars, sun, and moon.

The Different Classes of the Druids

Within the Druid's sector, they had different classes of Druids and these reflected their standing or learned experience. The Druids class was represented by the color of the robes they wore:

- The Arch-druid, or Chief-druid, wore gold robes. He was also usually the eldest and most experienced Druid.
- The Druid below the Arch-druid wore white, and they acted as priests, judges, and mentors.
- The Druids who performed sacrifices wore red robes.
- The Druids who were the artists, scribes, and translators wore blue robes.
- The Druids who were learning wore black or brown robes.

Legendary Celtic Druids

There are quite a few legendary Celtic Druids of ancient times. A lot of wizards were thought of as Druids, in Irish legends, there were even female Druids.

Bodhmall

Bodhmall is a female Druid who appears in Irish legends in the Fenian Cycle. She was one of the caretakers of the famous Fionn mac Cumhaill (Finn MacCool) when he was a child.

Bodhmall was also a fierce warrior, and was one of the women charged with raising Fionn when he was sent away after his father was killed.

Merlin

Merlin is usually depicted as a powerful sorcerer or wizard. Merlin is based on a poet who was deemed a madman named Myrddin Wyllt, or in English Myrddin the Wild. He has appeared as Merlin throughout many Celtic myths and legends, including Arthurian. Merlin is probably one of the best known Druids of all the Celtic Druids.

Amergin Glúingel

In the Irish Mythological Cycle, Amergin was the Chief Ollam of Ireland. Amergin was a poet, bard, and a judge for the Milesian people. During the Milesians' conquest of Ireland and the battle of the three kings, Amergin acted as an impartial judge, laying down the laws of engagement.

Mug Ruith

Mug Ruith was a very powerful Druid on the Island that could change his size. He could grow as big as a giant, and his breath had the power to call up a storm or turn men to stone. He drove a chariot that at night would be as bright as the sun and was pulled by a band of oxen. It was believed that he could fly by means of a contraption called the Roth rámach, or oared wheel in English.

Tlachtga

Tlachtga was a powerful Druidess and the daughter of Mug Ruith. She had long fiery red hair and went everywhere with her father, learning his magical secrets and forging her own path. She gave birth to triplets upon a hill that was named for her called the Hill of Tlachtga in Ireland County Meath. Her triplets were said to be from different fathers after she was raped by three men. These three men were the sons of Simon Magus the sorcerer.

The Celtic Holidays, Festivals, and Celebrations

The Druids were a well ordered sect and were concerned with nature. Trees were sacred to them and they followed many of nature's patterns as their way of life. Their season cycle ran in line with the lunar and solar cycles, which is why they had eight main holy days of worship.

Samhain

Samhain was the ancient Celtic equivalent of the current New Year's Day. It fell on the 31st of October each year. It was a day for many celebrations because it was the day that the last of the harvesting would be done. It was also the day when the veil between the living and dead was said to be at its thinnest. This meant that the living and dead would be in close proximity to each other.

Yule

Yule was the celebration of the winter solstice. It was the night that the Druids would sit on sacred mounds for the entire night so they would be reborn again with the first rays on the sun.

Holly was associated with the long cold winter months, where people would hang it in their houses. It was a sign of hope and encouragement to push through the long dark days into the bright light of the summer.

Holly and mistletoe were sacred to the Druids, who were said to cut the trees six days before the winter solstice with a golden sickle. These two plants are still to this day a symbol of Christmas and winter in the Northern hemisphere.

Yule fell on the 21st of December, which was the longest night but the shortest day. For the Celts, winters were harsh and they did not have the luxury of central heating or goose down duvets. They tried to survive the long bitter winters as best they could.

Yule marked the return of the sun to a frozen land so they would rejoice by gathering and having large bonfires.

The wine and ale flowed freely, while some of the livestock that had survived would be slaughtered, gathered, and rotated on large spits to feed the masses.

Imbolc

Imbolc is the holiday that marks the halfway point between winter and the coming spring. The celebration starts on the 1st of February and lasts until sundown on the 2 February. It usually follows the start of the animal breeding season, and is why the Celts celebrate the fertility Goddess Brigid on this day. It was a time of hope and the promise of the warmer spring days to come.

The celebration would be held by the Celts lighting a huge effigy of the Goddess which was made from bundles of rushes and oats. The Celts would have a huge celebration in the honor of the Goddess, and light various lamps and bonfires. By the end of the celebration, offerings of fruits, vegetables, and oats would be left.

Ostra

Ostra was the spring equinox and was celebrated on the day that the night and day are of equal length. This usually happens on or around the 20th of March and celebrates the Goddess Ostara. Ostra is a Goddess of fertility, and she's where the name "Easter" comes from. This was another day of celebrations where wine and ale would flow freely. Bonfires would be lit and feasts would be spread for all to enjoy.

Beltane

Beltane was the start of summer celebrations for the Celtic people. Beltane welcomed the change of seasons. The Celts did this with bonfires, feasts, and merriment to enjoy the warm bright weather of the season. This celebration usually took place on the 30th of April or 1 May.

Litha

There is a legend that during the winter and summer equinox the Holly King and the Oak go to war. At the time of the winter equinox, the Holly King wins and rules the dark cold days of the winter. During the summer equinox, the Oak King wins and rules the bright warm days of summer.

Litha is the summer solstice holiday and the day when the Celts would celebrate the Oak King's victory over the Holly King. It is also the longest day and shortest night that was celebrated on the 21 st of June.

Lughnasa

Lughnasa celebrated the first harvest of the year and took place in the autumn months on the 2nd of August. This day and holiday were associated with the God Lugh, to whom the Celtic people would offer the first pickings of their harvest in tribute.

Mabon

Mabon was the holiday that celebrated the autumn equinox and harvest moon. It was celebrated during the time in autumn when once again there was an equal time during the day and night. It was a celebration of balance, abundance, and sharing that took place on the 21 September.

Conclusion

Mythology can and has been depicted in many ways through the ages. All the interpretations we have today are from scripts or tales handed down from generations past. A lot of the scripts have been written in ancient languages that are also open for misinterpretation by the translator. Even the stories handed down from generation to generation would have been added to or told differently to what was told. Most everyone at some point in their life comes across the old game of broken telephone or Chinese whispers; the story whispered at the start of the telephone chain never comes out the same at the end of it. Handing down mythologies and legends is the same.

In our modern-day world, we are lucky enough to have scholars and advanced technology to help them dig a bit deeper into what we know as historical truths. It is thanks to these scholars, as well as the Celtic people keeping their heritage alive, that we get to become a part of their world. To have a better understanding of who we are, it is essential to know where we came from and the cultures that were our past. Learning about Celtic mythology, the folklore, fairy tales, druids, royalty, gods/goddesses, and all they entail keep these cultures alive for future generations.

In this book, we covered all the basic gods/goddesses, great legendary kings, and both fair and evil queens. We looked at some of the more popular fairy stories of the Celts and celebrated their most well-known heroes and heroines. You were introduced to bards and some of the most powerful druids, and learned about the Celtic culture, their mythical beasts, magic, festivals, and sacrifices. There is a lot more to Celtic mythology than presented here, as there is only so much a writer can squash into one book. But hopefully, this one book has inspired you to want to delve deeper into the adventure that is Celtic mythology. Even great writers like Shakespeare were inspired by the rich folklore of the Celts.

Many great books have been translated from the older texts that you can read and a host of information in various libraries on the subject. Of course, one of the best ways to find out more would be to take a trip to some of the heritage sites attributed to these myths and legends. These places always have vast treasure troves of information about their respective legends. It is when you visit these places that you realized just how diverse Celtic mythology truly is. The six nations that still hold a tribute to their Celtic heritages are Scotland, Ireland, Wales, Cornwall (Conaulles), the Isle of Man (Manx), and Brittany (North West Gual) in France. There are also parts of Galicia in Spain that still maintain parts of their Celtic heritage along with quite a few Celtic heritage sites.

Some good books having to do with Celtic mythology, folklore, and legends are:

- *Cath Maige Tuired*
- *The Cattle-raid of Cualnge (Tain Bo Cuailnge)*
- *Heroic Romances of Irelands (there are two volumes)*
- *Of Gods and Fighting Men*
- *The Books of the Takings of Ireland*
- *Cuchulain of Muirthemne*
- *VIII: The Battle of the Trees*
- *The Lament of the Old Woman of Bear*
- *Beira, Queen of Winter*
- *Part II Book IV: The Hunt of the Slieve Cuilinn*
- *Fairy and Folk Tales of the Irish Peasantry*
- *Fairy Legends and Traditions of the South of Ireland*

- *Pagan Celtic Britain: Studies in Iconography and Tradition*

We live in a world that through modern-day advances a lot of what most myths and legends were built on can be explained. However, there is still a lot that cannot be explained by science or technology. Even though the four corners of our world have been discovered, there are still many layers of it that have not. Strange and wondrous things are being discovered every day that makes us stop and go "Oh wow!" Maybe one day the things that were unexplained to us will go down as future generations' myths and legends.

I hope you enjoyed this journey through the romance, lure, battles, and wonders of all that is Celtic mythology as much as I enjoyed writing it for you. You should now have your own piece of the Celts' mysterious, ancient past to regale others with such as the bards once did. Unlike the bards, however, we have the power of the internet to help us spread their wonderfully creative and magical tales. Through books like this one and the interest of all its wonderful readers, these myths and legends will stay alive well into the future.

References

Ankou. (n.d.). Wikipedia. https://en.wikipedia.org/wiki/Ankou

Ashliman, D. (2013). *Tristan and Isolde.* Pitt.edu. https://www.pitt.edu/~dash/tristan.html

Blue Men of Minch. (n.d.). Britain Explorer. https://britainexplorer.com/listing/blue-men-of-minch/

Breton Myths & Legends. (n.d.). Gites and More. http://www.gitesandmore.co.uk/Legends%20of%20%2 0Brittany.htm

Brittany. (n.d.). Britannica. https://www.britannica.com/place/Brittany-region-France

Bugul Noz. (n.d.). Wikipedia. https://en.wikipedia.org/wiki/Bugul_Noz

Celtic Mythology. (n.d.). Myths and Legends. http://www.mythencyclopedia.com/Ca-Cr/Celtic-Mythology.html

Changeling. (n.d.). Britannica. https://www.britannica.com/art/changeling-folklore

Classic Authors Writing About the Ancient Celts. (n.d.). People. https://people.stfx.ca/mlinklet/ClassicalAuthors.htm

Danu (Irish Goddess). (n.d.). Wikipedia. https://en.wikipedia.org/wiki/Danu_(Irish_goddess)

Fairy Bridge. (n.d.). Transceltic. https://www.transceltic.com/isle-of-man/fairy-bridge

Jacobs, J. (n.d.). *Jack and His Comrades.* Fairytalez. https://fairytalez.com/jack-comrades/

Johnson, B. (n.d.). The Kelpie. Historic UK. https://www.historic-uk.com/CultureUK/The-Kelpie/

Lady of The Lake. (2019, September 2). Encyclopedia.com. https://www.encyclopedia.com/literature-and-arts/literature-english/english-literature-1499/lady-lake

Lavandière de Nuit. (n.d.). A Book of Creatures. https://abookofcreatures.com/2015/04/17/lavandiere-de-nuit/

Lloyd, E. (2016, November 28). *Mythical Submerged City Of Ys – Europe's Own Sodom And Gomorrah.* Ancient Pages. http://www.anciehttpsntpages.com/2016/11/28/mythical-submerged-city-of-ys-europes-own-sodom-and-gomorrah/

MacQueen, D. (2018, March 24). *Finfolk, the sinister creatures of the deep and the hidden islands of Orkney.* Transceltic. https://www.transceltic.com/scottish/finfolk-sinister-creatures-of-deep-and-hidden-islands-of-orkney

MacQueen, D. (2018, April 20). *Wulver: Shetland's kind and generous werewolf.* Transceltic. https://www.transceltic.com/scottish/wulver-shetlands-kind-and-generous-werewolf

Merlin. (n.d.). Fandom. https://questforcamelot.fandom.com/wiki/Merlin

O'Regan, A. (2018, October 02). *The Dearg Due - How a revengeful young lover became Ireland's most famous female vampire.* https://www.irishcentral.com/culture/entertainment/dearg-dur

Owen, J. (2009, March 20). *Druids Committed Human Sacrifice, Cannibalism?.* National Geographic. https://www.nationalgeographic.com/news/2009/3/druids-sacrifice-cannibalism/#:~:text=Recent%20evidence%20that%20Druids%20possibly,of%20Druidic%20savagery%2C%20archaeologists%20say.

The Black Dog. Also known as Cu Sidhe or Coinn Iotair. (2011, June 14). Mayo Folk Tales. https://amayodruid.blogspot.com/2011/06/black-dog-also-known-as-cu-sidhe-or.html

The Three Crowns. (n.d.). Fairytalez. https://fairytalez.com/the-three-crowns/

Who Were Celts? (2019, October 24). History.com. https://www.history.com/topics/ancient-history/celts

Wright, G. (n.d.). *Celtic Gods.* Mythopedia. https://mythopedia.com/celtic-mythology/gods/

Norse Mythology:

Explore the Timeless Tales of Norse Folklore, the Myths, History, Sagas & Legends of the Gods, Immortals, Magical Creatures, Vikings & More

Table of Contents

Introduction

The first world that came into existence, before the beginning of time, was Muspelheim, a realm of fire, flames, and heat. To the north lay the realm of ice and frost, Niflheim, and separating the two contrasting lands was Ginnungagap, the world of chaos, a great abyss of void and nothingness. But, as Ginnungagap met both the world of ice and the land of flames, it linked the two. The venomous waters of Niflheim flew into the void, stuck in a perpetual cycle of freezing and thawing caused by the hot winds that blew into the vast nothingness from Muspelheim. The water drops that came from the union of the two natural elements, ice, and fire, built up and took the form of the frost giant Ymir, the first of his kind and the earliest form of life in Nordic mythology.

The birth of Ymir marks the beginning of the mythical world of the Nordic people, and it paves the way for all the myths and legends that are to come; stories of the clever and driven Odin, of the courageous Thor and devious Loki, characters that we are all more or less accustomed to. Lately, the fascination with the Vikings, their beliefs, and their way of life is at its peak. We see mythological Norse heroes and gods in popular movies, we have TV shows starring fearless Vikings and their historical conquests, and we have comics and video games that allow us to follow along with the adventures and legends of the old Nords.

And yet, all these mediums take artistic liberties, and at the end of the day, we are left striving for more. We want to get to know the people behind the fantastic stories. We want to understand where these legends are coming from and what they meant for the Nordic civilization. This desire to learn more and understand the culture that created the gods and heroes we love, and to discover characters, creatures, and legends that didn't get the "media treatment" they deserved, needs an outlet. I hope that this book can become yours.

I am Sofia Visconti, a mythology expert, and an Amazon bestselling author. I can wholeheartedly say that the success of my books comes solely from my passion for the subject. I'm an absolute mythology freak, and there's nothing I love more than introducing people to the wonderful world of gods, legends, and breathtaking creatures. What makes mythology so fascinating is not the stories in themselves, although some are truly a feast to the eyes, but how they came to be and what they mean for the people that live by them. Mythology is nothing more than a creative expression of a culture. It embodies the beliefs, way of life, and values of a civilization, representing its identity. That is why each mythology is unique, and it can't exist apart from its culture. This also applies to Norse mythology. To understand it on a deeper level and connect with it, we must first get to know the Nords and how they saw the world they lived in. I can't wait to go on this adventure with you and show you the great and exciting world of the Vikings!

By the end of this book, you will be more familiarized with the gods and legends of Norse mythology, as well as the people who created them. You'll know who the Norse were, how they lived their lives, their beliefs, their faith as a civilization, and how they influenced the modern world. And, of course, you'll know more about your favorite gods, such as how Odin became the ruler of the Aesir gods, how Thor got his famous hammer Mjolnir, and who Loki's children are. I hope that the magical creatures of the Norse world and the peculiar characters of the Nordic tales will conquer your heart as it did mine!

Now before we start, if you're a beginner into the endeavors of mythology, there is something you should keep in mind: expect the unexpected and don't be discouraged when things appear to not make sense. I admit that most stories tend to be quite weird or have mystifying elements. Take that as part of the old' mythology charm and don't dwell too much on the unexplainable. I will do my best to analyze the myths and explain their origins and meanings, but not everything has scientific answers, and that's ok.

Another thing to keep in mind is that Nordic gods and heroes are not perfect beings. They have human characteristics, making them charmingly flawed. They get angry, make mistakes, act on the spur of the moment, and can be very cruel at times. However, that is what makes the Norse gods so appealing. We can relate to them and connect with them on a deeper level. They don't represent untouchable standards. That's why the Norse people were so close with their gods and saw them as role models as well as fearful forces subjected to whims and tempers.

With everything out of the way, let's imagine ourselves following into the steps of the great Odin. He sought knowledge, and in order to get it, he was willing to sacrifice anything. And so he did, by handing himself from Yggdrasill, the tree of life, to get the runes of knowledge, and by giving up one of his eyes to drink from the Well of Knowledge. Odin's hunger for wisdom is evident in many of the stories that involve him, and I invite you to share his willingness to let go of your reality and jump into the mysterious world of the old Norse.

Let's drink from the Well of Knowledge and jump into a realm of wonder, where nothing is as it seems!

Chapter 1: A Brief History of the Norseman

The Norse people, commonly known as Vikings, were seafaring warlords and warriors from the pagan Scandinavia. They had such a great impact on Europe's history that the time in which they raided, colonized, and conquered European soils, from around the ninth to the 11th century, was named after them: "the Viking Age." When we hear the word "Vikings" we can't help but imagine an army of barbarians who bowed to no gods and who only took pleasure in plundering and raiding. Honestly, we are not to blame for having this mental image. That's just how Vikings are usually portrayed, and the concept is stuck somewhere deep in our subconscious mind. But is this image close to the historical truth? Let's see!

The Origins of Vikings

Vikings came from Sweden, Norway, and Denmark, many hundreds of years before they were recognized as stand-alone countries, and they were mostly land-owning farmers and fishermen. They lived in villages ruled by chieftains or clan leaders, and they had few towns. Chieftains often fought for dominance over the lands, and with a seemingly inexhaustible arsenal of strong men who sought adventure, it was fairly easy for skillful leaders to organize armies and fearful bands. Historians are unsure what prompted Vikings to leave their lands and become seafaring pillagers, but they do propose a couple of theories.

The political instability caused by the frequent clashes between clans makes a good motive for branching out. Another would be localized overpopulation, which led to families owning smaller and smaller lands that could no longer provide sustenance for all the family members. Additionally, around the seventh and eighth centuries, the Vikings refined the way they constructed ships and vessels, adding sails and modifying their structures to sustain longer voyages. These longships were swift and shallow, allowing them to go across the North Sea and land on the beaches of unsuspecting lands. If we consider shipping advances, the troubled socio-economic situation of the Vikings at the time, the adventurous nature of these warrior-spirited people, and the tales of riches brought along by merchants, it's not hard to understand why one day they decided to raid the coasts of Europe.

The Start of the Viking Era

The first historical account of a Viking classical hit-and-run raid dates back to the year 793, when a monastery in Lindisfarne, England was plundered of its sacred, golden religious artifacts. Though, as a side note here, it is unlikely that this was the first time the Vikings attacked England. Evidence shows that English coastal villages had started to organize defenses against sea attacks earlier in the eighth century, suggesting that there were Viking raids or at least attempts before the attack on the Lindisfarne monastery. Many medieval English documents refer to them as "seagoing pagans" for their tendency to target holy places, which, to be fair, were full of unarmed men and gold, so who can blame the Vikings for taking the opportunity? The term "Viking," which is derived from the old Scandinavian word *vikingir* (pirate) or from the word *vik*, which means "bay," was popularized closer to the end of the historical Viking Age. Terms such as *Dani* (inhabitants of present Denmark), *Normani* (Northmen), and simply *pagani* (pagans) were more generally used when referring to the Scandinavian warriors by the European people who were unlucky enough to face their wrath.

From the year 793 forwards, Viking bands consisting of freemen, retainers, and young, adventure-seeking men led by chieftains had gone on to further attack England and its surroundings, especially Scotland, Ireland, and France. Additionally, some accounts from the latter years of the Viking Era speak of Viking attacks or sightings in the Iberian Peninsula, Ukraine, Russia, and even the Byzantine Empire. Originally, the raids were pretty small-scale. There were only a handful of ships, and the Vikings would happily return home when they collected enough booty or if they encountered a resilient defense. But from the 850s, the Vikings began to double down on the force and organization of their raids, establishing bases in the newly conquered lands and starting to dominate the surrounding island areas.

Viking Raids in England and Scotland

In 865, England was struck by the *micel here* (the great army) of Ivar the Boneless and Haldfan, a pair of brothers and the sons of Ragnar Lothbrok - a renowned Viking warrior. They attacked the Anglo-Saxon kingdoms one-by-one, capturing the ancient kingdoms of Northumbria, Eastern Anglia, and most of the kingdom of Mercia. By the year 878, only Wessex, a southern kingdom led by the inexperienced King Alfred, was standing. In January of that year, the Viking forces led by Guthrum attacked Alfred by surprise at his royal estate in Chippenham. The king of Wessex barely made it out alive, but he managed to gather an army and defeat Guthrum at Edington.

Despite Alfred's victory, most of England was controlled by Vikings. They held the north and the Midlands, and for the next 80 years, the territory remained divided between Alfred's successors and Viking kings. Eirik Bloodaxe, the last Viking ruler of England, was killed by Eadred, King Alfred's grandson, in 954, putting an end to the Viking control and uniting England. Other Viking attempts at reconquering England were only briefly successful, with England being for a while part of the empire of Canute, another Scandinavian king. In 1042, England's Viking Era ended, with the restoration of its native ruler, William I. Although no longer under Viking control, the seafaring warriors left deep marks on the area, influencing the social structure, dialects, and customs of England. Fun fact, William's great-great-great-grandfather was Rollo, a Viking. So, the Viking influence over England goes deeper than we might imagine.

Scotland was struck in 794, and the Vikings took control of the Hebrides, Shetlands, and the Orkneys. Their hold on Scotland was long-lasting, and they remained in control of Orkneys well into the 11th century.

Western Dominance

In the west, the Viking expansion was ruthless. They invaded Iceland, Greenland, and they even attempted to settle in North America (which they called *Vinland*, a name that roughly translates to "the land of wild grapes"). The Norse saga "*Eirik the Red's Saga*" credits Leif, son of Eirik the Red, as the accidental discoverer of North America, while "*The Saga of the Greenlanders*" claims that Bjarni Herjolfsson, a Viking explorer, was the first to lay eyes on Vinland. Although we can't know for sure who the Scandinavian Columbus was, we do know that Vikings made it to North America, thanks to the discovery of the L'Anse aux Meadows archeological site. The archeological remains of ancient houses were found in the 1960s by Helge Instad, a Norwegian explorer, and his wife Anne Stine, an archeologist. Although the site is unlikely to have housed the main Vinland colony, it still confirms the epic Viking sagas.

Viking raids in Ireland began around the year 795, and, despite valiant resistance from the natives, the Vikings managed to establish kingdoms and fortified ports. Waterford, Limerick, and Dublin were under Scandinavian control, and in 1014 there was a failed attempt to unify Ireland under the Scandinavian rule. Even so, the Vikings remained dominant even early into the 12th century, when the English invasion started.

Viking Attacks on France and the End of the Viking Age

Viking raids on France started a bit later, in 799, and the Scandinavian powers benefited a lot from the political turmoils of the Frankish kingdom. Their powers grew exponentially, and in 885, they almost conquered Paris. However, the Carolingian empire was too great of a foe for a nation of raiders and pillagers, no matter how skilled they were. Thus, the Scandinavian power never reached its peaks in France, at least not on the scale it did in England, Ireland, and Scotland. As the Viking Era went on, there were numerous raids, but none of them led to permanent victories. The greatest manifestation of Scandinavian influence in France remains a couple of small settlements established on the Seine River in the tenth century.

Eastern Europe was a different affair for the Vikings. There were raids, but nothing too violent, and no Scandinavian kingdom was established through armed forces. Nonetheless, Vikings made it into the heart of Russia, where they were subsequently "absorbed" into the native Slavonic population, calling themselves "the Rus" (Russians).

At the end of the 11th century, the raids began to stop and Viking leaders became a thing of the past. Norway, Sweden, and Denmark became united kingdoms. The first two were done with adventures, while the latter, Denmark, became somewhat of a force to be reckoned with and managed to amass its unruly, young, adventurous men into their royal military. The last historical Viking leader who adhered to the old tradition was Olaf II Haraldson, who lost his "title" in 1015 when he was crowned king of Norway.

The Other Side of Viking History

The writers and chronicles of the Viking Era had no qualms when it came to demonizing and denigrating the Scandinavian people who ravaged their land. Clerics, such as Alcuin of York, were especially dramatic in their account of Viking raids on monasteries and places of worship, describing the carnage in minute detail and painting the assailants as demonic beasts rather than people. No matter the artistic liberties that were taken by Anglo-Saxon clerics, we can't deny that Vikings carried out violent and destructive attacks. But reducing the Vikings only to their warrior ventures is a grave mistake.

These Scandinavian men were indeed great fighters and military tacticians, but they were also merchants, explorers, artists, storytellers, and poets. They came from a rich and complex culture that they shared and left behind in the numerous lands they conquered or settled in. The Vikings' maritime voyages seem to have always been driven by two factors. One is the raiding and the plundering, and the other the sheer sense of adventure and desire to discover new places. This led them to venture into the Faroes, around the eight century, which they used as a *longphort* (a fortified port) to advance across the Atlantic.

In 872, Viking colonists led by Ingolf Arnarson settled on Iceland, where they established a unique, independent society. This Icelandic settlement went on to become a republic, ruled by the Althing, an assembly of chieftains that is considered to be one of the earliest parliaments. From this Scandinavian settlement, we also have some of the earliest Viking-written history pieces, the *Islendingabok* - the history of Iceland and the *Landnamabok* - an account of the first Icelandic Viking settlers and the land lots they took as their own. Besides these historical pieces, the Vikings who colonized Iceland also kept a written account of the tumultuous relationship they had with Iceland's natives. In the *Islendingasogur* (The Icelandic Family Sagas), the Vikings speak of the feuds, betrayals, allegiances, and conflicts that marked their first 150 years of settling in Iceland. The tales from the *Islendingasogur* are today considered to be some of the most important pieces of European literature from the Middle Ages, and they show the Vikings' proficiency in composing prose of great power.

Iceland also served as a platform for further exploration. In 982, Eirik the Red, a chieftain with a fiery temperament was exiled from the Icelandic colony for his involvement in a murder case. Unphased by this development (perhaps due to his history of being an exile from Norway for another murder-related affair), Eirik decided to take to the sea, and he sailed west in search of a rumored land. A 300-kilometers voyage brought Eirik's longship to Greenland, a lush land that exceeded his wildest expectations. With this discovery on hand, Eirik the Red returned to Iceland, filled 25 longships with colonists, and established his own settlement in Greenland, one that would survive well into the 15th century. Eirik's son, Leif, a name you are probably familiar with by now, outdid his father as an explorer, sailing further west and discovering Vinland, but as a colonist, he wasn't as prolific as Eirik. Leif tried to replicate his father's strategy, however, the hostility from the Native Americans was too much for the small number of Viking settlers to handle, and Vinland was subsequently abandoned.

Regardless of his success at colonizing America, Leif Eirikson has garnered the reputation of a great discoverer and explorer, and for a Viking, few things mattered more than one's reputation. Sure, attributes such as bravery and intelligence were sought after in a Viking warrior, but leaving a legacy behind and being remembered was the icing on the cake. An aphorism from the *Havamal*, a collection of Viking sayings, goes something like *"Everything dies, we, our cattle, our families, but one thing that never dies is a dead man's reputation."* The language used in the *Havamal* is a bit more sardonic, but I tried to give it a modern twist to better reflect the idea.

And this concludes our brief look into the Viking's history. Now you have a timeline for the Viking Age, and you have a better picture of who they were, where they came from, and the many places they settled in or conquered. Before we move on to take a more in-depth look at the Viking way of life and what it entailed, I thought it would be a great idea to say a few words about some famous Vikings who, just as Leif, managed to leave their mark on history and garner a reputation that would last throughout the ages.

Famous Vikings and Heroes

Ivar the Boneless is part legend and part historical character. You might remember that he and his brother Haldfan were the leaders of the great army that took Northumbria and Eastern Anglia by storm. Ivar also led attacks in Ireland and he is considered a founding father of the Viking rule in the kingdom of Dublin. Not much is recorded about him after the year 870, but it is presumed that he led attacks and ruled in the Islands of Man, Ireland, and other places around the Irish seas.

In Viking sagas, Ivar is the son of Ragnar Lothbroke, and his attack on Northumbria is an act of revenge against its king for killing his father. As for his peculiar nickname, its clear origin is unknown. Some historians believe that it stems from his fighting style and flexibility, which gave the illusion of him being "boneless," while others think it's a sly remark regarding his masculinity (alluding to him being impotent). An Irish annal notes the year 873 as the date of his death.

Sigurd is a legendary Norse hero who appears in many stories. Although different sources propose variations regarding his character and fate, he is usually portrayed as being strong, courageous, and successful in his endeavors. In earlier accounts, Sigurd is described as being of noble lineage, which might hint at a potential historical origin and his connection with an old Scandinavian ruler. In the *Prose Edda,* we find one of Sigurd's most famous legends - the slaying of the great dragon Fafnir. The saga speaks of how Sigur stabbed the beast and tasted its blood, gaining the ability to understand the language of the birds. This allows him to find out Reginn's plan to murder him to acquire the dragon's treasure. Thus, Sigurd kills Reginn and keeps the gold for himself. He then marries the daughter of a king and helps his brother-in-law, Gunnar, ask for the valkyrie Bruhild's hand in marriage. But in doing so, he tricks the valkyrie by taking Gunnar's form to complete Brunhild's challenges. This whole plot ends up leading to Sigurd's demise when Brunhild takes her revenge for being tricked. In a different version, Gunnar kills Sigurd when he believes that the hero had slept with Brunhild.

In many stories of Sigurd's life, Brunhild is the one that inevitably gets him killed, in one way or another. But other legends see the courageous hero becoming a king of the Franks or learning the magic of the runes from the valkyrie Sigrdrifa (which is another one of Brunhild's names). Due to all the variations, we can say that Sigurd's tale is open-ended, leaving space for interpretations and choosing which version better suits our preferences.

Eirik Bloodaxe is often portrayed as the stereotypical Viking fighter, with an overly Viking nickname. His accomplishments include being the king of Northumbria as well as the king of Norway. However, this last honor came to him in a rather dishonorable way. To become first in the line of succession he and his wife, Gunnhild, killed five of his brothers, earning Eirik his nickname "Bloodaxe" as well as the ire of his people. When Hakon the Good, another brother of his, rose to fight him for the throne, Eirik received no support whatsoever from the Norway people, and he chose to flee for his life. Not a very Viking-like action for him. Rumors at the time praised Eirik for his abilities as a fighter but condemned him for being dominated and too easily influenced by Gunnhild. So, despite his accomplishments, Eirik is not very close to the classical Viking hero.

Cnut the Great definitely beats Eirik when it comes to his Viking reputation. He was the son of a Danish king, Svein

Forkbeard, who had managed to conquer England in 1013. But Svein's luck was tough, and he died shortly after asserting his claim over the lands. His oldest son, Harald, inherited the Danish throne, and poor Cnut received the mission to reinstate Viking control over England, which was already back in Anglo-Saxon hands. The young man rose to the challenge, and in 1016, he conquered England and married the last king's widow to cement his position. In the years to follow, Cnut also became king of Denmark (apparently through peaceful means) and the king of Norway (which he conquered in 1028). Thus, Cnut became the ruler of the largest North Sea empire of the Middle Ages.

Although Cnut would use the good old' Viking tactic of warfare to keep England in check, he was arguably a good ruler. Under him, the towns became important administrative and economic centers. Denmark flourished with material wealth and an influx of innovative ideas. Cnut also developed a coinage system, firmly established the Christian Church, and is known for going to Rome on a peaceful pilgrimage to meet the Pope in person. From this point of view, Cnut can be seen as closer to an Anglo-Saxon king than a Viking ruler and conqueror. Ironically, Cnut's ability to adapt to different circumstances and cultures makes him, to some degree, the ultimate Viking, for this flexibility allowed the Scandinavians to be so successful in their European endeavors.

Helgi Hundingsbane is another legendary Norse hero that may or may not be based on a real historical figure. It is said that on the night of his birth, the Norns had foreseen a great future for Helgi, decreeing that he will become one of the greatest princes that will ever exist. This is perhaps why his parents Sigmundr and Borghildr had named him Helgi, after another famous epic hero, Helgi Hjotvarosson. It is also theorized that our Helgi was the reincarnation of the late eponymous hero because their fates ended up being strikingly similar. Back to our story; when he was a youngster, Helgi disguised himself to explore the court of king Hunding, an enemy of his father's. He almost got caught, but he managed to escape, and Helgi later killed Hunding, earning him the name "Hundingsbane." Then the Valkyrie Sigrun called for his aid to help her escape an unwanted marriage.

Helgi fought for Sigrun and came up victorious, even though Sigrun's father and brother were slain. He then married her, and the pair had many children. All was fine and well until Dagr, another brother of Sigrun, had called for Odin's aide to avenge his fallen brethren. Odin listened to his plea and offered him his mighty spear, with which Dagr killed Helgi. However, Odin had picked him to be part of his honorable warriors in Valhalla. Helgi and Sigrun had one last final meeting before his departure for the realm of the honorable dead. It is said that Sigrun's sorrow was so deep that she too perished, not long after her beloved.

Aud the Deep-minded and **Freydis Eiriksdottir** are two famous Viking women with very different stories but a similar fiery spirit. For the most part of her life, Aud was the poster wife and mother. She married the king of Dublin, Olaf the White, in the mid-ninth century and gave birth to their only son, Thorstein the Red. After Olaf's death, she and Thorstein moved to Scotland, where he established himself as a great warrior. Thorstein ruled over most of Scotland before dying a Viking's death in battle. Aud understood that she could not recover her importance in Scotland without her son, so she took her grandchildren and fled for the new Iceland colony, which seemed very promising. Aud took her family, friends, and a couple of Irish and Scottish slaves (who she later freed to garner their loyalty). She chose a large piece of Icelandic land for her and her entourage. She is considered to be one of the great founding colonists of Iceland, and many great medieval Icelandic families could trace their ancestry back to Aud the Deep-minded. She was definitely a strong, Viking woman who knew how to take the opportunities that life gave her and make the most out of them.

Freydis's fate was strikingly different. She was the daughter of Eirik the Red and, consequently, Leif's sister. Freydis was deeply involved in her brother's attempts to colonize Vinland.

She was part of the group that initiated contact with the Native American population. At first, their relationships were friendly, but soon the natives turned on her men. Freydis was a true Viking warrior and, despite being in the later terms of her pregnancy, she picked up a sword and was ready to smite her attackers. Thankfully, at the sight of a murderous pregnant woman, the natives ran for the hills to save their lives.

On a different account, we see Freydis's bad side. During another attempt to conquer Vinland, she discovered that the group she traveled with had brought more people aboard her ship than she had agreed to. Furious, she pushed her husband and his men to slaughter all the unwelcome crewmates. And so they did, except for the women, who they did not want to kill. Then Freydis took the gnarly task upon herself and killed the understandably frightened women. She also forced her men to take an oath that what happened on the ship would never transpire on their return to the Greenland colony. Not much else is known about Freydis, the daughter of Eirik the Red, but from what we know, we can guess that she either died in battle or went on to die a more peaceful death.

Einar Buttered-Bread is well-known for a tale of treachery from the *Orkneyinga saga* in which he played a simple pawn rather than the leading role. I wanted to end the list of the famous Vikings with him because Einar has a rather unique story. He was the grandson of the Earl of Orkney, Thorfinn

Skullsplitter, and he was tricked by Ragnhild, Eirik Bloodaxe's daughter, to take part in the fight over the Orkney earldom. Ragnhild was a smart, driven woman who knew how to manipulate others into her schemes. She was first married to Thorfinn's heir, Arnfinn, but she had him killed, and she made his brother Harvard Harvest-Happy earl in his stead. She went on to marry Harvard, after which she immediately started to conspire with Einar, to get him removed. Ragnhild promised Einar to make him earl of Orkney if he killed Harvard, who, let's not forget, was Einar's uncle.

Einar Buttered-Bread completed his part of the deal, but Ragnhild had other plans. While her second husband was getting murdered at her orders, she instigated Einar's cousin, Einar Hard-mouth to kill him and become the earl. But the web of treachery goes even deeper! Hard-mouth himself was then killed by Ljot, yet another cousin, who went on to claim both the earldom and Ragnhild as his. Was this Ragnhild's plan all along? We have no way of knowing, but I like to think of it that way.

As for poor Einar, that's where his story ended. The only mystery that remains is that of his peculiar name. After all, Butter-Bread is not really a tough Viking warrior name that inspires fear and awe. But this mystery, just like Ragnhild's plot, is to remain unsolved.

Chapter 2: The Viking Life

We've seen the power and force of this warrior civilization. Still, the Viking way of life can't be reduced to naval endeavors and great battles. In fact, a closer look at the Vikings' daily lives shows a far more ordinary picture than we'd like to imagine.

Typical Settlements and Agriculture

Most Vikings lived in rural areas, where their main focus was agriculture. The settlements themselves were relatively small, and they consisted of somewhere around fifteen to fifty farms per village. Trade towns existed, but they were so far and few between that only an incredibly small percent of the population lived there. Additionally, isolated farms built-in remote areas such as mountains, forests, or fjords were pretty common, and so were villages that comprised only two or three farmsteads. Cemeteries were placed right at the edges of villages or farmsteads, serving as a morbid representation of one's claim over the land (because their ancestors had lived, worked, and died there). Not very poetic but rather successful at showing your legitimacy of owning the said plot of land.

Men would occupy themselves with taking care of the land, involving themselves in fertilizing the soil, sowing, and plowing while women took upon themselves tasks that were performed mainly inside the house, such as cooking and producing clothing and alcoholic drinks. Harvesting the crops usually fell on the entire family since it was a laborious task that required all hands on deck. The care for farm animals was also divided between men and women. During the summer the men would take the cattle and the sheep out to graze and watch over them, and during the winter, when the animals were kept inside to protect them from the cold, the women would cater to them, milking them and keeping their enclosures clean. Speaking of farm animals, horses were cherished by Vikings. They represented the main form of transportation of both men and their goods, even in the coldest parts of Scandinavia where the snowfall was substantial. In such areas, horses would pull sleds and be fitted with spiked footwear to allow them to cross frozen lands and bodies of water.

Back to farming, Vikings plowed their lands using an almost-vertical, wooden scratch plow that was pulled by oxen or slaves. The wooden spike did the job of breaking up the soil, but it didn't turn it. That is why Viking fields were cross-plowed, by plowing a second row of lines intersecting with the first. Because the plow was wooden, it would often break after a few days of wear, and it would have to be replaced - iron plows came after the end of the Viking Age. The Norsemen practiced crop rotation, alternating which fields were sown to allow them to rejuvenate naturally, and they used animal and human waste as fertilizer. To harvest, men used scythes to cut the crops and women had rakes to expose the grains. Then men would prepare the grains with precise club-strikes, and hand mills were used to ground them. Once the process was done and over, women could use the resulting material for baking, cooking, and making beer or other alcoholic beverages.

Ironworking was practiced on farmsteads, and it was reserved to fulfill the needs of the household. Professional smiths would practice their craft in the few urban areas, and they would often trade their goods in exchange for food. Most physically demanding tasks were carried out by the slaves that the Vikings captured during the raids or in battles for supremacy. Although one can look at this farming-centric life through rose-colored glasses, it was far from an idyllic situation. Sure, Vikings had slaves to carry out the unpleasant tasks or do hard work, but taking care of the land still required incredible effort and labor to accomplish even the easiest tasks. Besides that, these Viking farmers lived in constant fear of famine, natural disasters, or raids that would deprive them of their crops and, consequently, their means of living. Diseases were rampant at the time, and famine loomed over the lands. It wasn't uncommon for children to die before reaching adulthood, and the image of the strong, muscular Viking warrior may not be as close to the truth as we think it is.

With their at-home situation looking so grim, it's not hard to understand why raiding and establishing settlements on other lands became such a big focus for Vikings. They just wanted a better life for themselves and their families. And they were willing to do anything to accomplish that.

Social Classes

The Vikings had three main social classes: the slaves, the free men, and the earls. Their social hierarchy was similar in nature to that of other European civilizations of that time.

The slaves were the lowest class of the Viking society. There were three ways in which one could become a slave. One was, as I already mentioned, being captured in a war or raid. Vikings believed that the ones who they had spared in battle needed to pay them back with their freedom for being allowed to live. From the Vikings' point of view, this was a fair trade, and that's how they justified slavery. The second way to become a slave was to be born to a slave. The descendants of slaves were also slaves, a logic justified by the same "your freedom for the gift of life" principle. Lastly, one could become a slave if they went bankrupt. A poor person could give up their freedom to someone who was of higher status in exchange for gathering that person's protection. More often than not, that was the only choice these poor people had, especially when debts were involved. They simply had nothing else to give but their freedom, so they would willingly become someone's slave to have their material needs (such as food, clothes, and shelter) taken care of. It was a steep price to pay, but it was a better alternative to dying of hunger or at the hands of creditors.

Slaves were mainly used for farm work, but it wasn't uncommon for masters to sell their slaves into the slave trade business that was already flourishing in Europe. There are also a few accounts of slaves being sacrificed after their master's death, following the beliefs that they had to continue to fulfill their roles in the afterlife. From being subjected to inhumane amounts of labor to being sold into the slave trade network or being sacrificed during their master's funerary rites, it's more than fair to say that Viking slaves had few prospects.

Mostly, the Viking society consisted of free men. These were farmers (the wealthier ones had their own land, and the less fortunate worked the other's lands in exchange for permission to harvest a plot for themselves), merchants, craftsmen, and warriors. The majority of Vikings who took part in raids and great battles were free men. In the Viking society, the older a son was, the more he would inherit from his father, so the younger children would often be left with scraps. That's why

Viking warriors were mainly young men, with nothing tying them down to a place, looking to make a name and material situation for themselves. They sought silver and plots of land for farming in the areas that would become colonies and settlements. These young men simply wanted something better than the little they had at home and, because they enjoyed the protection of the law and had the means to improve their financial situation, there was nothing that could stop them from doing so.

The *jarls* (earls) were at the top of the Viking social hierarchy. They were mostly chieftains who became wealthy through plundering and raiding. In the later years of the Viking Age, earls were closer to what we call aristocrats, serving as the king's subordinates and appropriating as much land as they pleased.

Viking Politics

Throughout most of the Viking period, the political power was in the hands of clan leaders and chieftains, who exerted their control over small groups of people. They led bands in raids and vicious attacks while also competing with other fellow chieftains for power and dominance. To assert their position, chieftains needed to find great and loyal warriors that would stand by his side and bring him great success. And earning the loyalty of Vikings was no easy deed. A chieftain had to be fearless, generous with his man, always victorious in battles, and he had to have a good reputation. Success in battle was pretty much the means to everything, and the wealth they gained allowed them to be generous and "inspire" poets and storytellers to build up their reputation. These stories and epic sagas would then reach young men who wanted to fight under such a famous chieftain, growing the numbers of the warlord's armies and thus helping him be more successful in battle. It was an efficient cycle that smart chieftains knew how to work in their favor.

Wealth during the early Viking period was not expressed through coins. Warlords dispensed silver, gold, and arm rings, which ranged from simple to exquisitely ornate. Plots of lands were also commonly used as a trading coin since having land was a fundamental element of Viking success. Chieftains would reward their men by throwing great feasts, that were usually intertwined with religious elements. The generosity of the chieftains came at a simple but essential price: loyalty. This attribute was very important in Viking society. One of the greatest honors for a warrior was to die in battle alongside their chieftain, proving that their loyalty is not only tied to economic gain. Sure, wealth was an incentive, but Viking warriors wanted more. They sought honor and a sense of belongingness, which a great leader could artfully provide.

Besides these warlords who held control over particular regions, the power was held by a legal assembly. This institution ruled through laws, and it was highly respected. Legal assemblies were held in outdoor areas, and during these gatherings, free men would recite, amend, or make new laws. Slaves didn't have the right to participate, and women could only contribute when serving as representatives for male relatives. By modern standards, these Viking assemblies had legislative and judicial functions, but on a smaller scale. It was perfectly possible for two Nordic villages to have different sets of rules because the assemblies were local and had only local power. Since the assemblies had no executive branch, the decisions were enforced by the victorious party (for disputes) or by the community. If, for example, someone was fined and they refused or failed to pay, they would become outlaws. As an outlaw, you were no longer under the protection of the law, so anyone could kill you. Because this system was efficient enough, the assembly did not need an executive branch to carry out their dirty work. The Icelandic Althing was a more developed form of legal assembly with deep roots in politics, making it more similar to the form of government we have in the present days.

Speaking of politics, as chieftains became more and more influential, the battle for supremacy intensified. The most successful leaders in battle amassed greater armies of good, loyal warriors, and soon enough some armies grew large enough to conquer others. The most powerful leaders declared themselves kings over wide areas, to the terror of Medieval Europe that would now face greater, more organized attacks. The transition from warlords to kings didn't happen at once in the Scandinavian region. Denmark came first, followed by Norway, and Sweden, where the process went beyond the historical Viking Age. The switch from chieftains to kings was more than a power shift; it was also a shift in role and tradition. Viking kings, such as Cnut the Great, had more in common with European rulers than traditional warlords. The great scale of power made it impossible for kings to maintain that close, loyalty-based relationship with their men. Things were now more structured and bureaucratic. There were also rules in place regarding governance and succession and taxes were introduced. Interestingly, this shift in politics happened at the same time as the one in religion, with the Norsemen converting to Christianity (more on this in a later chapter!), so we can wholeheartedly say that this was an era of change for the Vikings.

With the introduction of Christianity, the relationship between the people and their king was formulated in religious terms. They were to serve their king unconditionally, just as they did God, swerving even further from the traditional Viking chieftain-warrior relationship. Although the rise of kings made Vikings a more organized and successful military force, it also represented the "death" of the old Viking way of life, leading to the end of the great Viking Age.

Commerce

The Norse people had one of the greatest trade networks of the Middle Ages, stretching as far as Baghdad and Asia. This feat is even more extraordinary if we look back at the simple way of life of early eight century Vikings. They were farmers who rarely produced more than their household needed to survive, and few people lived in urban areas where trade was common. But these "trade towns," regardless of how small they were, propelled the Scandinavian people into the vast Eurasian trade networks, starting a new age of commerce. With trade towns on the rise, people began to specialize in crafts, understanding the huge opportunity that foreign trade represented. Jewelers, blacksmiths, antler workers, and many more migrated to the trade towns where they would produce their goods mainly for export.

The most cherished Scandinavian trade items were by far furs. The cold Nordic climate was home to animals with thick, warm pelts that were coveted and prized abroad. Another pillar of the Viking trade was slaves, as it was for many civilizations in Eurasia at the time. The Viking slaves were, let's not forget, people that were captured in raids. And since it was not uncommon for Vikings to raid other Viking settlements, many of the slaves that were traded were Norsemen themselves. To the Vikings, it didn't matter much whether you were a foreigner or a Scandinavian, a Christian, or a worshipper of the Norse gods. All that mattered was your market value. The Vikings were very pragmatic in that way. Additionally, since trade towns were flourishing at the time, the abundance of valuable trade goods made them alluring targets for potential raids. Commerce was a brutal affair in the Viking age, even between Norsemen themselves.

For Viking chieftains of that time, trade was simply a way to garner more wealth and luxury goods. These gave them status and allowed them to be very generous with their men, strengthening loyalties and their power as leaders. For the Viking farmers, the rise of the trade towns gave them an opportunity to buy commodities in exchange for food or whatever goods they produced on their farmstead. Around the year 1000, due to the changes in politics and the switch to kings, the luxurious trade towns almost vanished, leaving space for market places that mainly focused on commodities and that were more accessible to the regular people. This is yet another way in which the shift to a more European type of society had negative repercussions for the Viking civilization.

Gender Roles in the Viking Age

We've gone through quite a few aspects of Viking life, and I've presented two outstanding Viking women, Aud the Deep-minded and Freydis Eiriksdottir, who held important positions in the Scandinavian society. But did the Vikings have an equal society? Were the Viking shield-maidens a reality or a figment of our feminist desires?

Well, the Viking society, just as many others of the time, gave men a higher social status than women, and they judged someone's worth based on how well they fulfilled their designated role. Men had to be manly, great warriors and/or farmers, and women had to ace housekeeping duties. The societal role of women was traditional in the sense that they were expected to be wives and mothers. On the bright side, a woman who could fulfill her role was greatly appreciated by her family and Viking society. But their appreciation never quite reached the level of the respect and reputation that men could garner. Great women had no stories made about them, no poems to speak about their deeds, and no songs to sing their accomplishments. But at least they got some recognition, which is more than many women in the Middle Ages could hope for.

Viking women didn't have much of a say when it came to marriage; the proposal came from a man, and the bride-to-be's family negotiated terms on her behalf and decided if the proposal was to be accepted or refused. Yes, the poor woman had no say in this. Adultery was also a capital sin for women, as their husbands were allowed by law to kill both their cheating wife and her suitor if they caught them in the act. Some Viking settlements had laws for men caught committing adultery, but the punishments were more lenient, as it was somewhat more socially acceptable for a man to cheat than a woman. It was commonplace for warlords and kings alike to have multiple wives and maybe some concubines on the side, but the women were expected to be loyal to their husbands. A pretty standard idea for the Middle Ages.

Women did, however, have the right to divorce their husbands. Women who found themselves in unhappy, abusive, or otherwise bad marriages, and who could prove their husbands' wrongdoings, were allowed to divorce them and would receive monetary compensation, to ensure that they could provide for themselves. When it came to careers though, women couldn't aspire to anything else except for being housewives. Only men could work the land, hold political power, speak in assemblies, become warriors, and leave their homeland. Sure there are stories of women going into battle alongside their men, and some artifacts showing that women were skilled in warfare and owned weapons, but as of now, we don't have enough scientific evidence to say this was the norm. They could have been exceptions to the norm. As of the mythical valkyries - the winged female warriors who took men to Valhalla, their historical counterparts were most likely sorceresses and not female fighters. The sorceresses were women who, allegedly, could use magic to aid Vikings in battle. But their magic could only influence the outcome of the wars, so their presence on the battlefield was not necessary.

Since we brought magic to the mix, that is one thing that belonged only to women. It was socially acceptable for women to practice *seidr* (Norse magic), but men that delved into such practices were deeply despised and sometimes even killed for their affinities. For some reason, Vikings saw magic as something akin to homosexuality, which brought dishonor for the overly masculine Norse warriors. And since women were seen as weak and, obviously feminine, they were free to flaunt their magic powers in bright daylight without anyone giving them the stink-eye. So, that's one point for the women, I guess?

These would be the generalities on gender roles, but as with any rules, there were exceptions. High-status women did exist in the Viking Age. Most of them had garnered this status through marriage or being born in an aristocratic family, but they had status nonetheless. Women could also inherit properties, if there were no male heirs, and indulge in artistic endeavors such as poetry - although there are few accounts of female poets. While Viking women did not have it good, they definitely had more liberties and overall better quality of life than their contemporaries in other nations, who were treated pretty much as a man's property and were considered disposable.

Food, Clothing, Jewelry, and Weapons of the Viking Age

Although not as captivating as other subjects, I think it's good to have at least some idea of these aspects of a Viking's life.

Starting with the food, different parts of the Scandinavian region offered different resources. Speaking on general terms, the most cultivated grain in the Viking world was barley, which was used for bread loaves and bread buns. Other plants and grains that would be added to the traditional bread recipe include oats, flax, rye, and pine bark. A Viking's diet also included plentiful dairy products, because they had sheep, goats, and cattle. The proximity to the sea made fish a common element of Viking foods, with the favorites being herring and cod. And of course, we can't forget about meat - the Scandinavians had many options when it came to this dietary element. The meat came from farm animals such as pigs, cows, and chicken, as well as from hunting. The Vikings hunted a wide array of beasts from deer, rabbits, and wild boars to seals and whales. The latter two were considered delicacies and their oils were used for cooking or as butter substitutes.

Because they were strong warriors, they did not skip on fruits and veggies. Vikings cultivated cabbage, peas, beets, and beans, and they gathered from the wild blackberries, strawberries, pears, cherries, hazelnuts, and others. Another interesting aspect of Viking meals is that they loved spices and aromatic herbs. Their meals often included parsley, garlic, thyme, mustard, cumin, salt (extracted by boiling salt water), and honey (as a sweetener). The staple Viking beverages were mead and beer, made from honey and barley. These alcoholic beverages would usually be drunk from cattle horns or wooden cups (if they wanted to enjoy their drink). Vikings also made fruit wines, but because they didn't know how to distill alcohol these were pretty tame. Luxury wines brought from abroad would usually be served in silver bowls or imported glass vessels, for a touch of refinement.

Viking clothing was mainly made from wool and flax (from which comes linen), to provide warmth, and was worn in layers to protect them from the harsh climate. Women produced the clothing by spinning the materials and weaving them into garments. It was a long and arduous process, which is why richer families would buy commercially-made fabrics. Linen was preferred for undergarments because it felt nicer on the skin, and fur was typically used for cloaks and decorative trimmings. Natural dyes were used to spice up the simple, white clothing (because the Scandinavian sheep were predominantly white) but they were of low quality and they faded quickly.

Calfskin and goatskin were used for boots. Linen or silk bands were used as hair ties for both men and women.

The clothing itself was pretty typical, with shirts, breeches, and tunics for men and linen chemises and woolen dresses for women. Silks, adornments, and fancy embroideries were reserved for the wealthy. As a side note here, the popular portrayal of Vikings as being unkempt is far from the truth. They valued their physical appearance and they used utensils such as razors, combs, and tweezers to take care of themselves. They also didn't live in huts, but in halls that were maintained by the women and would house feasts whenever there was a reason for celebrating.

Jewelry for the Vikings served two purposes: to show one's status and to act as forms of payment if the need arose. They consisted of rings, necklaces, brooches, pendants, and amulets. The most popular amulets of the time were representations of Thor's hammer, miniature thrones (which were linked with the worship of Odin), and crosses (when Vikings switched to Christianity).

In the Viking Era, all free men had the duty to own weapons. Swords were the staple weapons of the Norse society, and only the elite had the honor of carrying one. Many poets and song-writers would mention the swords of warlords in their works, using artistic metaphors such as "flame of Odin." At the start of the eighth century, most swords were single-edged, but as the Viking age went on, iron double-edged swords became more popular. Axes were the weapons of choice for the common people. They served both as tools and weapons, and they were simply made. All that distinguished one ax from another was the shape and size, which varied a lot. Viking spears were either for throwing or thrusting, and they were a staggering half a meter long. Bows and arrows were used for both hunting and war, although those taken to the battle were rudimentary and simply put together.

Viking shields were made from wood and they were heavily decorated with mythical motifs of colorful symbols. Chainmail was reserved for the wealthy, but helmets were worn by the great majority of Vikings. They were made from leather or iron and were rounded, with simple designs. So no, they didn't wear horned helmets, mostly because they were impractical in combat. The more you know.

The Old Norse

The Vikings spoke the Old Norse language, and all the texts that we have from the Viking Age are written using it. Old Norse evolved from a northern dialect of the Proto-germanic language, and it is part of the Germanic family of languages like modern German and English. By the beginning of the Viking

Age, around the year 750, the dialect had transformed into Proto-Norse, becoming a new language altogether. Even so, because the Vikings were spread all around Europe and in many other regions, the Old Norse had many regional dialects that were still pretty close to each other. The Old Norwegian and the Old Icelandic were about as different as North American English is to British English. Something to note here would be that, because most of the texts that survived from the Viking Era come from Iceland, what we presently refer to as Old Norse is actually the Iceland dialect of Old Norse.

From a grammatical point of view, the Old Norse had a free word order, with few rules regarding positioning, such as an object had to follow a verb. Only pronouns had separate dual forms, and verbs were inflected for mood, number, tense, and person. The first syllable of a word was always stressed, and the following could be either short or long. For written texts, the Vikings used the Younger Futhark alphabet, a runic script that was later replaced by the Latin alphabet when most of Scandinavia converted to Christianity.

Old Norse is considered to be the parent language of modern Icelandic, Norwegian and Faroese.

Valhalla and Viking Individualism

Valhalla or the Hall of Slain Warriors was pretty much the Viking interpretation of Heaven. If a Viking died an honorable death, in battle, he would be taken by a Valkyrie into Valhalla, where Odin himself would welcome them. Depiction of Valhalla in Norse literature describes it as an incredible hall, with golden shields adorning the roof and rafters made of spears. There, the warriors would fight all day to keep their skills sharp and feast all night to celebrate their great deeds. Feasting and fighting do sound like a Viking's greatest pleasures, right? These honored dead men, known as *einherjar* would spend their afterlife preparing for *Ragnarok* (the end of the world) and feasting from the meat of Saehrimnir, a boar that came back to life every night to satisfy the men's hunger and drinking Heidrun's mead (a goat that produced the finest alcoholic beverage).

However, out of the warriors who died in battle, only half made it to Valhalla. The ones that were not chosen by the mighty Valkyries would go to the field of Freya, where they would spend their afterlife offering their company to women who died as maidens. Some would argue that this sort of afterlife is more appealing than being stuck in a perpetual cycle of fighting and feasting, but again these are Vikings and to them, Valhalla was the ultimate goal. The Vikings who died of sickness or old age would go to Hel (the Underworld, also referred to as *Niflheim*).

This place is not equivalent to our concept of Hell, but rather a less satisfying version of Valhalla. The dead were being taken care of by Hel, the goddess of the underworld. But there was a special place in Niflheim for adulterers, murderers, and other evil-doers, where they would pay for their bad deeds and where a dragon ate their corpses, an imaginative punishment.

Now, something that I felt I should touch on before we dive into the Norse mythology is the character of the Vikings. We tend to see them as a somewhat patriotic civilization who put loyalty above personal gain and interests. But the Vikings were pretty selfish. They put themselves first, even if that meant betraying their own kin, just as we've seen in the case of Vikings enslaving other Norsemen to sell them on the slave market. The Norse idea of self only existed in relation to one's actions and social standing. The way you acted and the relationships you had made you who you were, so Vikings were somewhat constricted to be loyal to family, friends, and their leaders to not risk being considered unhonorable. Even so, the Viking society was permissive and it allowed people to choose their social relationships. That gave Vikings the liberty to refuse or accept obligations, for the most part. Their society was not as lenient on women, and certain obligations such as those for family and one's chieftain could not be refused.

The men who achieved greatness would be celebrated by name, in songs and poems, making them immortal in a sense. The graves of Vikings were individual, and they were decorated according to the person's life and achievements, another measure to ensure that someone's valiant deeds would not be forgotten. Remember, reputation was everything to the Norse people. The selfish individualism of Vikings is also apparent in their relationships with the higher beings, the gods. The Scandinavians worshipped them, and "served" them in the same way that they served their warlords, to garner favors and riches.

These are the Vikings; they treasured the ideals of honor and loyalty but what they ultimately desired was personal glory and immortality through great reputation. From this point onward in the book, we'll go into the mythical world of the Vikings and we'll discover the Norse gods and how the Northmen worshipped them. It's finally time to drink from that Well of Knowledge and meet Odin and his entourage of gods and goddesses.

Chapter 3: The Norse Myth of Creation

One thing I learned in all my years of studying mythology is that the best way to get into a new mythological realm is to start with the beginning, and that is the myth of creation. All cultures and religions have their version of how the world came to be and the Vikings make no exception. In fact, this book had actually started with the first few lines of the Norse creation myth, to give you a little taste of what was to come later and get you into the mystic atmosphere of the Viking mythos. How about we pick up from where I left it in the Introduction, and then we'll establish some basic notions about Nordic mythology.

The Birth of the Giants and the Aesir Gods

Ymir (the Screamer), the first living creature, born in Ginnungagap from the melted ice of Niflheim, was a giant and a force of destruction. He was also a hermaphrodite who could reproduce on his own. As he slept, the giant started to sweat, and from the sweat of his armpits, a man and a woman were born, while from the sweat of his legs emerged another man. This is how the first frost giants were born into this world. From the ice that was still melting in the void, another creature was brought into being - the cow Audhumla. She would lick salty ice blocks for nourishment and she graciously offered her rivers of milk for Ymir to feast on and grow.

While liking the salt, Audhumla found and uncovered a man - Buri (the Progenitor), the first of the Aesir gods. Buri was a strong handsome man, and he had a son called Bor. He then married Besla, the daughter of a frost giant. This unlikely pair of god and giant had three children: Odin, Vili, and Ve.

The Creation of the World and the First Men

One day, Odin and his brothers killed Ymir. The amount of blood that poured from Ymir's wound was so tremendous that it flooded Ginnungagap, drowning almost all the frost giants. Only Belgemir and his wife managed to escape, and he fathered the giants that came after. Odin, Vili, and Ve carried Ymir's corpse to the middle of the void and they built the world from his carcass. They made seas, oceans, and lakes from Ymir's blood, they used his muscles and his skin to brandish the Earth, from his hair they made trees and vegetation, they constructed mountains from his bones (except for the skull, that comes a bit later) and from his teeth, they made pebbles and rocks. A bit hard to imagine but bear with me. The gods then turned the creatures that fed on Ymir's body into dwarves. They would become great craftsmen that could create anything, from jewelry to magical weapons, such as the legendary hammer Mjolnir.

The gods used Ymir's skull to create the sky, and they placed a dwarf at each corner (north, south, east, and west), to keep the skull floating above the Earth. For clouds, they used Ymir's brains, and for stars, they gathered flying embers from Muspelheim. The newly created Earth was surrounded by waters, and the sons of Bor gave the land that was close to the sea to the giants, to settle and live there. But since the giants were hostile beings, the gods wanted a place to protect them from the creatures' fury, so from Ymir's eyebrows (or eyelashes in some versions), they created a stronghold inland, far from the sea. They called this citadel Midgard. A side note here, this great sea was also the abode of *Jurmurgandr*, the giant serpent who is said to have been so enormous that it could coil itself around the entire world. Yet another reason to keep humans away from the waters.

While walking around the shores, Odin and his brothers found two trees from which they decided to create a man and a woman, the first humans. Odin gave them the spark of life, Vili gave them consciousness, and Ve gifted them with clothes and identities. The first man received the name Ask, and the first woman Embla. The sons of Bor built a fence around Midgard and gave the stronghold to the humans, to keep them safe while they grew in numbers.

One human, called Mundilfari, had two children who were so radiant that he named them Sol (Sun) and Mani (Moon). When the gods found out about Mundilfari's arrogance (yes they saw him being proud and giving fancy names to his children as arrogance) they punished him by taking Sol and Mani and putting them in the sky, to light it up during the day and respectively night. They both rode chariots and were pursued by two wolves, Hati (Hate) and Skoll (Treachery). At Ragnarok, the end of the world, it is said that the wolves would catch and eat the sun and moon. In a different version of this myth, Mundilfari is replaced with the giant Norvi, who had only a daughter called Nott (Night). She had a son named Dagr (Day), and the pair would ride chariots across the sky to bring day and night. The two wolves Hati and Skoll are present in this version of the myth, still chasing the chariots in hopes of devouring the sun and the moon.

Asgard and the Aesir

Odin and his brothers now wanted to build a place for their own kind, so they went to the middle of the world and created Asgard. Many stories in the Norse mythology happen in Asgard, and there lived almost all the important gods we'll later discuss. Asgard had a great hall called Hlidskjalf, where Odin sat on a high chair, kind of like a throne, from which he could see the whole world and understand everything that was going on.

Odin went on to marry Frigg, and their descendants, known as Aesir, would inhabit Asgards and its kingdoms. Because he created men and fathered the Aesir gods Odin is also known as the "All-Father." His first child was the mighty and powerful Thor, who dominated every living creature with his strength. Other remarkable Aesir gods are Loki, Baldr, Tyr, and Heimdall. The main sanctuary of the Aesir is the tree of life, Yggdrasil, where they hold their court and their feasts. Yggdrasil is said to have been the greatest tree that ever existed, with branches that reached the heavens and spread out over the world. Its roots reach all the other realism, including that of men and that of giants, *Jutunheim*. Nidhogg, a dragon of death, feeds from the roots of Yggdrasil while the Norns (the three fates) decide the fates of the humans at the base of the great tree.

The Aesir and the Vanir

Odin might be the father of the Aesir gods, but not all Norse deities are part of this family. There is a second, smaller family called the Vanir, which contains fertility deities, gods of climate, and deities of harvest. For obvious reasons, the Vanir gods such as Freyja, Freyr, and Njord were very popular in farming communities, while the Aesir, who were usually connected with government and war, were mainly worshipped by kings and warriors. In Norse mythology, the two families are portrayed as being in a constant state of conflict, to the point of there being numerous Aesir-Vanir wars.

However, these wars always end with peace and with the deities fusing their families together. This peace reflects the Viking concept that society needs both social classes, the farmers and the warriors, to function and prosper.

Analyzing the Myth of Creation

As fascinating as it is, the Norse myth of creation is, unceremoniously said, weird and it requires a closer examination of its themes if we want to understand the concepts that lay hidden at its core. One of the first things we are introduced to in this story is the abyss Ginnungagap and the frost giant Ymir. These are both personifications of the idea of the chaos that comes before creation and its limitless potential. They are "nothingness" in the sense that they don't represent something material, but they contain what the gods need in order to create everything they want or need. After all, Ymir, a crude personification of chaos, is the creator of the first beings, and the sons of Bor use his body to build the world as the Norse saw it.

In Viking mythology, the frost giants are always characterized as beings who want to corrupt the world and destroy the order created by the Aesir gods. They are chaotic in nature, just like Ymir was, and they instinctively seek destructions. But, they also present the potential to create great things. The giants are described as having great abilities such as that to brew ale, craft enormous cauldrons, create runes and meads with magical properties, and so on. In many stories and legends, the gods recognize the resources that giants possess and they attempt to steal them for personal use or to benefit the Norse culture. In a way, we can say that the Aesir gods see giants as nothing more but raw materials, that they can mold and shape to their own advantage. Ymir is simply the first mythological account of this concept of gods using the chaotic potential of giants.

Another interesting thing about Ymir is that he is characterized as being a hermaphrodite, that can reproduce on his own. That is mostly because the differentiation between sexes did not exist at that point - it is a concept invented and created by the gods. This is yet another way in which Odin and his brothers polished and used the raw chaotic energy of Ymir. Even the name Ymir (the Screamer) alludes to the idea that the Aesir took a scream, a wordless means of communication, and transformed it into language, giving it an elevated form.

As with many other creation myths, the Norse interpretation of the origin of the world is focused on the theme of conflict. Ymir is created as a result of the conflict between ice and fire. The world comes into being as a result of the sons of Bor killing and dismembering Ymir, the conflict between chaos and order. This primordial murder is not interpreted as a sin, as it would have been in a Biblical myth. The slaying of Ymir is a necessity, an act that had to be done for the sake of creating the world and bringing honor to the gods' name. This myth taught Vikings that they needed to do what it takes to garner a good reputation and that they should specifically engage in honorable aggressions.

The Norsemen believed that their gods were the forces that impaired sanctity and order into the world, and that held the cosmos together. This is why there are many stories about the gods interfering in Earthly affairs; it is their role to maintain order in the world, a role that would only end when the world itself would perish. But the Norse believed that giants too were able to intervene in the human world. Everything that was created came from Ymir and aspects of his, such as his ruggedness, his might, his fluctuating character, were still present in the world of mortals, despite the gods shaping all that existed to fit their personal agenda. For the Vikings, the conflict between the gods and the giants was a never-ending ordeal, and they, the humans, were right in the middle of it, presenting characteristics from both worlds: the order and honor of the gods but also the wickedness and chaos of the giants. The resolution of this fight will be Ragnarok, the end times, when all will be destroyed and nothing will remain of the old world. Then, a new world will rise from the seas, and the cycle of life will start again.

Mythology in Viking Society

Despite having a collection of stories through which we can look at a different side of Viking society, Norse mythology is a hard subject to pin down. In the Old Norse, they refer to it as *siour* (custom), and each individual declared their devotion to a deity that they connected to, on some personal level, and the worship of said god became an integral part of that person's life.

Norse gods were complex beings with distinct personalities, and many were venerated by entire communities. Scandinavian settlements had temples and places of worship where they would make sacrifices to garner the favor of the gods in times of war or celebrations. We don't know much about the exact rituals or customs they had, because much of their religion was passed down orally, from a generation to another, and not written. We should also keep in mind that the Norsemen were extremely flexible, even when it came to their traditions and worship. Their religion transformed with time and it had multiple variations across the vast Viking world. They shared the belief in the divine powers but each settlement assigned them their own functions and attributes. Even when they shifted to Christianity, Vikings remained polytheistic, mostly adding to the list of divine beings they believed in rather than replacing one with another.

Besides the families of gods and the giants, the Norse people also believed in *Disir* (female deities who were worshipped by specific families or individuals, kind of like the household deities of Roman, Greek, and other cultures), elves (who were separated into dark elves and light elves), dwarves, trolls, draugar (the undead), dragons and many other fantastic creatures. So it's a rich mythological world with plenty of supernatural beings, most of them representing certain fears or beliefs of the Norse population of that time.

With all being said, let's jump right into meeting the most powerful and important Norse gods and discover who they were and what they meant for the Norse people through their most iconic stories.

Chapter 4: The Aesir Gods

Most of the popular Norse gods belong to the Aesir family. In this chapter, we will cover some notable Aesir gods along with their iconic myths and their potential interpretations.

Odin the Allfather

Odin is regarded as the ruler of the Aesir gods, and he is one of the most complex characters in Norse mythology. He is attributed to a number of contradicting traits that make him a hard to understand deity, especially if we look at things from a Viking's perspective. Odin is both a god of war, justice, and law but also a selfish seeker of knowledge who dwells in poetry and doesn't care for communal values such as fairness. He is worshipped by those who look for honor and prestige but he is also a patron of the outlaws. Even his name, *Odin* (the Master of Ecstasy) alludes to a unity between the multiple aspects of life respectively wisdom, war, magic (which is weird because as I mentioned before, Vikings had little respect for men who had magic abilities) poetry, sovereignty, and death. So, in what manners does Odin reflect these often contradicting aspects? Let's take them one by one and see.

War is perhaps the aspects that Odin is most predominantly linked with, in our modern portrayals of him. We often see him represented as an honorable commander, leading his armies into battle. But this portrayal is more suitable for deities such as Thor or Tyr. Odin, on the other hand, was adept at inciting strife between peaceful people, for his sheer enjoyment. He was, for the most part, concerned with the chaotic energy of war and the frenzy that came with it. As for those he affiliated himself with, Odin kept closer to rulers and berserkers, rather than the average warriors. Only the greatest fighters and heroes were deemed honorable enough to gain Odin's favors. As for the berserkers, they were special warriors who had the ability to tap into the spirits of ferocious beasts, such as bears and wolves, and use their power in battle. Since Odin too dabbled in shamanisms and other such spiritual practices, it's not hard to see why he was a patron of the warrior-shamans.

Sovereignty and leadership is another aspect that's closely tied in with Odin's identity, mostly because he is the archetypal ruler and the chief of the Aesir gods. So it was natural for the Norse chieftains and kings to claim themselves to be Odin's descendants or his protegees. But Odin is not the only Norse divinity associated with the Scandinavian rulers. Few know that Tyr was also a patron of kings, with the difference being that Tyr represented the lawful, virtuous, and just ruler while Odin was associated with cunning, devious, and inspired rulers. Let's not forget that Odin patronage outlaws, especially those who were exiled for heinous crimes. These men were strong-willed but they, just like Odin, defied societal norms. They were warriors but also poets at heart, and they sought to carve their own path into the world. The men that garnered Odin's favor were creative, intelligent, and unstoppable when it came to getting what they desired. Only luck and circumstances deemed them either rulers or outlaws. In fact, Odin's popularity among criminals is said to have led to his banishment from Asgard for ten years, because the other gods didn't want to be associated with his vile reputation. Thus, being a ruler that served Odin didn't always speak wonders of your character.

Wisdom and magic (or shamanism) are perhaps the two aspects that the Vikings attributed most frequently to the Allfather, and we seldom find them in modern portrayals of Odin. Unlike the Christian God, who is all-knowing, Norse deities are limited by their particularities. Odin makes no exception to this, which is why many stories of him present him in the role of a seeker, for wisdom, knowledge, and power (usually magical power). Odin is a driven individual who is ready to go the extra mile to surpass his limitations. In Norse legends, Odin is always on the look for new means of gaining knowledge and power. He speaks to wise people, he uses his two ravens, Munin (Memory) and Hugin (Thought), to gather news about what's happening around the realms of Norse mythology, and his throne, Hlidskialf, lets him see everything that's going on, without him having to leave Asgard. His desire to know all there is to be known also stems from his dread for the ever-approaching Ragnarok when he is doomed to perish alongside the other gods. Let's see the iconic Norse myths that speak of Odin's thirst for knowledge.

Odin's Sacrifice to Learn the Magic of the Runes

The story of how Odin learned the magic spells from the rules is rather well-known. It is said that Odin pierced himself with his own spear, Gungnir, and hung himself from a branch of the World Tree, Yggdrasill, above the Well of Urd (that was guarded by the Norns) to garner the wisdom of the runes. You see, only the dead to those who were deemed worthy by the Well of Urd were allowed to learn the magic of the runes, so he put a noose around his head and he hung himself for nine days and nine nights, managing to learn nine spells - a great accomplishment considering that he allegedly only saw the runes for a split second before falling from the branch. The number nine has a special significance, and it is mostly associated with magic. During his time in the tree, Odin forbade any deity to aid him in any way.

The ninth night is when Odin ritually died. All light extinguished to mark the god's death and the magical powers of the spirit world reached their peak. The last night of the ritual coincided with the celebration of Walpurgis Night when large bonfires are lit to celebrate this moment of great power. Odin's death was however short-lasting, and after midnight the light returned to the world, and with it the Allfather who now knew the mighty spells of the runes as well as how to perform incredible feats. For example, Odin learned how to heal all wounds, to wake the dead, to free himself from any type of constraints, to win and keep the love of anyone, and many other things. With this knowledge, he became one of the wisest beings in the Universe.

Thematically speaking, Odin's sacrifice is of himself to himself, and his lower self (that died) to his higher self (the Odin who gained more knowledge, becoming a better version of himself) ringing true to that selfish sense of individuality characteristic of Viking civilization.

Odin and the Well of Mimir

The Well of Mimir, most commonly referred to as the Well of Knowledge, was near Yggdrasill's root that extended over to Jotunheim (the world of the frost giants) and it was guarded by Mimir. He was the wisest of the Aesir gods, specifically because he often drank from the Well of Knowledge. But the price he requested out of those who wanted to gain knowledge was not cheap. Heimdall, the Norse god who guards the Bifrost (the rainbow bridge that links Asgard to Midgard) had to give up one of his earlobes to drink from the well and Mimir didn't make any special offers for the ruler of the Aesir. On the contrary, he asked for one of Odin's eyes. It is unknown whether Odin immediately accepted or bargained for a more suitable deal, but in the end, he did sacrifice his eye, becoming the One-Eyed-God.

The fact that Odin's sacrifice is one of his eyes is a meaningful detail. The eye was always seen as a symbol and metaphor, both in poems and in everyday expressions. It is the window of the soul and the physical representation of one's perception of the world. Here, it seems like the latter concept is more suitable, meaning that Odin traded the way he saw the world for wisdom, which allows for a different perception. For Odin, this trade must have seemed fair, since for him all that mattered was to become his "higher self" and gain the wisdom of the divine.

In a separate myth about one of the numerous Aesir-Vanir wars, Mimir's head is cut off and sent to Odin. The Vanirs felt cheated when they were given Vili as an advisor, only to find out that he wasn't very bright and all his good advice was actually from Mimir. Vili was Odin's brother so they didn't dare to touch him, but Mimir was fair game. Odin however, was not one to waste a good opportunity. Mimir was, after all, the wisest of the gods. When he received Mimir's head he embalmed it, with his special herbs so it would not decay. Then, he used one of the spells he learned from the runes to bring Mimir's head back to life. From then on, Odin would often use Mimir's advice in times of need. This is yet another way in which Mimir provided Odin with knowledge, albeit we could argue that Mimir got the short end of the stick here, becoming a talking head and all.

Magic and Poetry

Odin and Freya are the greatest shamans of the Norse gods. Shamanism is a form of magic in which practitioners can contact spirits or interact with the spirit world to accomplish a purpose. Odin is especially known for his spiritual-journeys, while his body remained in Asgard, appearing to others as if he was asleep. Such an instance is when he visited the underworld, on Sleipnir (an eight-legged horse attributed to shamanic trances) to find out what was Baldur's fate. As a practitioner of shamanism, Odin is surrounded by plenty of animal familiar spirits, such as his ravens, the wolves Geri and Fleki, and even the Valkyries (even though they are maidens, they are still spiritual beings that serve the Allfather). The ritual of death and rebirth that Odin underwent in order to decipher the runes is also part of shamanic practice, if there was any doubt left regarding the god's abilities.

Shamanism is a part of the traditional *seidr,* the form of magic that was considered acceptable for only women to master - that is why Freya is a patron of it. Men who practiced seidr were scorned and even banished from society if the animosities ran deep. Odin's affinity for shamanism made him a target for ridicule and taunts. His 10-years exile from Asgard is said to have been in part due to his preferences in "doing a woman's work." To say that magic tarnished Odin's reputation would be an understatement. It questioned his honor and his ability to perform his "manly" duties. However, to Odin, the idea of honor was not everything, and he gladly discarded the concept if it meant he could indulge in ecstatic practices.

Odin's connection to poetry goes back to the time when he stole the mead of poetry, a drink made by the dwarves from Kvasir's corpse. Kvasir was the wisest man to ever live, and anyone who consumed the mead made from his body gained knowledge and the ability to compose poems. Of course, Odin was interested in possessing this mead, and he acquired it through trickery; by seducing the giantess who guarded it. But Odin, in an act of generosity, decided to share the gift of poetry with humans, gods, and other beings, making him a patron of scholars, poets, storytellers, and composers. To flaunt his poetic abilities, it is said that Odin only speaks through verses.

Death

We may not think of Odin as a god of death, but the Vikings clearly believed him to be deeply connected to the dead. He is, after all, the one who presides over Valhalla, the Viking Heaven, and a fine connoisseur of the spiritual world. His ability to speak and interact with the dead makes him sort of a necromancer, although his purpose is solely to garner as much knowledge as he can.

Perhaps to honor this aspect of Odin, his worship consisted of frequent human sacrifices, especially notable ones such as enemy rulers or nobles. These sacrifices were accomplished with the use of a noose or a spear, elements that allude to Odin's self-sacrifice to learn the magic of the runes. Although Odin is not the stereotypical Norse god or a personification of the Viking ideals, he is the vital force of all vital forces and the ruler of all gods. He represents inspiration, fury, ecstasy, selfishness, and the drive to accomplish the goals he has set for himself, regardless of how others might judge him for it.

Odin presides over the most fundamental aspects of a Viking's life, and for that, even though he was fundamentally flawed, he was the most worshipped and honored of all Norse deities. A far cry from our idea of a ruler of the gods, but at least he was a relatable figure that the Norsemen could connect with on a deeper level.

Thor the God of Thunder

Thor is the son of Odin and one of the most prominent deities in Norse mythology. He is the ideal Viking warrior, a role model for all young Norsemen, sporting virtues such as honor and unshakable loyalty. These qualities come in handy because he is the defendant of Asgard, protecting the gods from the ever-present threat of giants and whatever enemies might come their way. No one can measure in strength with Thor, and to double up his forces he wears a special belt of power and yields the famous hammer Mjolnir (Lightning) that never misses and always comes back to his owner. Whenever there was a lightning storm, the old Scnaidnavians believed that it was Thor battling with the giants in Asgard, as he rode in his chariot drawn by goats. As a side note here, the Vikings didn't believe that Thor was actually riding in a chariot pulled by real goats, they are just a symbol for the invisible and incomprehensible world of the gods. Many elements in Norse mythology are not meant to be taken literally.

Although Thor is the greatest slayer of giants and, subsequently the greatest keeper of peace and order, he is ironically described as having giant proportions and coming from a giant ancestry. Let's not forget that Odin is half-giant, and Thor's mother, Jord, is of pure giant blood. This is just to show that relationships between the gods and the giants were not as simple as we'd like to believe, and many gods were in some way or another of giant lineage. Nevertheless, Thor's greatest foe is Jumurgandr, the great sea serpent that's coiled around the human world. It is said that the two will face each other at Ragnarok when both will day of the other's "hands."

The Creation of Mjolnir

The story of how Thor got his favorite weapon is quite funny. It all started with Loki, the god of mischief, who, on a particularly boring day decided to pull a prank on Sif, Thor's wife, and cut her beautiful golden locks. Understandably, Thor didn't appreciate Loki's sense of humor, and he threatened to break every bone in Loki's body if he didn't fix the situation. The trickster god pleaded for his life, and he came up with the idea to go and ask for the help of the crafty dwarves. Surely, they would find a way to give Sif a new head of golden hair.

In Svartalfheim, the home of the dwarves, Loki found what he was looking for, but he also managed to get himself into even more trouble. You see, he first approached the sons of Ivaldi and told them that the gods were holding a contest to see who could create the most marvelous gifts. They crafted Sif's hair, alongside two other great artifacts: Gungnir that would become Odin's spear, and Skidbladnir, the greatest ship in the world, that was gifted to Freyr. Loki however, also approached the dwarven brothers Brokkr and Sindri, and he taunted them saying that they could never create marvels as incredible as those of the sons of Ivaldi. The brothers took the bait, on one condition - if the gods preferred their gifts, Brokkr and Sindri would receive Loki's head. Against his better judgment, Loki accepted the wager, but he was also not adept at playing fair. To sabotage the brothers, he transformed himself into a fly and he pestered Brokkr who tended to the fire while Sindri worked on the gifts.

Despite Loki's involvement, the first two pieces ended up being flawless. The first marvel was Gullinbursti, a boar with golden hair, who was faster than any horse and who lit up in the dark - he was gifted to Freyr, the god of the harvest. The second wonder was Draupnir, a magic ring that would create eight golden rings of similar weight and value every nine nights (again notice the use of number nine in relation to magic). This ring of wealth went to Odin, the Allfather. But for the third marvel, Loki's sabotage prevailed, and Mjolnir, the greatest hammer to ever exist, ended up having a rather short handle. Sindri and Brokkr were unhappy with the hammer, but they were still pretty confident in the quality of their gifts, so they made their way to Asgard to present them to the gods.

The gods were extremely happy with everything they got. Sif had recovered her wonderful golden hair, Freyr had two new tools to help him complete his duties, Odin had a mighty weapon and a ring that produced him more wealth, and Thor had the perfect item to help him smite giants - he couldn't care less about the short handle. To Loki's horror, Brokkr and Sindri were declared winners, and they were eager to claim their prize. But Loki was as clever as he was devious, and he pointed out that he had not promised them his neck, thus there was no way for them to take his head. The dwarves then decided to sew Loki's mouth shut, and they returned to Svartalfheim empty-handed but content. That is the story of how Thor got his hammer, a myth that speaks more of Loki's character than of Thor's.

Thor's Role in the Viking Society

Besides his role as a divine guardian, Thor is known for his activities in the human realm. He was called upon whenever there was a need for protection, comfort, and purification, especially of a place or event. The hammer, Mjolnir, is said to have had both smiting and blessing powers (in the sense that it destroyed evil forces), and many runic inscriptions that speak about Thor invoke him to bless places, plots of lands, and weddings. A peculiar demonstration of Thor's ability to purify and bless is the myth of him eating his goats and blessing their hides with his hammer to bring them back to life.

Thor's association with agriculture and fertility, in general, comes from him being a sky god - one that could invoke rain as he pleased. Historians believe that his golden-haired wife Sif was a personification of good harvest, her locks symbolizing fields of grains, thus their marriage being a portrayal of prosperity through the union of the divine spirits of the sky and those of the Earth.

But Thors's principal role in the Viking society remains that of a role model for warriors. If we add his affinity to the farming class to the mix, it is not hard to see why Thor was such a beloved god for the Norsemen. In many ways, Thor is the perfect opposite of Odin. He is the god of the common people and the fighters, and he values honesty and loyalty. This is why Thor's popularity skyrocketed throughout the Viking Age, to the point that he surpassed Odin, with the most telling example of this preference being the Icelandic Viking colony. The Norsemen of Iceland venerated Thor, in part because they were mainly a farming settlement, but also because they had experienced first-hand the oppressions of the noble class (who happened to worship Odin). To farmers, settlers, and colonists,

Thor is seen as a protector and a true leader, one that rules with honor and blesses his people.

Thor's cult also saw a peak when Christianity first came to the Scandinavian world. This new religion sought to annihilate the traditions and beliefs of the Norsemen, and Thor became a symbol of hostility towards these invading forces. Vikings of that time who refused to give up on the old gods would wear pendants brandished to resemble miniature hammers - small Mjolnirs, to show their allegiances, a retaliation to the cross amulets worn by Christians.

Loki the Trickster God

Loki is a very peculiar character of Norse mythology, with a similarly strange lineage. His father, Farbauti, is a giant and his mother, Laufey, is of unspecified descent in Norse lore. She could have been a giant, a god, or even a human. Loki himself has fathered a complicated family. His proper wife was Sigyn, a goddess of victory, with whom he had a son called Narfi. But Loki also had an entanglement with the giantess Angrboda, with whom he had three children, Hel, Fenrir, and Jumungandr, each being more monstrous and destructive than the other. Jumungandr and Fenrir alone have rather prominent roles to play at Ragnarok, and Hel is the goddess of the underworld.

Leaving his perplexing family ties aside, Loki is a deity that defies most Viking societal norms. He has little to no regard for his fellow gods, he is malicious, cowardly, extremely selfish, and almost every action he takes is with self-preservation and mischief in mind. Loki also defies the laws of nature in an instance by being the mother of Sleipnir, the shamanic horse with eight legs. That was possible when he turned himself into a mare to seduce Svadilfari's stallion, stopping him from winning a bet with the gods that would have granted him the sun, the moon, and the goddess Freya as a bride. We've already seen Loki's character in the Creation of Mjolnir, but another story that speaks volumes about his treacherous character and his lack of loyalty towards any faction is that of the Kidnapping of Idun.

The Kidnapping of Idun

Idun is a primordial goddess of Norse mythology, and she is the keeper of the fruits of immortality, which allow gods to remain young and strong. Whenever a god felt like they were starting to age, they would go to Idun and she entrusted them one fruit- that was enough to ward off old age and give them their youth back. So, what happened to her?

Well, one day, Loki, Odin, and Hoenir went on a perilous journey. There was little to eat in the desolate regions they traveled through, but they managed to find an ox and kill it. But no matter how long they kept the meat over the fire, it wouldn't cook. It turns out that Thjazi, a giant, was using magic to prevent them from cooking their meat, and he wanted a piece of the ox for himself in exchange for letting them prepare their dinner. The gods reluctantly agreed, but when the giant came down, taking the form of an eagle, and snatched the biggest, juiciest piece of meat, Loki got angry. He launched a thick branch at the eagle, but Thjazi fought back and took Loki to the sky. Loki, terrified that Thjazi would drop him, pleaded for his life, and the giant relented. But his price was high, to say the least. He wanted Idun and her fruits of immortality.

Loki spent what remained of the journey thinking of a plan to trick Idun into being captured by Thjazi. Of course, he found a way. He told her that he had seen incredible fruits - yes, even more, incredible than hers, beyond the walls of Asgard, and that he would bring her to these fruits if she wanted to compare them by herself. Poor Idun was fooled, and when they reached the wood she was taken by Thjazi, to his abode situated in the highest mountain peak of Jotunheim. Without Idun and her fruits, the gods grew old and sick. They quickly discovered that Loki was behind the goddess's disappearance and they threatened to kill him if he didn't retrieve her. Loki then took

Freya's hawk feather cape, which allowed him to turn into a hawk and he flew to Jotunheim.

He was lucky enough to find Idun alone and unsupervised, and he wasted no time. He turned her into a nut and flew back to Asgard with her in his talons. But Loki didn't make it back home before Thjazi found out, and he turned into an eagle and caught up with the treacherous god. Fortunately for Loki, the gods from Asgard were on the lookout and they built a wooden barrier around Asgard. After Loki made it back, they lit the barrier, killing Thjazi who didn't have time to turn back and plunged right into the flames. However, the story doesn't end there. Skadi, Thjazi's daughter soon came to Asgard to demand restitution for the murder of her father. Her request was for the gods to make her laugh because the death of her father had saddened her deeply.

Loki, the trickster god, was the only one who could accomplish such a feat. He tied one end of a rope around his male parts and the other one around a goat's beard, creating an absurd spectacle that even the frost giant couldn't gaze at without laughing. That is how Loki both caused and solved Idun's kidnapping and how he made up for the death of Thjazi to his daughter, Skadi.

The Deity Without a Cult

There are countless legends in which Loki commits crimes against the gods, and he ultimately pays for his wrongdoings. To punish him, the gods tie him down, with his legitimate son's entrails, to three rocks. The number three is sacred in Norse myths, and it is usually linked to royalty and divinity. In this case, it signifies Loki's divine punishment. It is said that a poisonous snake sits above Loki, dripping poison in his eyes. Sigyn, his wife, stays by his side and holds a bowl above his face, to catch the poison. But every once in a while the bowl gets full and she has to go and empty it while Loki writhes in agony. Loki will be freed at Ragnarok, to witness the end of the world at the hands of his children (mostly Fenrir).

Loki's identity was questioned by the many Scandinavian tribes. Some recognized him as a god, others considered him a giant, and a few cults believed him to be a different kind of mythological being. Similarly, there is confusion regarding the meaning of his name. If we go by the popular theory that Loki means *tangle* or *knot* then that is very telling of his character. His schemes tangle the deities in dangerous situations, and he himself can be considered the knot or the flaw in the cosmos that causes the end of the world. What's certain is that Loki is a traitor, a schemer, and a complete antithesis of the traditional

Viking values. Thus it is to no surprise that, as far as we know, there was no cult or following around him. There is no record speaking of Loki worshippers, nor of celebrations or sacrifices in his name. So, ironically, Loki is one of the most important characters of Norse legends and the element that causes or triggers most Norse myths, but there is no worship or cult around him. In the end, it seems that Loki's biggest joke was himself.

Baldur the Beloved God

Baldur is the son of Odin and Frigg, and he is the deity beloved by all beings and creatures that have a physical form. He is often described as being handsome and cheerful, but his name which roughly translates as "bold" also alludes to Baldur's war-like character. The most well-known myth about Baldur is that of his death.

The Death of the Beloved God

The story starts with an ode to Baldur's character and how much he was appreciated by the other gods for his ability to bring joy to anyone's heart. But, at some point, the young god starts to have ominous dreams about his death, making everybody in Asgard worry about his fate. The gods appointed Odin to look into the matter and find out what Baldur's dreams meant. And so he did. Odin disguised himself, took Sleipnir, and embarked on one of his shamanic journeys to the underworld where he knew of a wise seeress who could clarify the matter. When he got to the cold realm of Niflheim he was surprised to see the halls decorated, as if some great celebration was about to occur. He hurried to the seeress and inquired her about the preparations only to find that the distinguished guest for whom all the underworld was decorated was no other than Baldur.

Odin returned to Asgard and shared the sorrowful news. That's where Frigg, a devout mother, stepped in. She was prepared to do anything to potentially spare her son from this horrible fate. In a desperate attempt, she went to all the living and nonliving things in the universe and extracted an oath for them, to not harm Baldur. Frigg was very thorough in her mission but she made a fatal mistake - she skipped the mistletoe. To her, the small plant looked harmless, and there was no point in asking. Surely, there was no way that the mistletoe would bring any harm to her beloved son. When Loki got wind of this, he saw the opportunity for mischief.

While all the other gods made somewhat of a sport out of Baldur's invulnerability, by throwing rocks and sticks at him and laughing when they bounced off, leaving no wound behind, Loki got to scheming. He carved a spear out of mistletoe and he approached Hodr, the blind god, with apparent kindness. Loki told Hodr that he understood that he felt left out and he offered to help him take part in the game and honor Baldur's invincibility. The trickster handed Hodr the mistletoe spear and he guided his hands in the right direction. All Hodr had to do was throw, and throw he did. The weapon pierced Baldur, killing him in an instant. Poor Hodr who just wanted to fit in was nothing but a pawn in Loki's game.

The gods remained still at the sight of Baldur's corpse, not just because they cared deeply for the god, but also due to the fact that his death was foreseen in the first presage of Ragnarok. Frigg was the first to snap out of the stupor and look for a solution. The only chance that Baldur had left was for someone to go to the underworld and bargain with Hel, the goddess of the death, for his release. Hermod, a brother of Baldur took on the challenge. He borrowed Sleipnir from Odin and off he went to the realm of the dead, while the other gods prepared a worthy funeral for their dear friend. Beings from all the nine realms attended this ceremony, from gods to giants, dwarves, elves, humans and even valkyries gathered to mourn the death of Baldur.

They turned Hringhorni, Baldur's ship, into a funeral pyre and they attempted to launch it into the sea. When the ship didn't bulge, they called for Hyrrokkin, the strongest giantess, to free Hringhorni from the sand. The giantess managed to launch the ship to sea, but Nanna, Baldur's wife, couldn't bear the sight of her husband being carried to his last voyage and she died of sorrow. They place her body next to Baldur's and then Thor lit the flames. As sacrifices, Odin placed his ring Draupnir in the flames, and Baldur's horse was led in the fire, to follow his master in the afterlife.

Hermod's journey took nine nights (the divine number) but he made it to Hel. The half-living, half-dead goddess of the underworld was a strange sight, and her popularity as a harsh and greedy deity did not honor her. And there, sitting in a chair next to Loki's monstrous daughter was Baldur, or what had remained of him - a pale and lifeless spirit who looked nothing like the joyous deity. Hermod pleaded for Baldur's life, telling Hel that all the living things in the world missed him deeply. Hel was not a cruel goddess, so she presented Hermod with a deal. If the gods could determine that all the living things wept for Baldur, the living world would get him back. If, however, even one being did not care for Baldur's demise, he would remain in the underworld, forever. Hermod hurried home with the good news, and the gods wasted no time in sending messengers to find out if everything wept for Baldur. And they all did, except for one giantess called Tokk, who showed no sympathy towards Baldur's fate. Tokk was none other than Loki himself, determined to see his devious plan to the very end.

Thus Baldur was doomed to remain in the underworld, and his joyous and glorious light never graced the land of the living again.

Baldur's Character

Although in his most famous legend Baldur plays a passive role, we should not forget that he is a Norse god, who adheres to Viking ideals of a role model. In different sources that mention him, Baldur is presented as a deity that's always eager to engage in war and lead others to battle, making him a similar figure to Thor, albeit on a much smaller scale. Baldur never quite matched Thor's popularity, and because most of the sources that speak of Norse mythology are fragmentary in nature, we don't know a great deal about Baldur. What we do know is that the Vikings held him in high regard, for both his joyous personality and his war-like attributes, and they honored the memory of the beloved god of Asgard.

Tyr the God of War and Justice

When we think of important Norse deities, Tyr is not the first god to pop into our minds. He, like Baldur, is not present in many myths and legends, but it is widely believed that he was once one of the most cherished deities in the Norse pantheon, for his role as a war god and protector of justice. In epic poems, Norse heroes such as Sigurd, often invoke Tyr to garner victories in battles. Additionally, the part he plays in the story of the Binding of Fenrir, speaks volume of his just and heroic character.

The Binding of Fenrir, Son of Loki

Fenrir the wolf is the third son of Loki and the giantess Angrboda. Just as with his brothers, the gods had terrible premonitions regarding Fenrir's fate. He is said to be the one who will devour Odin at Ragnarok, allowing chaos to reign free and destroy the cosmos. Out of all Loki's monstrous children, the gods feared Fenrir the most, so they took him while he was still a pup to grow in Asgard, under their watchful eyes. The deity who took upon himself the responsibility to feed and care for the infant wolf was Tyr, the most honorable of the gods.

As weeks turned into months, Fenrir grew bigger and bigger, and the Norse deities understood that they had little time to find a way to contain the beast. They attempted to bind him with various chains, by tricking Fenrir into believing that they were but challenges to test his strength. With each chain that the beast shattered, the gods cheered to not garner the wolf's suspicion, but their anxiety grew with every failure. Finally, in the last attempt, the gods asked for the dwarves' help. They were, after all, the greatest craftsmen in the nine realms, surely they could create a chain that could bind even the fearsome Fenrir. This final attempt proved successful when the dwarves created Gleipnir, a chain made out of things that don't exist, such as the beard of a woman and a fish's breath.

But Gleipnir was a light and dainty-looking chain, and upon seeing it Fenrir suspected foul play. The wolf beast was not stupid, he agreed to try the chain only if a god or goddess would put their hand in his mouth, as a symbol of good faith. Of course, no deity rushed to fulfill Fenrir's demand, as it meant losing a limb. And yet Tyr, the brave, volunteered to put his hand in the wolf's jaw, for the sake of the world. You'd think that Fenrir would have a moment of hesitation to bite the proverbial hand that fed him, but he didn't. When he realized the gods' treachery, he chomped off Tyr's hand in an instant. Fenrir's story ends with him being tied to a boulder and transported to some sordid place. There, with a sword in his jaws to hold his mouth open, Fenrir awaits for Ragnarok, when he will be freed to carry out his destiny.

This myth is the most telling portrayal of Tyr as a divine upholder of the law. He sacrifices his hand not only to save the world from Fenrir's threat but also to offer just compensation for the gods not maintaining their side of the oath. His act fulfills the deities' end of the bargain, bringing justness and order to this whole affair. This instance mimics that of Odin sacrificing his eye for wisdom, showing that he is the foremost deity of wisdom, with the difference that, through his sacrifice, Tyr proves that he is the greatest god of justice and law.

Tyr's Roles in the Norse World

It might seem weird that a god of justice is also one of war, but for the Vikings, these two aspects were deeply entwined. From the Norsemen's point of view, war was not simply a chaotic bloody business, but somewhat of a lawful duel, where the gods decided who won and who was defeated. In many cases, the dates and places of the battles were chosen beforehand by both armies, and the Vikings had precise rules in place to prevent good war conduct. Similarly, the law could sometimes be used to gain victory over an enemy, just like war, so it makes sense to have the same deity handling both law and war.

Even though there are few surviving records of Tyr, it is clear that he was, at some point, a cherished deity of justice, before whom people swore oaths, but also a patron of honorable warriors. His worshippers valued him deeply and considered him to be on par with the mighty Thor and Odin, the ruler of the sky. It goes to show that if a deity of the time wanted the people's respect, all they had to do was sacrifice their hands to a monster of destruction that would one day bring the end of the world. Tough crowd, right?

Bites of Aesir Gods

Because few written accounts of Norse myths and legends have survived through the ages, there are plenty of Viking deities that we know little about - so little that I don't even have enough information to give them their own separate subchapter here. So, instead of allowing these gods to be forgotten, here are some "bites of the Norse gods" with some interesting things we know about the more obscure Aesir deities.

Heimdall

Heimdall is the son of Odin and the guardian of Asgard, who sits at the top of the Bifrost. He is said to have keen eyesight and hearing, which he uses to detect potential intruders. Heimdall holds the horn Gjallarhorn, which will ultimately signal the arrival of giants at Ragnarok. Heimdall's biggest enemy is Loki, and they are destined to kill each other at the end of the world, much like Jumungandr and Thor. Some Old Norse poems speak of Heimdall as being the one who created mankind and established the Viking society. An interesting fact about the guardian of Asgard is that he was born from nine different mothers, a miraculous feat to say the least.

Vili and Ve

Vili and Ve are Odin's brothers, and they are credited both for the construction of the universe and for the creation of the first two humans (both feats were done in collaboration with the Allhather). Despite being founding deities, there are few mentions of Odin's two brothers in myths and poems, except for a small note that they had slept with Frigg during Odin's 10 years of exile. Even so, they must have been extremely important to the Vikings at some point for their simple kinship to the ruler of the Aesir if for nothing else. In the Old Norse, Vili roughly translates to "will" and Ve to "temple," suggesting that the pair were associated with the sacred and the holy. Other interpretations are that the three brothers represent the basic forces that distinguish the existing world from chaos, respectively inspiration, intention, consciousness, and the sacred.

Some Old Norse texts allude to the fact that Vili and Ve are nothing more than different representations of Odin, a theory that complicates the family ties of the Aesir gods.

Ullr

Ullr was the son of Sif, and he is said to have been a great hunter and archer. Although he is an obscure deity, some surviving accounts of him describe Ullr as being a handsome war-deity, who was frequently invoked before duels. The mention of "Ullr's Blessing" in an epic poem suggests that Ullr was a deity of great importance in the Norse pantheon. His name can be translated as either "temple" tying him to the sacred, or "glory" linking him furthermore with war and war-like abilities. Some historians suggest that Ullr was a deity of law and justice, connecting him with Tyr, but there is little to no evidence to prove this supposed link. Other theories are that Ullr was actually part of the Vanir tribe, because there is a mention of him crossing the sea at some point, and many Vanir deities were associated with the iconography of water. But that is also just another theory about the enigmatic son of Sif.

Hoenir

Hoenir is another god with an enigmatic existence. He is often portrayed as the travel companion of Odin and Loki, but most accounts about him are confusing, to say the least. In some stories, he is credited with having a role in the creation of Ask and Embla, the first humans, while other legends speak of him as if he is an extension or identity of Odin (mostly because ecstasy was his gift). Hoenir is described as being a swift god, a fearful deity, and a handsome man. In fact, during an Aesir-Vanir war, when he and Mimir were offered as hostages from the Aesir, the Vanir were taken aback by Hoenir's beauty and they made him their chieftain. The rest you already know, although in that story Hoenir was replaced with Vili; the Vanir discovered how dim-witted Hoenir was and in a rage, they decapitated Mimir and sent his head to Odin, as a retaliation. But this characterization of Hoenir being a timid and dim-witted deity is contradictory to other portrayals in which he resembles Odin in abilities and characteristics. Was Hoenir nothing more than a pretty face or was he a powerful and important Norse deity? We'll probably never know.

Chapter 5: The Vanir Gods

There is a lot of debate when it comes to the Aesir-Vanir classification of the Norse gods. What sets the Vanir apart from the Aesir is a tendency towards having a closer connection to mankind and their affinity for agriculture as a whole. But even these attributes aren't always singular to Vanir gods. Take Thor, for example. Besides his roles as guardian and warrior, he is also a god of fertility and harvest, and his connection with the Viking people is perhaps one of the most significant out of all Norse deities. And yet, he is undeniably an Aesir god. Additionally, the word "Vanir" is rarely used in Old Norse texts that precede the Christian conversion of Vikings. So, at the end of the day, the whole Aesir-Vanir matter is pretty confusing.

Regardless of the controversies, three deities are commonly assigned to the Vanir family: Freya, Freyr, and Njord. According to Norse myths, they lived in Vanaheim (the realm of the Vanir), a place that is said to have been closer to nature than Asgard but still within the Aesir realm territory. The existence and descriptions of Vanaheim are just disputed in the historical world as those of the Vanir family.

Freya

Freya is one of the most important Norse goddesses, and the most prominent Vanir deity (although she became an honorary Aesir after an Aesir-Vanir war). She is the sister of Freyr and the wife of Odr, a god of inspiration and ecstasy. Freya is frequently portrayed as being beautiful, joyous, gentle, and very fond of material possessions as well as the elusive concept of love. Many stories speak of her romantic endeavors with other gods and creatures of the Norse mythology, including elves. But let's not forget that to Asgard and the old Norsemen, Freya was much more than a fun-loving deity with a fondness for the finer things in life. She is the goddess who presides over Folkvang, the afterlife realm for unmarried maidens, and one of the greatest practitioners of seidr (and the one who brought magic to gods and humans alike).

I mentioned seidr a lot throughout this book, but I never took the time to explain its nature. It is a form of magic combined with shamanism, that serves the purpose of finding out the course of one's fate and changing it by adding new events. Thus seidr could be used in a great number of ways. In the Viking Age, the women who practiced seidr were known as *vola*, and they would perform acts of magic in exchange for goods, food, or accommodation. The Vikings' sentiments towards volas were mixed. They respected them and celebrated them, but they also feared them and treated them as outcasts. In the historic period that preceded the Viking Age, it was customary for a war chief's wife to be a practitioner of seidr, and her role was to foresee and influence the outcome of a plan of action through her magic.

How Freya's beauty Led to Mjolin's Theft

The most popular stories of Freya revolve around her beauty. She was often the object of desire for antagonists, such as the giant Svaldifari who wanted to marry her (and get the moon and the sun) in exchange for building an impregnable wall around Asgard. Thankfully for her, Loki took one for the team and sabotaged Svaldifari by seducing his horse.

But another, more mainstream legend that speaks volumes of her reputation as a rare beauty is that of the theft of Mjolnir. The story goes that one day, Thor woke up to find that his precious hammer was gone. This was bad news for Asgard since without his weapon Thor couldn't fight off potential giant attacks. Freya lent Thor and Loki her falcon fathers to look for Mjolnir, and they quickly deduced that the perpetrator was Thrym, a giant. When confronted about the theft, Thrym made no effort to hide his crime, and he had the insolence to ask for something in return. Of course, this wouldn't be a story about Freya's beauty if the giant hadn't asked for her hand in marriage. The gods of Asgard, especially Freya, were livid, and they gathered to find a solution. The proposed plan quickly turned this otherwise classic myth of honorable gods versus the treacherous giants into a quirky legend: Thor was to disguise himself as Freya and go to the realm of giants to attend the wedding and get back his hammer. Somehow, all the gods agreed that was the best course of action.

And so Thor, dressed in a bridal gown, and Loki, disguised as his maid of honor, made their way to Jotunheim. At the welcome feast, Thor almost gave himself away with his insatiable appetite and his piercing gaze, but thankfully Loki was there to find unbelievable explanations that mitigated Thrym's suspicions. Then, at the ceremony, Mjolin was brought to bless the union, as the traditional custom required. But when the hammer got to Thor, he took it and wasted no time to slay his groom along with all the wedding attendees. Thor then returned home with his precious weapon and all was, once again, well and good in Asgard.

Freya or Frigg

Although most sources present Freya and Frigg as being distinct deities, many elements connect the two. For one, Freya's husband, Odr, is virtually Odin. The names themselves are a dead giveaway (Odin and Odr have the same root) but Odr's association with inspiration and ecstasy is truly the nail in the proverbial coffin. There is even a story that portrays Freya as being Odin's concubine. If we also take into account the tales that speak of Odr's frequent journeys, it becomes very evident that Odr and Odin are the same deities, or at least that Odr is an extension of Odin. That in exchange means that Freya and Frigg are either the same goddess or different sides of the same deity.

Let's not forget that Frigg herself had somewhat of a bad reputation of being an arduous lover, who even went as low as sleeping with Odin's brothers while he was exiled from Asgard. That sounds pretty similar to Freya's tales of romantic endeavors. Additionally, Frigg is frequently associated with the practice of magic, which comes to light through her proficiency in weaving and her extensive knowledge of the fate of all beings. The names of the two goddesses are also very peculiar. Freya or *Freyja* roughly translates to "lady" which sounds more like a social title than a name. Meanwhile, Frigg in the Old Norse meant "beloved," tying her to attributes such as love and desire, which are frequently used in portrayals of Freya. So in a weird twist, Frigg's name describes Freya's identity, while Freya's name describes just a social status rather than a unique characterization.

No matter how we look at this, it's impossible to not conclude that Freya and Frigg are ultimately the same people. Their husbands, their use of magic, their portrayal as sensual women, and their significance in the Norse pantheon, make it crystal clear that they share an identity. And yet, in many myths and legends they are portrayed as different individuals, one the Allmother and one a Vanir goddess of magic and fertility. Where is this separation coming from and what purpose does it serve? Unfortunately, we have no way of knowing that.

Freyr

Freyr is a god of peace, masculinity, good weather, and prosperity. He is Freya's twin and one of the most beloved deities of the common Norsemen who were farmers and settlers. Since his blessings were usually good harvest, fertility, prosperity, and health, it's not hard to understand why he was held in high regard and was often the recipient of sacrifices, especially during harvest festivals and weddings. Fortunately, his sacrifices were often boars and not humans, because that was Freyr's favorite animal, perhaps in reference to Gullinborsti - the golden bristled boar he had received from the dwarves Sindri and Brokkr.

Although he is a Vanir god and an honorary Aesir, Freyr lives in Alfheim, the realm of the elves. That could mean that he was a ruler of the elves or he had deep connections with the elusive creatures. Freyr is also known for his famous ship, Skidbladnir, that could be easily folded to fit in a bag and that always had a favorable wind. Skidbladnir is considered to symbolize the ritual ships used by the Scandinavian people during funeral rites or celebrations and not their long-ships. For on land transport, Freys is said to have used a chariot drawn by boars, his preferred beasts. During harvest celebrations, Freyr worshippers would put a statue of the god in a chariot and travel through the lands with it. All the settlements would welcome the procession and the festivities would ensure, overseen by the kind and peaceful presence of Freyr (or at least his statue).

We can understand the magnitude of Freyr's importance for the Norse people simply by the amount of information that we have regarding his worship and cult. As you've probably noticed by now, not much is known about the spiritual life of the Vikings, and yet for Freyr, we have details regarding not only sacrifices but also celebrations in his name. That's pretty huge! On top of that, the deity is credited with being the founding father of numerous royal lines and tribes.

Freyr's Wedding

The most well-known and one of the only surviving stories of Freyr is that of his marriage to the giantess Gerdr. It's a touching myth of how Freyr one day saw the woman of his dreams when he sat on Hlithskjolf, Odin's throne. Freyr then was overcome with sadness, because he couldn't be with that fair woman. His father, Njord noticed his son's depression and sent a servant, Skirnir, to tend to his needs. Freyr told Skirnir about his plight and he implored him to find Gerdr and ask for her hand in his name. Skirnir accepted the task but he asked for something in return - Freyr's magical sword, that fought on its own. Freyr complied and soon enough he and Gerdr met for the first time and they became a happy couple.

The myth is sweet in nature, but Freyr's sacrifice was perhaps bigger than what he bargained for. Without his sword, Freyr encountered many hardships in fights with various giants. It is said that at Ragnarok he will perish at the hands of Surtr, specifically because the sword is no longer in his possession.

Njord

Njord is the father of Freyr and Freya, and he is a Vanir deity associated with fertility, wealth, and the sea. Considering that seafaring was an important aspect of a Viking's life, it's safe to say that Njord held an important place in the Norsemen's hearts. And yet, one of the only historical accounts that we have of him is the story of how he married Skadi.

Skadi was Thjazi's daughter, who came to Asgard to avenge her father's death at the hands of the Aesir deities (although Thjazi himself was not so innocent, by kidnapping Idun and stealing the gods' immortality). One of her requests was for the gods to make her laugh, which Loki accomplished with his parlor tricks. Another wish of hers was for her father to be honored, and to do so Odin took his eyes and transformed them into stars in the night sky. Lastly, to appease Skadi, she was allowed to choose any god she wanted for marriage with the catch being that she could only choose them based on their feet. Her personal preference was Baldur because he was the most beloved of the gods, and she chose the pair of feet that she believed to be the fairest -worthy only of Baldur. But the gods with the fairest feet ended up to be Njord. Thus the two got married.

Their marriage however was short-lived because they couldn't agree on where to live. Skadi found Njord's home, Noatun (a place near the sea) to be too sunny, and with noisy seabirds that didn't let her sleep. Njord hated the cold of Skadi's home, Thrymheim, and the sounds of the howling wolves. They ended up parting ways after only 18 nights spent together.

Njord seems to have been widely worshipped at some time in the Vikings' history, but we'll never know to what extent or how he was honored by his worshippers.

Chapter 6: Viking Spirituality

Just like all complex religions, Norse spirituality had two main elements: rituals and mystical knowledge that allowed people to understand the inner workings of the universe and how to find their purpose.

When it comes to rituals and other practical ways of worshipping the deities we don't have much to refer to. It is obvious that the Norse gods had a devout religious following which served the social, spiritual, and psychological needs of the Vikings, but the myths and legends do little to explain how the actual worship of the gods played out. Historical evidence speaks of the Norse *blot*, a ceremony through which Odin and other important deities were celebrated. The blots were usually performed at temples or special "blot houses" and they involved sacrifices, of both the human and animal kind. Enemy rulers or noblemen were frequently sacrificed to honor Odin, while animals were used wherever the specific deity had an animal that they could be linked to, such as Freyr with boars. The animals would be killed and consumed by the religious practitioners, in a ceremony that somewhat resembles a modern Christian communion - meaning that the animal was seen as an embodiment of the god.

Blots were a central part of Vikings' lives, and the month of

November was named after the divine ceremonies "Blotmonth" or "Bloodmonth." Old Anglo-Saxon writings speak of en masse sacrifices of cattle and horses, where the blood was gathered in special vessels to be consumed and "splashed" over the attendees of the ceremonies. A priest would then bless the meat, vessels, and goblets used at the feast and they would ensure the celebrations. A goblet was ceremoniously emptied to honor certain gods. First Odin, to bless the ruling class, then Freya and Freyr to bring peace and good harvest. Attendees could also empty a goblet to honor their departed.

Viking sacrifices were seen as gifts to the gods, to show appreciation for their blessings and for maintaining order and peace in the cosmos. For the Norsemen, their deities were not perfect or all-powerful. They too were governed by fate and by the laws of the world. Vikings saw them first and foremost as protectors of order, that kept the evil forces in check and seldomly intervened in the events that happened in the mortal world. If we consider how dangerous and harsh the Viking world was, it's not hard to see why the Christian portrayal of a loving and omnipotent god didn't flourish in the minds and hearts of Norsemen. They worshipped their gods with the hopes that they would, in exchange, bless and protect their families and communities. That was all.

Most of the mystic knowledge of the Vikings came from their myths and legends. Through these tales of the realm of the gods and how the cosmos came to be, the Norsemen can easily find ideals, role models, and goals to strive towards in their lives. Odin is a model for kings, knowledge seekers, and fathers alike. Thor is the ultimate Viking - warrior, loyal, and determined to fulfill his duty to the very end. Freya and Frigg are symbols of motherhood, the joy of life, and Norse magic. Freyr is the personification of wealth, peace, and prosperity. And the symbolic peace that is established between the Aesir and the Vanir tells Vikings that all the aspects that the deities represent and equally important to lead a happy life and have a successful society. Norse tales are also full of numerology and hidden elements that only the wise and knowledgeable can decipher. These people who were wise enough to see beyond the apparent could practice divination and seidr, to foresee and influence someone's fate.

There's no doubt that Viking spirituality ran deep, and was a lot more complex than Anglo-Saxons of the time believed. And yet, close to the end of the Viking Age, the Norsemen started to give up on their gods and traditions and embrace Christianity. There are many dramatized stories speaking of forced conversions and even of saints or angels that aided Christian clerics in their mission to bring God to the Viking pagans. But in reality, Christianity came to the Viking world naturally and progressively. Vikings were very flexible with their beliefs, and they started to incorporate Christian elements in their religion as soon as they set foot on European soil. Sure there were a few traditionalists who clung on to their Mjolnir pendants, but most of the Scandinavian population was open to inclusion, though they opted to accept one element at a time rather than make a full 180 degrees conversion. Old Norse iconography mixed with Christian symbols and customs to create hybrid religions. It was perfectly acceptable for baptized Norsemen to still invoke Thor's protection in their times of need.

The conversion to Christianity of the Norse population was slow, and it started way before Christian missionaries officiated it. The challenge clerics had was not to teach Norsemen the values and practices of Christianity, but rather to convince them to embrace only these Christian elements, and give up on all remnants of their pagan beliefs. The conversion to Christianity didn't happen on its own as a singular event. It came together with the "Europeanization" of Vikings, which led to the Norsemen giving up on traditional values and norms. They made the switch from chieftains to kings, they adopted the Latin alphabet, and little by little the Viking world adhered to European standards.

But what triggered the conversion to Christianity, in the first place? Well, although we can't know for sure, the most plausible reason is the selfish character of the Vikings. Remember, they worshipped their gods in hopes of garnering protection, blessings, and prosperity. But there were things the Norse gods could not provide. Norse deities were ambivalent and not prone to forgive. They did not offer the salvation of one's soul, and they were not always in the "mood" to listen to mere mortals. The Christian God, however, was kind, ever-loving, and forgiving. For the Vikings, all that mattered was who could offer more, thus Christianity was an easy pick. The benefits that it bought were deemed enough to merit worship and loyalty. Viking kings and rulers were usually first to convert because it helped them make powerful alliances. And if the king went first, his people would usually follow. As time went by, Christianity slowly became the default, and the once pagan Vikings became devout followers of God.

Chapter 7: Mythological Creatures

Norse mythology presents a rich and complex world of spiritual and supernatural beings. These beings lived among the gods or humans and carried out their specific roles. The dwarves, for example, are often called upon by the gods for their unmatched talents of crafting incredible weapons and tools. Dragons are fearful beasts that have a special love for material things, especially gold. Such an example is Fafnir, the great dragon that was slain by the Nordic hero Sigurd, to avenge his father's death and obtain the dragon's treasure. Only the most honorable and brave could kill these magnificent and malevolent beasts. And the Valkyries are Odin's familiars and the ones who choose who goes to Valhalla. But there is not much to say of these creatures, at least nothing new or exciting. So, here in this chapter, I'll cover some more elusive sprites of the Norse mythology, some of which will give us a better understanding of the Viking civilization and the values and beliefs they held dear.

Elves

Elves, or *alfar* as they were called by the old Norsemen, were divine beings that were above the human race. They were often described as being tall genderless or androgynous-looking beings, with a pale complexion and light-colored hair. Elves were renowned for their beauty and their ability to use magic, and some stories go as far as to call them gods or demi-gods due to their powers and affiliation with the Norse deities.

As a side note here, we must understand that the way in which the Norsemen classified their mythological creatures was kind of confusing and it left a lot of room for interpretation. For example, there are no clear distinctions between the gods, elves, dwarves, and other beings, and the boundaries between the classifications are blurred further due to the apparently free-handed use of terminology. Some sources describe the Vanir gods as being elves, with Freyir being their lord and ruler, while other texts consider them separate beings. Another result of this confusing classification comes to play when describing the nature of the elves. A long-held belief was that elves were beings of light and goodness, who could heal or aid humans (in exchange for offerings or sacrifices). But in reality, it seems like elves were rather ambivalent, and it wasn't uncommon for them to use their magic to cause illness and misfortune to humankind.

Although this ambivalence was common in Norse belief, Christianity couldn't wrap its head around the concept. So, in an effort to categorize the elven race, 13th-century historians divided them into classes of dark and light elves, drawing inspiration from Christian concepts of angels and demons.

Ijosalfar were the elves of light, who personified the good attributes of the human race, while the *dokkalfar*, the dark elves, became demonic beings who brought upon temptation and destruction. The distinction went as far as to ascribe a separate realm for each type of elves, with the light elves living in Alfheimr and the dark elves in Svartalfaheimr. It's worth mentioning that these post-Viking Era historians misunderstood many of the Old Norse writings. Such an example of misinterpretation could be the use of the term dokkalfar to refer to the dark-elves. The Vikings used *dokkalfar* when they spoke of the dwarves. Additionally, the realm of the dwarves was called Svartalfar, which is conspicuously similar to Svartalfaheimr, the realm attributed to the evil elves. Thus, the dark-elves of the 13th-century writings may be nothing more than the old Norse dwarves.

In many senses, the early Vikings worshipped elves as they did their deities, in the hopes of winning their blessings. Humans who accomplished great deeds in their lives were believed to become elves after their demise, an element that ties in the worship of elves with that of the ancestors. Perhaps because the elves were somewhat closer to the human realm, so much so that cross-breeding was an option, the worship of elves had ultimately outlived that of the gods, disappearing entirely only when the conversion to Christianity of the Viking world was completed.

Huldra

The Scandinavian space has always had plentiful forested areas, and it comes as no surprise that the dark and mysterious-looking woods sparked the imagination of the old Norsemen. From witches to trolls and shapeshifting monsters, there was no end to what could hide among the trees of Norway, Sweden, and Denmark. Tales of forest spirits are very common in areas with lush greenery, but no spirits are as interesting and treacherous as the Nordic Huldra or Skogstra. These are female spirits who ruled over the vast forest of the Viking world, sowing fear and perhaps curiosity, in men's hearts.

In the early days, forests were seen somewhat as separate realms, that hid both perils and wonders, violence and beauty. It was a place for outcasts and forces of evil, where dangers awaited at every step. And they were not wrong. Without maps or modern navigation equipment, a wrong turn or a slight shift in the weather could lead to someone getting lost, increasing their chances of bumping into dangerous forest beasts such as bears and wolves. Many people who ventured into the forest of the old Norsemen never made it out alive, which is most likely why tales of forest sprites were so popular. They served as explanations of why loved ones failed to return, but also as a warning for children and adventurous youngsters. At the time, blaming natural events such as disappearances on fantastic creatures was more appealing than finding a reasonable and logical explanation. Most mythological creatures are born as a result of this tendency towards fantasizing the "unexplainable."

Our Huldra or Skogsra was a forest spirit who usually took on the form of a young, beautiful maiden with a fox or cow's tail. Because the Scandinavian world was rather big, the creature has many names, and there is a lot of variation when it comes to her descriptions and the stories revolving around her. She would lure young men, make love to them, and then eat them alive, much like the popular tales of the sirens and mermaids who caused shipwrecks and feasted on human flesh. This anthropomorphic being is often portrayed as a stereotypically seductive creature that roams the woods naked and can barely carry her large breasts. Other portrayals of the Huldra describe her as being an animal-human hybrid, that looks beautiful from the front but it has a backside that resembles a rotten tree-trunk. Whatever the version, Huldra is undeniably an anthropomorphic representation of nature itself, that is about alluring and dangerous.

Some tales, however, speak of female forest spirits that gave birth to half-monster half-human babies, alluding to forbidden relationships between young men and the Huldras. Indeed, not all forest spirit-human interactions led to death and misfortune. Men who willingly became a forest spirit's lover would receive the Huldra's blessings and aid in times of need. A Huldra could ensure that your arrow always reached its mark or that you would survive perilous situations. These relationships would often lead to the human counterparts being looked down upon or even punished by the church. Of course, there were also situations in which the humans would refuse such an intimate relationship, and they could allegedly safely do so by burning the private parts of the spirit. Because most stories of the Huldra and the Skogsra are sexual in nature, they likely have, in part, originated from erotic fantasies of men who spent a lot of time in the woods.

Draugr

Draugr are the undead of the Norse mythology, who would rise from their graves to kill and terrorize the living. These creatures would maintain the physical abilities that they had during their lives, with an added element of magical powers such as the ability to increase their size, superhuman strength, and knowledge of the past and future. Draugr were violent and very hostile towards the living, which is why the Norse people feared them and took many precautions to prevent their dead from coming back to life. One such method was the creation of a special "corpse-door" through which the corpse of the recently deceased was carried to their burial place. You see, the

Norsemen believed that the undead could only enter a house by using the door through which their body had last left the house. So they dismantled a part of the walls to use as a "corpse-door," that would quickly be repaired after the funeral was completed. Another way of keeping the dead at bay was to build walls around gravesites, although if the Draugr had the power to grow as tall as they wanted, I don't think that method was too successful. A more strategic approach was to bury the dead with blunt weapons or broken weapons, so the dead couldn't use them or to place a large boulder over a person's grave.

But what caused the dead to come back to life? Norse people, just like other civilizations of the past, had a very deep connection with the afterlife. The fate of the dead was often more important or real for Vikings than their life in the world of the living. Dying an honorable death and being chosen to go by Odin's side was pretty much the goal of a Viking's life. However, death is a complicated concept, and the Norsemen didn't see the bodies of their deceased as being "dead." Reanimation was a real fear, especially because it could happen to anyone. Sure, things like practicing magic, being an outlaw, or being buried outside a graveyard court would make it more likely for the dead to come back to life, but so was dying of an accident. That could happen to anyone, especially in an age and geographic region as dangerous as the Viking one.

Draugr were dangerous creatures that killed any humans they laid eyes upon. But there are also stories and accounts of weird acts done by the undead and specific Draugr that featured in Norse tales. Starting with the first, a quirky thing that the Draugr were said to indulge in was "riding roofs." That means that they would climb on people's roofs at night and stomp on them, to disturb the sleep of the inhabitants. Having a Draugr "riding your roof" was surely preferable to being killed by one, but it was still a way of terrorizing the living. Famous Draugr include Glamr, an extremely aggressive sprite that was killed in a wrestling match by the Norse hero Grettir, and Thorgunna, a Draugr lady who came back to life because the men carrying her to her grave did not treat her body with respect. You'd think that Thorgunna's body was reanimated to get its revenge but you'd be mistaken. In exchange, she came back to cook for them, naked. The men, pleased with Thorgunna's cooking and perhaps impressed with her attire (or lack of) buried her a second time, in a churchyard.

Some Draugr were said to guard the treasure they possessed while they were living, kind of like the nefarious Fafnir who was obsessed with his gold. Apparently, the only correct way of killing a Draugr was by burning it, which is likely part of the reason why ship burials were preferred especially for kings and people of high status - they ensured the dead won't come back while the soul was making its way to Valhalla.

Fossegrim

Fossegrim is a troll or a water spirit that plays the fiddle from beneath waterfalls. This sprite shares many attributes with the Huldra such as its beauty, its alluring nature (the Fossegrim is said to play enchanting music), its apparent nudity, and its ambivalence towards humans. But there is one big difference that sets them apart - the Fossegrim is male. The music of the Fossegrim is said to be so enchanting that even the lame, sick, and old would dance to its tunes. Just as with the Huldra, the Fossegrim is a seductive spirit that can lead humans to their doom. He is more prominent in Norwegian folklore, although legends of the Fossegrim can also be found in Sweden and Denmark.

Some stories speak of women and children who were lured to bodies of water where they ultimately drowned. Again these stories are more likely just ways to rationalize drownings and warn the young ones about the dangers of lakes and rivers. Let's not forget that water is a force of nature, that brings both prosperity through fishing and agriculture but also death for those foolish enough to challenge the depths and currents. The more intimidating and awe-inducing an element was at the time, the more supernatural beings were attributed to it. Our Fossegrim just happens to be one of many such as water serpents and Krakens - the giant octopuses or squids that pulled ships downwards to their demise.

Other stories of the Fossegrim are more lighthearted. It is said that the sprite would teach you how to play the fiddle if you offered him a proper sacrifice. The requirements for the offering were pretty intense. For once, the sacrifice had to be a plump white male goat, offered in secrecy on Thursday evening. The goat had to be thrown into a waterfall, while the animal's head was turned away from the wall of water. Only waterfalls that flowed northwards were considered acceptable. Another type of sacrifice that suited the refined tastes of the Fossegrim was smoked mutton, but this too had a catch - it had to be stolen from a neighbor, on four subsequent Thursdays. If one would successfully make an offering to the water sprite, the Fossegrim would take the person's hand and play the fiddle until their fingers bled. After this harsh training, the person would gain the musical abilities of the spirit. If, however, the goat was too lean or the mutton insufficient in any way, the Fossegrim would only show you how to tune your fiddle.

Because the fiddle was so tightly linked to the legends of the Fossegrim, the instrument was banned from being used in churches, and those who played it were discriminated against in religious communities. This hatred resulted in many fiddles being burnt or destroyed, in an attempt to cast away the esoteric forces.

Kraken

Since I've mentioned the humongous beast, it seems fair to go into a little more detail about this Norse creature that was based on a very real fear of the sea. The Kraken is a species of sea monsters said to swell in the waters of Greenland and Norway. Many depictions of them describe the Kraken as being so huge that they could easily pass for islands, that, if you were foolish enough to dock for a quick exploration, would sink as soon as you set foot on "land" turning you quite literally into "fish food." This description ties the Kraken to another well-known sea creature, the island whale - a sea beast that was frequently mistaken for land and which took sailors to the depths as soon as they lit a fire on its back. In one way, we can think of the Kraken as the result of humanity's greatest sea-related fears. First, we have the unimaginable size, then the apparently neverending number of limbs and its violent nature. And of course, its preference for dragging ships to the bottom of the sea - a gruesome way to die. We can't really fault the sailors for believing in such stories, especially when they were presented with the perils of the sea on a daily basis.

For people in Medieval times, if you rowed too many miles into the Norwegian Sea, you were merely a few seconds away from becoming the victim of the greatest animal creation that ever existed. The first and foremost sign that you were close to encountering a Kraken was when you started to reel in an unusually large amount of fish. The sailors believed that the fish fled for the surface in an effort to escape the sea-monster, thus resulting in great luck for the fishermen. But escaping the Kraken was not impossible. If the rowers could flee the area in which their catch was suspiciously good fast enough, they could escape with their lives and see from a distance the enormous creature coming to the surface. The Kraken though is not a stupid sea-monster. It was known to form whirlpools with its giant tentacles, to draw in ships, and use small fish as bait for unsuspecting sailors. Nonetheless, many stories make note of the Kraken's appetite for fish and how, if left alone, it wouldn't go out of its way to harm humans. These stories tell the tales of how the creatures used its excrement (which is described in way too much detail as being thick and making the waters appear muddy) to lure fish directly over their mouth for a quick and efficient fish-snack.

I wanted to finish off the Mythological Creatures chapter with the Kraken for two reasons. One would be that it's an extremely popular mythological being that most of us have heard of, at least in passing, and second, it is one of the few fantastic beasts that is based on a real-life animal - the giant squid. These creatures are just as elusive as the mythical Kraken but they are without a doubt real, roaming the waters of the world in search of food and having epic underwater battles with their life-sworn enemies (and natural predators) the sperm whales. With this in mind, it's not hard to understand why so many European legends speak of the Kraken and its formidable nature.

Chapter 8: Ragnarok

In Norse mythology, Ragnarok is the end of the world, kind of like the Christian Apocalypse. It is a great cataclysm that will trigger the destruction of the universe and all its beings, including the gods. For the Vikings, Ragnarok, which roughly translates to "the Fate of the gods" was a prophecy that foretold the doom of all life, and it had a big influence on how the old Norsemen perceived the world around them. Although no one knows when the prophecy will happen, the story itself is very complex and detailed, including signs that foretell the beginning of the end, clear descriptions of the great battle between the gods and the giants, the outcome of the divine war, and what is to come after the apocalypse. Let's go through all of these aspects first and then we'll take the time to understand the impact that Ragnarok had on the Norse civilization.

The Signs of Ragnarok

The first sign included in the tellings of Ragnarok is one that has already happened in the mythological universe of the Norse people, and that is the murder of Baldur. We've covered the circumstances of his death and the deities' attempt to bring him back - for their sake and that of the universe since Baldur's resurrection would have meant the delay of Ragnarok. Then, at some point, the Norns, the three creatures that spin the fate of the cosmos (called Urd, Verdandi, and Skuld) will decree the coming of the *Fimbulwinter* (the Great Winter), a long a bitter winter unlikely any other than the world has seen before. The cold will be so great that the warmth of the sun could no longer reach the Earth, allowing the snow to fall without interruption and the temperatures to drop to unimaginable lows.

This great winter will be as long as three normal winters, with the exception that there will be no summer in between. Mankind will be at the brink of extinction, their desperation to survive chipping away at their morality. At its peak, the frenzy of survival will take control of them all, and the age of swords and axes will begin. No laws of nature or society will be able to stop the chaos of the human world. Fathers will slay their sons, sons will kill their fathers, and brother will turn against brother in hopes of surviving the end times. This situation will only worsen when the two wolves, Skoll and Hati, will finally catch and devour the moon and the sun bringing darkness into the world. The stars too will vanish, leaving behind a black void. Yggdrasill, the great world tree, will tremble, causing the mountains and the trees to fall to the ground.

Then in Jotunheim, the realm of the giants, Fjalar (The All-knower) a red rooster, will warn the frost giants that Ragnarok has come. A second red rooster will announce to Hel and all the dead from Niflheim that the time of the final war is upon the world. And finally, in Asgard, a third red rooster called Gullinkambi, will warn the deities that the giants are coming. The number three, which is used to symbolize the sacred is heavily present in these tellings of the signs of Ragnarok. There are three Norns, Fimbulwinter lasts three winters, and we have three rosters that warn the gods, giants, and dead at the beginning of Ragnarok.

The Great Battle

As Ragnarock starts, all the beasts will run free and join the army of the giants. Fenrir's chain will snap, Loki will escape from his cave of torment, and Jumurgandr, the great serpent, will rise from the depths of the sea, spilling the waters over Midgard. The convulsions created by the coming of Ragnarok will free the ship Naglfar, which is made from the toenails and fingernails of all the dead in Niflehmein. Aboard this ship will be Hel and her dead, the giants, and all the forces of destruction and the captain of Naglfar will be none other than Loki, the god of mischief. With the world now engulfed by waters, the ship will easily make its way to the realm Vigrid, where the last battle will take place. As the great serpent will poison the Earth and the waters with his great venom, Fenrir will roam the Earth, with his jaws wide-open, devouring everything in his path.

While this whole procession will make its way to Vigrid, the sky will open and the fire-giants of Muspelheim will be led by Surtr the destroyer. This procession will march across the Bifrost, breaking the rainbow bridge. Then Heimdall will blow the Gjallarhorn, to announce the beginning of the end. The horn will be heard by Odin's honorable warriors, the *einherjar,* and Freya's *folkvangr,* and they will hurry to march into battle alongside their veneered deities. The fallen Aesir gods, Baldur and Hodr, will come back from the realm of the dead, to join the battle and aid their kin. Odin will consult Mimir's head, for one last time, before deciding to go to battle and fulfill their destiny. They will swiftly arm themselves and then they will follow the All-father, who will lead them to Vigrid, on the back of his trusty steed Sleipnir. With his spear, Gungnir in his hand, Odin will dive into the battle that he knows he is destined to lose.

The battle of Vigrid will happen as it was foretold. Odin and his warriors will fight valiantly but they will be eaten by the great wolf Fenrir. Vidar, a son of Odin, will avenge his father by holding open the wolf's mouth with one leg in which he'll have a special shoe made only from the leather that has been discarded by shoemakers, and sliding his sword in the beast's throat, killing him in an instant. Garm, the wolf of the underworld, and Tyr will kill each other. Loki will finally get his ultimate punishment by dying at Heimdall's hands, although the guardian deity will also perish in the process. Freyr will be killed by Sutr because he will no longer possess his sword. Thor will finally face his lifelong foe, Jumurgandr, and he will kill the beast with a blow of his precious Mjollin. But the snake's venom will end up putting an end to the mightiest of the Norse gods, and Thor will lie dead on the battleground of Vigrid after managing to take nine last steps. The number nine here shows Thor's connection to pagan beliefs and signifies the turning point of the battle.

In the end, most of the gods and giants will die, and the dragon Nidhug will feast on the corpses. Other dragons will come and their fire will destroy the world, and the waters will engulf what will be left of it. Thus, a new void will be created, and everything will be as if the universe from before had never existed.

A New World

Many believe that the tale of Ragnarok ends there, but the prophecy goes on to speak of a new beginning. A green and beautiful world will rise from the waters. The gods that will survive Ragnarok, which are Baldur, Hodr, Vidar, Vali, Modi, and Magni, will reinstate the realm of the deities, Ivadoll. Here they will build great houses with golden roofs and they will be ruled by a great unnamed leader. A man and a woman, Lifthrasir and Lif, who were lucky enough to hide in the Wood of Hoddmimir (or in the sacred tree Yggdrasil in some versions) will survive Ragnarok, and they will repopulate the realm of men. A new sun will adorn the skies, and new places will be established such as Okolnir (Never cold) and Namstrod (a shore of corpses). There will also be a new underworld, for murderers and thieves, where the great Nidhug will satiate his hunger for dead meat.

Not much else is known about this new era that will come after Ragnarok.

The Vikings and Ragnarok

The first problem that arises when we look at what Ragnarok meant for the Norse people is the fact that we have two versions of the story. In one, the world ends and all that remains is a void, and in the other one, the demolition of one world leads to the birth of a new one. The generally accepted explanation is that the second version, that in which rebirth follows destruction, is newer and it shows the shift in Norse belief brought by the introduction of Christianity in the Viking world. We can look at this as a representation of the death of the old gods and the birth of a new era, presided over by a mighty ruler, who could or could not be the Christian God.

But let's take a step back and look at the other version, which is more authentic to the Viking way of thinking. In one way, their belief in Ragnarok brought a somewhat tragic meaning to their lives. After all, who wouldn't feel like their life was meaningless if they knew that one day the universe itself will end and nothing and no-one can change or survive that? It is as if you grow up knowing that you are destined to die and disappear forever. However, in another way, the tale of Ragnarok taught Vikings how to act and what was expected of them. It taught them the importance of having a noble attitude and facing your fate with courage and honor. After all, if the gods can courageously march towards their doom and fight valiantly despite knowing that no matter what, they will fail, then so could humans. Thus, Vikings embraced the inevitability of death and focused on accomplishing great deeds and creating a name for themselves - one that would be passed down for all the generations to come.

And their reputation would live on until the arrival of Ragnarok when the world would end.

Conclusion

This marks the end of our Norse journey. We've seen how the Vikings transitioned from a peaceful, agriculture-focused society into a military force to be reckoned with, that made all the European world tremble in fear. But these people were far from our preconceived idea of barbarians, pagans, and mindless brutes. They were an advanced society with a rich culture and deep belief in the sacred and the divine. The Vikings had legal assemblies where they proposed and voted laws for settlements to live by. They were driven, courageous people who were ready to risk their lives for a chance at improving their social and financial situation, and garnering a good reputation. They valued their social bonds deeply and they honored their kin, and even if their ideas of gender roles were still private, the Norse women enjoyed liberties and luxuries that few of their European sisters could dare to dream of in Medieval times.

One of the most important aspects of a Norseman's life was worshiping and honoring their deities, in hopes of winning them over and receiving their blessings. The kings, rulers, and noblemen invoked Odin for guidance and inspiration. The warriors asked for Thor's protection in battle. The farmers celebrated Freya, Freyr, and the mighty Thor to ensure their harvest would be plentiful and that their family will prosper. Although most Norse rituals and traditions are lost to time, we

249

can't deny the deep connection these people felt with their gods. For them, deities were their role models, their guides, their protectors, and the answers to all their questions about life and its purpose.

The Norse also believed in mythological creatures that roamed the forests, waters, gravesites, and the other unseen realms of gods, elves, and giants. Most of these creatures, just as the Norse gods, were ambivalent in nature, able to bring both fortunes and disasters. Their belief in the mythical was so deep that people would take precautions against the living dead and they would banish any individual that seemed to be connected to the esoteric. This negative attitude towards the unexplained was only worsened when the Norse people renounced their faith in favor of Christianity. But that's not the only aspect of the Vikings' life that was changed by the Europeanization of the Scandinavian space.

The shift to Christianity also marks the end of Norse tradition and politics. War chiefs were replaced by kings, the loyal and honorable clans became armies, the trade-cities flourished and the Norse turned their back to their gods. These changes led to military and economic success, but it cost the Vikings their identity. Their pragmatic way of regarding their fate had softened, and even Ragnarok, the grim prophecy of the end of the universe, had changed to better fit this new mentality. It became a tale of hope and new beginnings, a fitting story for the new-generation Vikings, who renounced their old ways as soon as those no longer worked in their favor.

So who were the Vikings? How should we describe this flexible civilization that swept the European world like a storm? They were brave, strong, educated, driven, perhaps greedy, thirsty for adventure, and open-minded. They were warriors, discoverers, poets, story-tellers, and colonists. They took all the opportunities that life threw at them and they never looked back, no matter where their destinies brought them.

I hope you enjoyed our ride through the history, life, and mythological world of the old Norse people. Good luck with your mythological travels and don't forget to keep your eyes open for new discoveries! There is so much that we don't know about these forgotten civilizations and every new archeological finding brings us one step closer to understanding them and finding out who they really were.

References

Ager, S. (2017). Old Norse language, alphabet and pronunciation. Omniglot.Com. https://omniglot.com/writing/oldnorse.htm

Apel, T. (2019a). Freya. Mythopedia. https://mythopedia.com/norse-mythology/gods/freya/

Apel, T. (2019b). Freyr. Mythopedia. https://mythopedia.com/norse-mythology/gods/freyr/

Ashliman, D. L. (2010, February 17). The Norse Creation Myth. Pitt.Edu. https://www.pitt.edu/~dash/creation.html

Black, J. (2020, June 25). The story of Ragnarok and the Apocalypse. Ancient-Origins.Net; Ancient Origins. https://www.ancient-origins.net/myths-legends/story-ragnarok-and-apocalypse-001352

Encyclopedia Mythica. (2004, October 9). Helgi Hundingsbane | Encyclopedia Mythica. Pantheon.Org. https://pantheon.org/articles/h/hundingsbane.html

Encyclopedia Mythica. (2005, October 11). Helgi Hjörvarðsson | Encyclopedia Mythica. Pantheon.Org. https://pantheon.org/articles/h/hjorvardsson.html

Foster, J. (2020, August 31). Fossegrim and His Fiddle: The Troll at the Heart of Norwegian Music — The American Skald. Jameson Foster. https://www.theamericanskald.com/blog/fossegrim

Groeneveld, E. (2017, November 2). Norse Mythology. Ancient History Encyclopedia; Ancient History Encyclopedia. https://www.ancient.eu/Norse_Mythology/

Harasta, J., & Charles River Editors. (2015a). Decline of the Norse Faith - Odin: The Origins, History and Evolution of the Norse God. Erenow.Net. https://erenow.net/ancient/odin-origins-history-evolution-norse-god/6.php

Harasta, J., & Charles River Editors. (2015b). Legends About Odin - Odin: The Origins, History and Evolution of the Norse God. Erenow.Net. https://erenow.net/ancient/odin-origins-history-evolution-norse-god/3.php

Harasta, J., & Charles River Editors. (2015c). Norse Mysticism and Odin - Odin: The Origins, History and Evolution of the Norse God. Erenow.Net. https://erenow.net/ancient/odin-origins-history-evolution-norse-god/5.php

Harasta, J., & Charles River Editors. (2015d). Worship of Odin - Odin: The Origins, History and Evolution of the Norse God. Erenow.Net. https://erenow.net/ancient/odin-origins-history-evolution-norse-god/4.php

Joe, J. (1999). Odin Hanging From Yggdrasil (Search For Wisdom) Explained. Timeless Myths. https://www.timelessmyths.com/norse/wisdom.html#:~:text=Odin%20had%20several%20means%20of

Kuusela, T. (2020, July 16). Skogsrå and Huldra: The femme fatale of the Scandinavian forests. #FolkloreThursday. https://folklorethursday.com/folktales/skogsra-and-huldra-the-femme-fatale-of-the-scandinavian-forests/

Lloyd, E. (2020, May 24). Draugr - Vikings Feared This Ugly Living Dead With Prophetic Visions. Ancient Pages. https://www.ancientpages.com/2020/05/24/draugr-vikings-feared-living-dead-with-prophetic-visions/

McCoy, D. (2012a). Baldur. Norse Mythology for Smart People. https://norse-mythology.org/gods-and-creatures/the-aesir-gods-and-goddesses/baldur/

McCoy, D. (2012b). Elves. Norse Mythology for Smart People. https://norse-mythology.org/gods-and-creatures/elves/

McCoy, D. (2012c). Freya. Norse Mythology for Smart People. https://norse-mythology.org/gods-and-creatures/the-vanir-gods-and-goddesses/freya/

McCoy, D. (2012d). Freyr. Norse Mythology for Smart People. https://norse-mythology.org/gods-and-creatures/the-vanir-gods-and-goddesses/freyr/

McCoy, D. (2012e). Frigg. Norse Mythology for Smart People. https://norse-mythology.org/gods-and-creatures/the-aesir-gods-and-goddesses/frigg/

McCoy, D. (2012f). Heimdall. Norse Mythology for Smart People. https://norse-mythology.org/gods-and-creatures/the-aesir-gods-and-goddesses/heimdall/

McCoy, D. (2012g). Hel (Goddess). Norse Mythology for Smart People. https://norse-mythology.org/gods-and-creatures/giants/hel/

McCoy, D. (2012h). Hoenir. Norse Mythology for Smart People. https://norse-mythology.org/hoenir/

McCoy, D. (2012i). Loki. Norse Mythology for Smart People. https://norse-mythology.org/gods-and-creatures/the-aesir-gods-and-goddesses/loki/

McCoy, D. (2012j). Mimir. Norse Mythology for Smart People. https://norse-mythology.org/gods-and-creatures/others/mimir/

McCoy, D. (2012k). Njord. Norse Mythology for Smart People. https://norse-mythology.org/gods-and-creatures/the-vanir-gods-and-goddesses/njord/

McCoy, D. (2012l). Odin. Norse Mythology for Smart People. https://norse-mythology.org/gods-and-creatures/the-aesir-gods-and-goddesses/odin/

McCoy, D. (2012m). Odin's Discovery of the Runes. Norse Mythology for Smart People. https://norse-mythology.org/tales/odins-discovery-of-the-runes/

McCoy, D. (2012n). Ragnarok. Norse Mythology for Smart People. https://norse-mythology.org/tales/ragnarok/

McCoy, D. (2012o). The Aesir Gods and Goddesses. Norse Mythology for Smart People. https://norse-mythology.org/gods-and-creatures/the-aesir-gods-and-goddesses/

McCoy, D. (2012p). The Binding of Fenrir. Norse Mythology for Smart People. https://norse-mythology.org/tales/the-binding-of-fenrir/

McCoy, D. (2012q). The Creation of the Cosmos. Norse Mythology for Smart People. https://norse-mythology.org/tales/norse-creation-myth/

McCoy, D. (2012r). The Creation of Thor's Hammer. Norse Mythology for Smart People. https://norse-mythology.org/tales/loki-and-the-dwarves/#:~:text=Loki%20immediately%20stung%20Brokkr

McCoy, D. (2012s). The Death of Baldur. Norse Mythology for Smart People. https://norse-mythology.org/tales/the-death-of-baldur/

McCoy, D. (2012t). The Fortification of Asgard. Norse Mythology for Smart People. https://norse-mythology.org/tales/the-fortification-of-asgard/

McCoy, D. (2012u). The Kidnapping of Idun. Norse Mythology for Smart People. https://norse-mythology.org/tales/the-kidnapping-of-idun/

McCoy, D. (2012v). The Marriage of Njord and Skadi. Norse Mythology for Smart People. https://norse-mythology.org/tales/the-marriage-of-njord-and-skadi/

McCoy, D. (2012w). The Mead of Poetry. Norse Mythology for Smart People. https://norse-mythology.org/tales/the-mead-of-poetry/

McCoy, D. (2012x). The Vanir Gods and Goddesses. Norse Mythology for Smart People. https://norse-mythology.org/gods-and-creatures/the-vanir-gods-and-goddesses/

McCoy, D. (2012y). Thor. Norse Mythology for Smart People. https://norse-mythology.org/gods-and-creatures/the-aesir-gods-and-goddesses/thor/

McCoy, D. (2012z). Thor the Transvestite. Norse Mythology for Smart People. https://norse-mythology.org/tales/thor-the-transvestite/

McCoy, D. (2012aa). Tyr. Norse Mythology for Smart People. https://norse-mythology.org/gods-and-creatures/the-aesir-gods-and-goddesses/tyr/

McCoy, D. (2012ab). Ullr. Norse Mythology for Smart People. https://norse-mythology.org/ullr/

McCoy, D. (2012ac). Vanaheim. Norse Mythology for Smart People. https://norse-mythology.org/cosmology/the-nine-worlds/vanaheim/

McCoy, D. (2012ad). Vili and Ve. Norse Mythology for Smart People. https://norse-mythology.org/vili-ve/

McCoy, D. (2012ae). Who Were the Historical Vikings? Norse Mythology for Smart People. https://norse-mythology.org/who-were-the-historical-vikings/

McCoy, D. (2012af). Why Odin is One-Eyed. Norse Mythology for Smart People. https://norse-mythology.org/tales/why-odin-is-one-eyed/

McCoy, D. (2013a). Shamanism. Norse Mythology for Smart People. https://norse-mythology.org/concepts/shamanism/

McCoy, D. (2013b). The Norns. Norse Mythology for Smart People. https://norse-mythology.org/gods-and-creatures/others/the-norns/

McCoy, D. (2013c). The Old Norse Language and How to Learn It. Norse Mythology for Smart People. https://norse-mythology.org/learn-old-norse/

McCoy, D. (2014a). Daily Life in the Viking Age. Norse Mythology for Smart People. https://norse-mythology.org/daily-life-viking-age/

McCoy, D. (2014b). Odr (god). Norse Mythology for Smart People. https://norse-mythology.org/odr-god/

McCoy, D. (2014c). Viking Clothing and Jewelry. Norse Mythology for Smart People. https://norse-mythology.org/viking-clothing-jewelry/

McCoy, D. (2014d). Viking Gender Roles. Norse Mythology for Smart People. https://norse-mythology.org/viking-gender-roles/

McCoy, D. (2014e). Viking Political Institutions. Norse Mythology for Smart People. https://norse-mythology.org/viking-political-institutions/

McCoy, D. (2017a). The Viking Social Structure. Norse Mythology for Smart People. https://norse-mythology.org/viking-social-structure/

McCoy, D. (2017b). Viking Trade and Commerce. Norse Mythology for Smart People. https://norse-mythology.org/viking-trade-commerce/

McCoy, D. (2018a). The Vikings' Selfish Individualism. Norse Mythology for Smart People. https://norse-mythology.org/the-vikings-selfish-individualism/

McCoy, D. (2018b). Viking Food and Drink. Norse Mythology for Smart People. https://norse-mythology.org/viking-food-drink/

McCoy, D. (2018c). Viking Weapons and Armor (Swords, Axes, Spears, Etc.). Norse Mythology for Smart People. https://norse-mythology.org/viking-weapons-and-armor-swords-axes-spears-etc/

McCoy, D. (2019). The Vikings' Conversion to Christianity. Norse Mythology for Smart People. https://norse-mythology.org/the-vikings-conversion-to-christianity/

McKay, A. (2018, July 19). Creatures in Norse Mythology. Life in Norway. https://www.lifeinnorway.net/creatures-in-norse-mythology/

Mythology Wikia. (2020a, September 25). Fossegrim. Mythology Wiki. https://mythology.wikia.org/wiki/Fossegrim

Mythology Wikia. (2020b, October 26). Sigurðr. Mythology Wiki. https://mythology.wikia.org/wiki/Sigur%C3%B0r

Parker, P. (2018, November 26). A brief history of the Vikings. History Extra; History Extra. https://www.historyextra.com/period/viking/vikings-history-facts/

Ramirez, J. (2015, August). "Vikings didn't wear horned helmets," plus 7 more Viking myths busted. HistoryExtra. https://www.historyextra.com/period/viking/historical-fact-check-vikings-myths-busted-did-wear-horned-helmets-violent-barbarians/

Short, W. R. (2019). Hurstwic Norse Mythology: The Story of Creation. Hurstwic.Org. http://www.hurstwic.org/history/articles/mythology/myths/text/creation.htm

Simon, M. (2014, September 10). Fantastically Wrong: The Legend of the Kraken, a Monster That Hunts With Its Own Poop. Wired. https://www.wired.com/2014/09/fantastically-wrong-legend-of-the-kraken/

Skjalden. (2011a, June 1). Creation of the World in Norse Mythology. Nordic Culture. https://skjalden.com/creation-of-the-world-in-norse-mythology/

Skjalden. (2011b, June 1). Ragnarok - The end of the World in Norse Mythology. Norse Mythology. https://norse-mythology.net/ragnarok-in-norse-mythology/

Skjalden. (2018, June 15). Important and Secret Numbers in the Icelandic Sagas & Norse mythology. Nordic Culture. https://skjalden.com/important-numbers-norse-mythology/#:~:text=Pagan%20%E2%80%93%20Magic

The Editors of Encyclopaedia Britannica. (1998, July 20). Old Norse language. Encyclopedia Britannica. https://www.britannica.com/topic/Old-Norse-language

The Editors of Encyclopaedia Britannica. (2009, June 4). Fafnir | Norse mythology. Encyclopedia Britannica. https://www.britannica.com/topic/Fafnir

The Editors of Encyclopaedia Britannica. (2019, September 19). Siegfried | Germanic literary hero. Encyclopedia Britannica. https://www.britannica.com/topic/Siegfried

The Editors of Encyclopaedia Britannica. (2020). Ragnarök | Scandinavian mythology. In Encyclopædia Britannica. https://www.britannica.com/event/Ragnarok

The Editors of Encyclopedia Britannica. (2018). Viking | History, Exploration, Facts, & Maps. In Encyclopædia Britannica. https://www.britannica.com/topic/Viking-people

V.K.N.G. (2019, January 21). 15 Scariest Norse Mythology Creatures [Monster List]. Norse and Viking Mythology [Best Blog] - Vkngjewelry. https://blog.vkngjewelry.com/creatures-of-norse-mythology/

Williams, G. (2016). Ivar the Boneless, Ragnvald of Ed and 6 more Vikings you should know about. HistoryExtra. https://www.historyextra.com/period/viking/8-vikings-you-should-know-about/

Winters, R. (2017, June 30). The Diverse Nature of Elves in Norse Myth: Beings of Light or Darkness? Ancient-Origins.Net; Ancient Origins. https://www.ancient-origins.net/myths-legends-europe/diverse-nature-elves-norse-myth-beings-light-or-darkness-008327

Zarka, E. (2019). Draugr: The Undead Nordic Zombie | Monstrum [YouTube Video]. On YouTube.

https://www.youtube.com/watch?v=VNM1Y8i8tuI&ab
_channel=Storied

Runes:

A Guide To The Magic, Meanings, Spells, Divination & Rituals Of Runes

Table of Contents

Introduction

There is evidence that many people these days want to learn runes. However, because it's ancient, there is no clear guide on how to go about it. There are many misconceptions surrounding the topic of runes. Some associate them with magic, spells, and divination. On the other hand, some only know them as a sacred alphabet. All these are right, but depending on the context of the user. The starting point for anyone wishing to learn and use runes is to understand the whole topic. Runes have been there since ancient times, and like many other things, they have evolved over time.

Did you know that similar to Hebrew letters, each runic symbol has a meaning? Well, for your information, each symbol has, in fact, a deeper meaning that goes beyond its function as a letter. In a nutshell, runes are practical, effective, and useful symbols that have a wide array of uses. Just to shed more light on this interesting topic, today, some of the most common application of rune lore is in areas of spell casting and divination. Also, the modern-day, Bluetooth logo is a combination of two runes. What this means is that there is a lot to learn and understand about runes before one can successfully apply them.

This book delves into the topic of runes to bring out what they are and what they are not. It focuses on the history of runes, runic alphabet, spell casting and divining, modern use, connecting with the sources of energy and future, exercises and descriptions, and lastly, rituals to accompany the study. We provide details and uncover what many do not know about runes so that anyone interested can have an easy time learning the ropes of runes. We do this knowing that the real power of runes comes from understanding their value. More specifically, we get the real power of runes when we find the wisdom in each runic symbol and internalize it within ourselves.

While the contents of this book may seem overwhelming at first, you will find it easy and enjoyable learning about runes. This book is, therefore, intended to be a guide to anyone interested in learning runes, how to use them, and their benefits. What we know is that runes can only help you if you understand them better and you can practice. As you read, you will gain knowledge, and more importantly, understanding the power and usefulness of runes. If you get things right, you might reap a lot, including unlocking your potential to connect with sources of energy, healing, and love. As an inspiration, some people have mastered the art and are gaining from the hidden power of runes. You can become one of them too.

Every chapter of this book brings out interesting ideas you probably didn't know. For instance, one of the chapters of this book explains how you can see your future with the help of runes. It explains how you can use runes by sending them into the Cosmo to help you consult as well as manifest a goal about a given situation. We hope that this and other interesting things you learn in this book will be useful. Without further ado, let's delve into the deeper meaning of runes and their application.

Chapter One: Ancient Origins

The history of runes is very vital for your understanding and how you can apply them. While there are a lot of historical facts worth knowing about runes, this chapter provides a brief history of context only. Before you understand what it is and how it works, it is important to know how runes developed.

Runes have a history that dates back to about 100 BCE in Northern European and about 1600 CE in Scandinavian countries. While most runes came from Germanic tribes, a couple of others were stolen from Greeks and Romans as well. Since then, runes have evolved. However, the fact is that despite the changes that have occurred over time, they have been consistently used for centuries.

Initially, runes were characters in several alphabets of Germanic languages used in the first century. As Christianity spread, runes were gradually replaced with Latin letters. However, despite the replacement, runes did not completely disappear. Those who understood their deep meaning kept and continued using them. They were then reviewed in the twentieth century when many ancient spiritual practices were making a comeback. While a lot has been said about runes over time, the complete story remains unclear. For this reason, there is so much variation when it comes to symbols, meaning, and their uses.

Origins

Runes stemmed from an ancient form of the alphabet that was widely used by Nordic and Germanic tribes of Northern Europe, Britain, and Scandinavia. While their primary use was in writing, runes were also used those times for magical as well as divination purposes. Although their existence came to the limelight in the 3rd century, there is a belief that they existed long before that time.

According to Norse Mythology, the word rune derived from the German word run whose meaning is secret or whisper. It is further believed that the first person to gain the knowledge of runes was Odin, the king of gods. He gained it to help him in war and give him the wisdom to lead the other gods well. History has it that in order to gain full knowledge of runes, Odin hung himself in the Tree of life for nine days. When the period was over, he had acquired so much wisdom that helped him to understand that, indeed, hidden powers existed in runes.

Overjoyed with the fact that there was so much hidden power in runes, Odin shared the knowledge he had gained with humanity. From there, it spread, and it has also evolved over time to what it is currently. It is, however, unclear whether or not Odin was taught the signs, or he developed them just to make it easier for humankind to understand.

A couple of years later, the rise of Scandinavian and Viking languages around AD800 led to the replacement of a couple of runic signs and alphabets. This might explain the existence of the various types of runic alphabets and the many changes that have taken place over time. This is evidenced by the remains of carvings that were created at different times and are still kept for reference to date. In ancient times, runic signs were carved into hard surfaces, including wood, bone, metal, and stone, among others. As of the 21st century, there were still people who still curved runes into surfaces just like it was done in ancient times.

Early Inscriptions

Early runic inscriptions dating back to around 150 AD have been found in many objects, including stones, weapons, and jewelry, among others. While most of these objects vanished as those who made them underwent Christianization, some uses of runes, especially for specialized purposes withstood the wave of change and remained up until the 20th century. In Northern Europe and Rural Sweden, for instance, runes were able to resist the change and remained since they had a special place in calendars and decoration activities.

From 150 AD to around 1100 AD, there were three best-known alphabets, namely the Elder Futhark, the Anglo Saxon Futhorc, and the younger Futhark. While there are many other runic alphabets, they are also descendent from these three ancient ones. In fact, even the Latin alphabet bears a great resemblance to the Elder Futhark. Many argue that a lot of exchange and borrowing happened during the times when Christianity was spreading to many parts of Europe, especially in the Northern areas that saw a massive change from their old lifestyles and religions to the Christian way of life.

Norse Beliefs

Norse beliefs are embedded in the very rich Norse Mythology, which is often called the Germanic Mythology. But what is this mythology all about? Well, it is not just a myth but is also a religion practiced by the Vikings as well as the Germanic people. Vikings were conquerors, raiders, traders, settlers, and explorers from current-day Denmark, Iceland, Norway, and Sweden. These are the people who spread the Norse Mythology. While there are many beliefs in Norse Mythology, not all of them are explored in runes books and inscriptions that have helped hand over the beliefs from old generations to the modern-day.

One of the famous Norse beliefs is the argument that there is not one world but nine, perhaps corresponding to the nine planets. It is also worth noting that the concept of luck came from Norse beliefs. Essentially, there was no Norse code of conduct since morality was based on family bonds and a concept known as 'weird,' which meant fate or luck. Other beliefs included those of rebirth after death. Other beliefs, including the killing of men in raids with the belief that those killers would be rewarded. Some of these beliefs were swept away by the wave of Christianity, but there are a few people who remained with them. They have been handing over from one generation to another to date, especially in Northern Europe.

Descriptions and Alternate Meanings

Learning runes in their original runic language can be an uphill task for people who might be used to a different language like English. The starting point for learning should, therefore, be understanding the alternate meanings of runes in other languages, mainly English. Without a translation, runes become more mysterious, not forgetting that there are already many mysteries surrounding runes and their use. It is thus imperative for every learner to understand the various descriptions as well as meanings of various runic signs.

Illustrated in the table below are alternate meanings of the runic signs used in the 12th century. They are the sixteen runic signs that stemmed from the original 24 signs of the Elder Furthark (explained later in chapter 2 of this book). Here we go:

Runic Name

Meaning

fé

wealth

úr

rain

thúrs

danger

ás

haven

reið

speed

kaún

disease

hágáll

hail

náúðr

need

isá

ice

ár

good harvest

sol

the sun

tyr

justice

bjárkán

spring

mádðr

humankind

logr

water

yr

endurance

The first step in learning runic languages should start with understanding the meanings of the various runes, mostly the sixteen, as they represent the recent signs that were finally picked after refining the old runic signs. After mastering these runic signs and their meanings, you can proceed to learn more about the special powers associated with each of these signs. You will also realize that there are different gods and goddesses associated with different runes. Remember that learning is only enjoyable when you understand what you are learning, and you can relate to a real-life situation.

When written in runic alphabets, runes tend to appear as strange things. But once the English meaning of the signs is given, it becomes easy to visualize what runic sign could be used for in real-life situations. As you will see later in this book, most runic activities, including rituals, practices, and exercises are things you can easily understand if you know their meanings. With the above table, you strange signs won't again strike you. Most importantly, you will be in a position to make translations from runic alphabets to English.

Gods and Goddesses Associated with Runes

Just as there are in many cultures in different parts of the world, there are gods and goddesses associated with runes. They are the drivers of the different forces responsible for different happenings or special powers. Here are the most common runic gods and goddesses:

Frey

Frey is associated with Ingwaz rune. He is the runic god of peace, plenty, happiness, sexual love, and abundance. He is also known as the protector of natural vegetation and fertility. Some writers and books call him the god of this world since most of the things he grants are seen as belonging to this world only and not the world of spirits.

Fry

Fry is associated with Perthro rune. She is the goddess of marriage, love, reconciliation, where there are a crisis, pregnancy, and childbirth as well. In a nutshell, she is the god of the family who takes care of different family affairs. Her desire to make sure that families are safe, protected, and have peace makes her a favorite goddess for families facing struggles and other problems that are a bit tough to solve.

Freyja

Freyja is associated with Gebo rune, and she is responsible for feminine beauty, sexual pleasure powers. Some books call her the lady as she is mostly concerned with showering ladies with beauty.

Baldur

Baldur is associated with Sowilo rune. He is the god responsible for light, joy, persuasion, and the power to reconcile warring parties. Since light is associated with the sun, rituals and gifts give to Baldur were mainly done on the day of the sun (Sunday).

Hands

Hands god is associated with Naudhiz, and he is the god of the moon. He was dedicated on Monday or the day of the moon. He is believed to preside over natural processes and timings just as different moon phases are used to make different timings or seasons. Hands can change cycles in favor of the needs of those who believe in him.

Heimdal

Heimdal is associated with Mannaz rune. He is the god who gives the ability to hear sounds, including the quiet ones that would go unheard. He is believed to have sacrificed his own ear to help his people get a unique power of hearing. Others also know him as the god who connects the earth and heaven.

Thor

Thor is associated with Thurisaz rune. He presides over deadly natural forces such as thunder and lightning. He uses these forces to keep the atmosphere free from chaos or any forms of distractions that tend to make it impure. Many believe that Thor uses a deadly hammer to keep things in order. The hammer is, however, not only for hitting wrongdoers, but it is also a sign of a hardworking god who helps men as they labor with their daily hassles.

Gefion

Gefion is associated with Jera and Fehu runes, and she is the goddess of virtue and women who are unmarried. She is also responsible for fertility and has the ability to shift shapes to match the different needs of those struggling with infertility. Her favorite colors are gold and green, which is a sign of fertility.

Sunna

Sunna is associated with Raidho, Ansuz, and Ehwaz runes. He is the god of powerful protection in times of need, inspiration, and general weather. Among all the gods and goddesses associated with different runes, Sunna is the most powerful and strongest of all. Just like Thor, he has the ability to wield a strong hammer that causes deadly lightning flashes upon the earth.

Many other runic gods and goddesses exist, but the ones discussed here are the most common ones who are often invoked for intervention in various human activities. Their special powers/forces and abilities to influence human activities positively is what makes them popular since the ancient times of Germanic people when runes were developed.

Chapter Two: Understanding Runic Alphabets

Traditionally known as futhark, the Runic Alphabet is believed to have stemmed from the Greek Alphabet. In fact, a couple of letters in the Runic Alphabet have a great similarity to those used in the ancient Greek version. However, that is not the only alphabet system that the Runic Alphabet bears resemblance with. It is also argued that it might have been developed from the ancient alphabets that were initially used in Italy. While little is known about the origin of Runic Alphabets, there is much that can be talked about when it comes to its development and change over time.

Types of Runic Alphabets

There are at least three different runic alphabets, namely Elder Futhark, Younger Futhark, and Medieval Futhark. While there are a couple of differences among these three alphabets, there are many similarities as well, bearing in mind that they are all Runic Alphabets. Their only major difference is the fact that they were developed at different times of history and have all had their own changes over time. To get a better understanding of each of these alphabets, here are the details:

Elder Futhark Runic Alphabet

Elder Futhark is the oldest Germanic runic alphabet. It was widely used in many parts of Europe until many years later when other alphabets came into existence. It is believed that all others that came after stemmed from the Elder Futhark. They emerged as a result of changes that occurred over time in the way the European people used their languages. Experts in the runic alphabet argue that the name Futhark was derived from the first six runes. Besides, there are 24 runic signs that represent different letters. The signs and the corresponding letters that the Futhark alphabet signs correspond to are illustrated here:

Regarding the origin of the signs used in the futhark alphabet, researchers seem not to have a consensus on it. In addition, the order of the letters used does not in any way narrow down to the usual letters of the alphabet (ABC...) since their development was independent of the already existing English letters of the alphabet. However, some scholars argue that the development of the elder futhark was inspired by the Etruscan writing as well as the Roman alphabet since those were the commonly used systems at the time.

A couple of Elder Futhark runic inscriptions have been found in many artifacts, some dating to as old as the 2nd century. The most common ones include runestones, weapons, and amulets, among many others. The inscriptions, of course, consist of twenty-four runes, but picked from the first six runes, namely

F, U, P, A, R, K. Later during the Viking Age, the Elder Futhark runic alphabet was simplified to match the phonological changes that had occurred in the Germanic languages. More specifically, the number of runes was reduced by 8 to 16 to form the Younger Futhark.

Younger Futhark Runic Alphabet

History has it that towards the end of the 8th century, the spoken language had encountered a lot of changes, and there was a need to reform the runes. To illustrate the change, it is reported that the number of vowels had increased from the initial 5 to 9. Seeing the changes, one runemaster decided to change the runes by reducing them to 16. Further changes occurred in the 9th century, and eventually, in the 10th century, the changes were accepted in Scandinavia. The acceptance is what can be said to have given birth to the Younger Futhark alphabet.

The Younger Futhark Runic Alphabet has two variants, namely, the Long Branch, which is also known as the Danish variant, and the Short Twig runes, also known as the Swedish & Norwegian runes. The difference between these two variants is said to be in their use. For instance, the Long Branch runes were mainly used when making inscriptions on stones. On the other hand, the Short Twig runes were mainly used when writing official as well as confidential messages. The authenticity of these differences in use is, however, a subject of controversy with no clear explanation of their development.

Signs used in the Younger Futhark alphabet vary between the long-branch runes and the short twig runes. The variation is not, however, large between the two. In fact, some differences are just as a result of the simplification of runes of the other variant. More precisely, nine runes in the short twig runes are a simplification of those of the long-branch. The other remaining seven are just similar. Here are the illustrations:

Long Branch Runes

ᚢ

ᚿ

ᚦ

ᛊ

ᚱ

ᚢ

ᛪ

ᛏ

ᛁ

ᛏ

ᚼ

↑

ᛒ

Ψ

ᚱ

ᛣ

f

u

þ

ą

r

k

h

n

i

a

s

t

b

m

1

Short-Twig Runes

ᚠ

ᛦ

þ

ᛦ

ᛦ

ᛦ

ᛦ

ᛦ

ᛁ

ᛦ

ᛁ

ᛦ

ᛦ

ᛦ

ᛦ

ı_

f

u

þ

ą

r

k

h

n

i

a

s

t

b

m

l

R

A couple of years later, the younger Futhark runes saw another change. Signs that were previously not there were introduced.

What exactly happened is that voiceless signs were introduced to denote their voiced counterparts. This essentially increased the number of runes from the original number that existed before the changed happened. The expansion of the existing runes is what gave birth to the next runic alphabet; the Medieval Futhark.

Medieval Futhark Runic Alphabet

The transition from the Younger Futhark to the medieval runic alphabet took place during the spread of Christianity in Scandinavia. It took place in the late 18th century, and it saw many changes occurring in the language system that was there previously. Although a lot happened at the time, runic masters argue that the change mainly involved the decoration of runes using Latin letters. Yes, it brought a new way of writing runes, but there were confusions, especially in the use of three letters, namely s, c, and z. In a nutshell, runes were Latinized to match the new Christian way of life that was rapidly spreading at the time.

While the wave of Christianity had a great impact on the use of runes, it didn't completely stop it from being used. Runes were, in fact, in common use side by side with the Latin system of the alphabet. In addition, a great interest in learning and use runes grew a lot in some areas such as Iceland after the 15th century. The tremendous growth is evident from the hundreds of

Norwegian runic inscriptions that have been preserved in many archives to date. Many have been discovered over time, with the greatest ones being the 600 that were discovered in the 19th century in Bergen. This reinstates the fact that despite the reality that runes alphabets have been there for centuries, their usefulness is still great.

Today, there are still many people who use runes for different purposes. Discussions are ongoing on the best way to store and pass on the unbroken tradition that has stood the test of time to its current status. A lot has been written in books about runes and the continued growth of interest to learn and use them among many even in the 20th century points out the fact that they still have a special place and use as well in modern-day activities.

Misconceptions

You've probably have come across stories detailing the common misconceptions that exist about runes. They have been there since ancient times, and they are not about to vanish any time soon. Well, in all honesty, anything that seems difficult to understand or uses strange signs often attracts different interpretations, including misconceptions about it. Runes are not spared either. Those who have tried to learn but and left it on the way or couldn't just connect the dots to make meanings out of runes have many stories and myths about runes. If you come across some of those stories, you may no longer move on with your quest to learn runes and use them to improve your life. Misconceptions surrounding them are no doubt misleading, let alone the fact that they are discouraging. The most widespread misconceptions about include the claims that runes are no longer useful, they have no powers, are used by Satanists, can attract bad omen, and others. All these are just baseless claims spread by those who do not understand what runes really are and their role in humanity.

The truth is that runes are totally different from the messages that these statements send out, especially to unknowing rune novices. To set the record straight, runes are primarily used for communication. Like any language, it uses signs, and it has evolved over time. Besides, the use or runes in everyday activities simply is for the purpose of serving the specific use and not any hidden or specialized function that cannot be understood as is often said by agents of misconceptions. Also, when spells are carved into runes, the power comes from the spell and not the rune. Similarly, all other functions where runes are involved do not necessarily imply that anything unusual is from the runes. It could be a different force. For instance, there are gods and goddesses associated with runes. Anything good or bad associated with them belongs to the forces (gods and goddesses) and not the runes. Runes only help in connecting with these forces or powers that have an influence on human behavior.

Chapter Three: Spell Casting and Divining

Runes are said to have magical properties/powers that can be used in spell Casting and divining. Since time immemorial, runes have been used for many other activities apart from general communication. In this chapter, we delve into the use of runes for spell casting as well as divining. Although there have been many changes over the years, the fact remains that runic signs are still useful in many ways.

Meaning of Spell Casting

Spellcasting is a practice that has been there for many years. However, it has been misunderstood by many, especially those involved deeply in spiritual work. So what exactly is this practice all about? Well, it is simple. Just as we bring different letters to do works that finally combine to make meaning, so does spell casting work. It is about stringing things together to make something great that can enhance life. Spell casting is not, however, necessarily about changing things but rather supporting what our minds can do.

Contrary to the general beliefs, spell casting is about bringing oneself into proper alignment with the inner purpose. Therefore, people spell craft to change their own lives and not to influence the lives of those around them negatively. Just to illustrate this, we can use spell casting in our lives to attract something to our lives, strengthen our character, increase our self-confidence, and benefit ourselves. These are the ways in which spells are used, although the practice of spell casting varies from one place to another.

Apart from spell casting to improve our lives, spells can also be used in meditation to connect with other beings. Besides, other people use spell casting as a spiritual tool or as a divine power to deal with daily life challenges. Other than these, spells can be used in many other different ways. In addition, there are different levels of spell craft that can be used. With that said, spell casting remains an ancient practice that has stood the test of time to become an activity that is still applicable by many in different parts of the world.

Types of Spells

There are hundreds of different types of spells. In fact, there are spells of almost every activity or imaginable task. Human needs are unlimited and endless, as well. Therefore, there are spells for almost every need that a human mind would want to achieve. These spells also vary from one place to another and from one culture to another. And since there are many different cultures across the world, you can imagine how many types of spells exist in this world.

Protection spells, loves spells, abundance spells, wealth spells, trick spells, health spells, life spells, beauty spells, luck spells, weather spells, fantasy spells, and spirit connection spells are just a few types. As it is evident, these types of spells correspond to the different activities that people do on a daily basis. People do different things to achieve what they want, and spell casting is just one of the ways people try to enhance their living environment.

The Connection between Runes and Spell Casting

Runes are letters or individual elements which when they come together, make words that eventually make meanings. They can thus be used in spell casting, and in fact, many people continue to use them in different parts of the world. When runic signs are brought together, they make words and meanings that can be attached to these different words. People, therefore, use runes or rune casting to strive to achieve their daily needs. More specifically, runes are used to create a cause-effect and predict a likely outcome in one's life.

Runes act as excellent tools for spell casting. Just to illustrate this, runes may be used to create writings, curves, paintings, or castings with special meanings or powers. People can then use them according to their needs. This practice has been there for centuries, and even today, spell casting people still use them for different purposes. It is, however, worth noting that spell casting using runes or rune casting as some people call it is so diverse. As such, there is no single formula for doing it. It all depends on what one is interested in achieving at the end.

One popular way of using runes for spell casting is working with an individual or even a set of runes that is inscribed into an object so as to access the power associated with it. Powers associated with such individuals or sets of runes include healing power, luck in work, protection power, and many others. Runes, therefore, whether written or carved into an object, act as marks of protecting, healing, love, and other aspects of life already outlined. While sometimes these practices are condemned as witchcraft or magical works, they have remained popular for many years. To date, many people are learning the different ways of using runes for spell casting.

Indeed, runes spells are powerful and very useful to some people. On the other hand, some look at it as mysterious and things that belong to witches only. The reality, however, is that an everyday person can use runes for spell casting without necessarily doing it for witchcraft purposes. People who know what spell casting and understand its role use it to draw the things they need in life. It has worked for some, and many others are inspired to explore the power that exists in using runes for spell casting.

As a way of wrapping it up, if you are interested in testing the power of spell casting using runes, then there is a lot to do. First, understand what it is all about since there are so many misconceptions about it. The fact is that there are so many good things worth knowing about runes and spell casting. In fact, spell casting might just be what you need to change your life and find it easy to meet your daily needs. Many testimonies are there about the success of runes and spell casting. It is, therefore, a matter of how you perceive and use it.

Rune Casting Techniques

While the art of casting runes has changed over time, the fact remains that it is all about using runes to find meanings of hidden things and changing one's life as well. It relates things to find a possible cause-effect relationship and a likely outcome. Some of the common types of rune casting practices include the following:

Simple Rune Casting

As the name suggests, simple casting is easy to carry out. It does not require anything that is too special or out of the ordinary. To do it, simply take your bag of runes, stir it around to mix them up, and pick up a bunch. Throw them on a white cloth then keenly monitor how they land on the place you have thrown them to.

Some runes will face up, others down, and others upright. The directions they face have a meaning, and that's what you should interpret. You can formulate a question that relates to the puzzle that you are trying to unfold. If a rune faces a give direction, then it means a certain thing.

Spiritual Nine-Rune Cast

This is often done by people who want to obtain deeper insights about an event or situation that is facing them. Why nine runes? Well, in Norse Mythology, nine has a meaning as well as magical significance. To do it, pick nine runes randomly then hold them between your hands as you think about the problem you want to solve. Scatter them on a piece of cloth, on the table, or even on the floor.

How the results of nine rune casting are interpreted is subjective. Everyone has their own way of making meaning out of the results obtained. However, although there is variation, there a general rule regarding the nine-rune-cast is the runes lying at the center are the ones who carry the greatest meaning and relevance. You should, therefore, focus on interpreting them to help you answer your questions.

Ground Casting

Unlike the earlier types, ground casting is a bit unique in a couple of ways. First, it uses rune tines such as sticks and twigs on which symbols of runes are inscribed. Also, its interpretation is a bit simple. You just cast them on the ground then look at those that land upright. Their positions in relation to each other are also important in interpreting the outcome.

Regarding meanings, if runes cross each other upon landing on the ground, it means they are in opposition. If they are lying in a parallel position, they are related. Also, those that group far away from the others imply something too. You should, however, note that interpretation techniques applied here rely a lot on intuition. So you have to build your own techniques that suit your needs and situation.

Divining

In the simplest terms possible, divination can be explained as the act of trying to discover hidden knowledge or foretell what is likely to happen in the future. It is a practice that has been there for many centuries, and it continues to exist to date. The history of divination dates back to about 200bc when the people of Mesopotamia, Egypt, Canaan, and Anatolia, just to name a few, communicate with their deities through divination. This practice did not, however, end at the time. It has evolved over time, and many people in different parts of the world still practice it mostly for religious purposes.

Intuitive forms of divination are the most practices. It simply involves people using natural or human phenomena to reveal hidden things or tell the future. One common example to illustrate this is an analysis of stars, weather, birds' behavior, moon, and entrails to derive the meaning of various happenings. Some people also speak to the dead, cast lots, shoot arrows, or drop oil in water, all in an attempt to predict the future or interpret the hidden meaning of things that are happening presently.

Types of Divination Methods

Different methods of divination exist, and people use them depending on what they want to achieve at the end. Some methods are also common in some regions of the world, while others are promoted for religious purposes. Even more interesting is the fact that people choose what works best for them, leaving the other types. While there is no specific number regarding the types of divination, the most common types include the following:

Rune Stones

Runes stones, otherwise known as Norse runes, are also used in divination. They are carved into stone, and those who understand and use them argue that they are sacred and holy gifts that human beings can use. More specifically, they are often used to help in finding out what the future has or what events are likely to happen. One, however, has to understand the runic language, including runic alphabets, in order to make use of this divination method.

Numerology

Numerology in divination is simply the use of numbers to help reveal the hidden meanings of different mysteries or unforeseen future. The belief behind the use of numbers is the fact that they have magical and spiritual significance. In addition, some numbers of particular combinations of numbers are believed to be more powerful than others. They are thus used for divination practices.

Use of Pendulum

The use of a pendulum is the most common method of divination often used in different parts of the world. Its common use can be attributable to the fact that it helps solve simple puzzles just as everyday life choices. This method uses a weight that is attached to a chain or string and calibrated to help answer simple yes or no questions. Users argue that it is the easiest method of divination.

Automatic Writing

This method is one of the most popularly used ones when one wants to get messages from the spiritual world. It simply involves holding a pen and allowing the spirit to relay messages about any events or circumstances. One requirement here is that one should not apply any effort or think about what to write. Instead, they should allow the spirit to relay messages through automatic writing.

Unique Intuitive Ability

Although it is a rare one and is only used by a few people, intuitive ability is also another method of divination. In this method, one uses an extraordinary ability to know things without being told. It has been there for years, and it still exists to date. Like the other methods, it also helps uncover hidden things or tell what will happen in the future.

While there could be other methods of divination, these five are the most common ones. They are still used in many parts of the world among people of different cultures and religious beliefs. Some have, however, changed over time, and they are no longer done the way they used to be done in the past. For instance, some practices have been mixed with Christianity and hence transformed so that they are done in an acceptable Christian manner.

Runes of Divination

As already explained previously in this book, runes are said to have magical powers that can be used to meet human desires. For instance, those who understand the runic language and its signs can cut runes to uncover a hidden thing or to cure a serious illness. Also, as part of the methods of divination rune, stones and signs can be used for different activities. Besides, there are different runic objects, including necklaces and other ornaments that are used as divinatory aids.

It is believed that Vikings (Inventors of runes) used runes for everyday activities, including divination. Although there is no clear evidence to support this, there are many runic activities and inscriptions that are connected with divination in many ways. For instance, runic readers believe that the future is not fixed. That is, one can change what will happen in the future by acting differently at present. Similarly, divination involves foretelling future events and changing behavior currently to avoid any future disasters. One can thus say that runes can be used for divination, especially when the intention is to explore the future and find out what it has for one.

One thing to remember is that although runic signs and stones can be used for divination, rune casting is not all about fortune telling as it is often made to appear like. It is simply a way of asking questions about the future or finding meanings of the present happenings that we would otherwise not understand without the use of runes. Most importantly, it is good to note that not all runic materials can be used for divination. The commonly used ones are stoned, pebbles, and inscriptions. Others, including bone, metal, and many other signs, serve other purposes. Either way, runes have a special role to play in everyday life and in the solution of human challenges, including the uncertainty of the future.

Take-Home Point

Rune casting, spell casting, and divination are not the same thing. Unlike the later, rune casting is not supernatural. Neither is it also superstitious. It is just about making use of your subconscious mind to connect things.

Chapter Four: The New World

The culture surrounding runes has been there for centuries, and it continues to find use even in modern-day society. To date, runic alphabets act as a symbolic representation of certain aspects of life. For this reason, those who understand it continue to apply it in many ways. However, there is another interesting thing that many people do not know. Almost everyone has used runes but most likely without their knowledge. In this chapter, we explore some of the technologies that make use of runes.

Bluetooth Technology

Let's face it! The Bluetooth technology has completely transformed communications and made work easier than it used to be. These days, we can easily connect to devices without having to use cables as they were in the past. Since its invention, billions of devices have created connections and shared data and information thanks to this amazing technology. Moreover, many other technologies have come as an improvement in technology. It has, therefore, acted as a base or reference technology for other inventors interested in adding features to what we are already enjoying.

Aside from the usefulness of Bluetooth technology, there is one interesting thing that many people do not know. Well, The

Bluetooth logo you see on your smartphone is a combination of two bind runes, namely Haglaz and Berkana. These runes are equivalent to letter "H" and "B," and they represent the initials of the name of King Harald Blåtand. He was the King of Denmark during the Viking age and tried to build connections across the borders of his country. Interestingly, almost everyone with a mobile device or smartphone has used Bluetooth to create connections and transfer files. However, not many people know the fact that the technology's name has a runic origin. Indeed, this is something interesting to explore if you like runes and would like to understand its applications even in modern-day society.

Why Bluetooth Is Named after Powerful King of Denmark and Norway

Bluetooth is named after Harald "Blatand," who was a king of Denmark and Norway. He is remembered for many things and especially his efforts beyond borders that sought to unify his people, including neighbors. While most of his subjects were pagans, King Harald embraced Christianity and worked tirelessly to spread the religion. He promoted the faith within his borders throughout his tenure. His main aim was to unify the people of Denmark and Norway. Perhaps Bluetooth is named after him because of the similarity between the work he did and what Bluetooth does these days. Well, the technology connects by going beyond the borders of a single device to help make communication easy.

According to some scholars, King Harald was got the name "Blatand," which means Bluetooth because he had a rare dental condition. He had a dead tooth that literally turned dark and bluish. That is what led him to get the name Bluetooth. How the name transferred to a telecommunications technology is, indeed, interesting. According to Jim Kardach, one of the founders of Swedish Telecommunications Company, Ericsson, the name Bluetooth was chosen for all the right reasons. The founders felt that Harald's ability to negotiate beyond borders and unite people was a great thing. They, therefore, saw it right to name their technology after the King since the intention of coming up with it was to 'unite" devices and make communication easy.

Since its invention and release, Bluetooth technology has, indeed, lived the life of the name it is named after. In fact, it had done much more than what the owner of the name did when he was alive. The technology has connected millions of smart devices worldwide and enabled communication. Most importantly, it has helped in the sharing of important files, documents, and anything worth sharing or transferring from one device to another. It is also great to note that other technologies have also borrowed from the features of Bluetooth to help develop other similar technologies to help share information and resources easily.

In modern English, the Bluetooth logo is simply a combination of letters H and B. These two letters are the initials of Herald Bluetooth, the kind who died centuries, but his spirit of communicating across boundaries and among different groups live to date courtesy of powerful innovation. Letter H and B were, however, not written in Viking language the way they are currently written in English. That takes us to a very interesting question.

Can Modern English Be Translated to Runic Language?

The truth is that it is easier to translate the Runic language to English than to do the vice versa. Taking English names and translating to runes is a complicated procedure. It is an attempt to transcribe words whose sounds never existed in languages from which runic alphabets were developed. But that does not, however, mean that it cannot be done. With research and more studies on phonology, there might come a time when it will be possible to write whatever we want in English then have it translated into runes. If that happens, a lot will be achieved, and people will be able to create more runic exercises, and practices in their own language then have it put in runes for originality.

Away from translation, the fact that runic signs are being used in modern-day technologies, writings, and even in-wall decorations affirms the power that exists in runic language. Despite many changes that have occurred over time in runic alphabets, runes still exist to date, and more people are continuing to learn it. One distinguishing trait that could possibly explain the uniqueness of runic signs is the use of the same signs for voiced and voiceless consonants, a trait that is not existent in modern English.

Chapter Five: Witness Your Future

Runes are still used these days in many ways by those who understand them and what they are capable of doing. In this chapter, we explain how runes are used these days to make predictions about the future. In a nutshell, runes can help answer questions about the past, what is happening presently, and, most importantly, what the future has for one.

How Runes Can Be Used to Predict the Future

Runic readers argue that you can unlock your ability to connect with the sources of energy, healing & love and be able to tell what is likely to happen. This does not, however, imply anything to do with fortunetelling. On the contrary, what rune casting or the art of using runes to predict the future does is that it gathers a couple of variables and offers advice on what one can do in the event that something occurs. Simply put, runes give you hints of what is likely to happen but leaves you with the freedom to decide what to do now.

According to the assumptions of rune casting, the future is not fixed and that if you don't like the direction you are following presently, you can at any time divert. The implication of this assumption is that individuals have the power to make their own decisions and follow their own path. So if there is something you fear that it might happen in the future, you ought not to fear anymore as you have the power to change it. You can take a different route and see the future you desire unfolding before your eyes.

When Should You Resort to Rune Casting?

You can use runes in many situations depending on your circumstance and what you are really interested to know about the future. A good example is when you have limited information about a future event, or you want to act, but you have an incomplete picture of what is likely to happen. At such instances, consulting rune readers can help unearth the hidden future, so you can act accordingly.

When you can use runes, you are ideally asking a question or thinking about an issue. The idea here is to focus your conscious and unconscious minds to help you make a decision. Runes can thus be said to be useful when you are in a situation of indecision. It is, therefore, right to say that rune casting helps to bring out the decisions already made but not opened to you. Casting runes can thus help you get a better picture of what awaits you in the future and what to do if what awaits you is not what you have been anticipating.

Runes Used to Discover the Future

There are twenty-four different runes that you can use to discover your future. Each of them has a runic meaning as well as its implication for your life. Most importantly, they help answer whatever questions you have about the future. Therefore, when you cast them, the order in which they fall has a meaning in your life. They also determine your fate. Although there are renowned runic readers, anyone can cast runes and interpret if they have the knowledge of rune casting.

Here are the twenty-four runes you can use to discover your future and their corresponding meanings:

i. Fehu Rune: money, wealth, and material goods

ii. Uruz Rune: strength & manhood

iii. Thurisaz Rune: a new start

iv. Ansuz Rune: a signal or message

v. Radio Rune: travel

vi. Kaunaz Rune: fire

vii. Gibo Rune: blessing

viii. Wunjo Rune: happiness

ix. Hagalaz Rune: chaos

x. Nauthiz Rune: pain

xi. Isa Rune: frustration

xii. Jera Rune: Fertility and harvest

xiii. Eihwaz Rune: barriers/protection

xiv. Perth Rune: hidden things

xv. Algiz Rune: defense

xvi. Sowelu Rune: perfection

xvii. Tyr Rune: victory

xviii. Berkana Rune: rebirth or a fresh start

xix. Ehwaz Rune: overcoming obstacles

xx. Mannaz Rune: humanity

xxi. Leguz Rune: motherhood

xxii. Inguz Rune: beginning

xxiii. Degaz Rune: sunlight

xxiv. Othela Rune: possessions

There are different ways of rune casting to discover the future. If you want to give a try, then do not go for complicated procedures. Simply find a quiet environment that can allow your mind to focus on the issue or question at hand. Have the runes preferably the stones in a box before you as you meditate. After meditating, cast the runes onto a cloth, or a pouch then read those that are fallen the right side up. Check the bearing and try to interpret the meaning, as already explained. This is one of the commonly used methods, but there are also other alternatives.

Can Runes Help Predict Future Misfortunes?

Future runes are not only aimed at discovering good. As already hinted, there are used to tell what the future holds. Runes tell the future whether it is good or bad for you. There are, in fact, runic signs that are a sign of unfortunate occurrences on the part of humans. Those are the ones that can help predict misfortunes likely to happen in the future. There are many runes that can help predict any unfortunate happenings that are likely to be experienced in the future. That means that as you learn about runes, you should be a good student of both good as well as bad runes as they all have an influence on your living.

An example of rune that represents dark forces acting against human is the Thurisaz. The meaning of Thurisaz is ogre, and from ancient tales, ogres are hostile gods that threaten to destroy humans. If you cast your runes and what you see is Thurisaz, then that could mean that you are headed towards something that might not be good for you. For instance, it could mean that your timing is unfavorable if you were preparing to start a project.

Is It Possible To Carry Out Past and Future Cleaning Using Runes?

Although it is a little bit confusing and painstaking process, it is possible to carry out the cleaning of your future from any damage that you are likely to face. Similarly, it is possible to use runes to restore your energy or health that might have happened to you as a result of magical effects. Many people say that it is hard, but the truth is that if you are determined to rid you're your past and future of any unfortunate occurrences, then it is possible to do it.

Runes are highly versatile, and they can be used for different roles and purposes, including cleaning. You can, in fact, do whatever you want with runes provided you know what you are doing. Most importantly, you ought to aggressive in learning the different runes and how to apply them to make your life better. The learning process should actually be continuous with the goal of finding out new ways of using runes to make your life worth living.

For future cleaning, you'll need to be familiar with rues of constructing the future or shaping it up the way you want. You can, for instance, seek the help of Sunna, the most powerful rune with the ability to transform anything. If you combine the power of Sunna plus a couple of others that have powers for transforming human life, then you can be sure to change your future and make live knowing that there is no misfortune awaiting you.

Regarding damage suffered in the past that is likely to affect your future, you can use certain restorative runic combinations to overcome the effects. If left uncured, they can easily cause physical weakness, indifference, and spiritual emptiness. At the worst, people who are victims of such magical effects at some point even contemplate suicide or anything that can easily take away their lives.

Glyphs, staves, and bandages are a combination of runes that are often used to restore as well as cleanse. The process of carrying out these combinations is also not that tough. Simply choose that which will help you get back to the status or health condition. Once you pick a combination that best solves your problem, carry it on yourself as a picture for a period of nine days. These days are ideally the length of cleansing time. At the end of it, and if you had picked the best combination, it is possible to completely rid your life of any past magical effect that has been affecting you.

Note that cleaning or restoring alone is not enough if you are a victim of past misfortunes, and you even fear that you are likely to face a lot in the future. You need to go a step further and look for a way of protecting yourself. Without protection, you risk going back to the former self or state of trouble that you have been trying to emerge from. That again calls for learning about rune protection and how you can apply it to stay safe now and in the future.

Runes That Can Be Used For Personal Protection Going Into the Future

Turisaz, Teyvaz, Algiz, and Isa are the four runes that you can use to protect yourself from the impact of your feared enemies in the future. These four runes have powers to stop bad energy and forces that are threatening to destroy your future. Apart from using these runes to protect yourself, you can also use them to protect your loved ones, your home, and even your workplace if you fear that there are threats there too.

To enjoy the security of runes of protection, use a marker or a ballpoint pen to draw these runic signs on the wall, objects at home, or on your body. You should, however, note that with time, drawings tend to fade. More specifically, those on your body are likely to be washed as you bath each day. Therefore, a more permanent way to have the lasting symbols is to make special amulets of the images you want. Curving the sign or symbol on wood or stone would be the best way to put your protection in place permanently.

For clarity about the runes of protection, Teyvaz is the best rune to protect your business, money, and general financial situation. It has the ability to send back negative spells send to your business and also resist any circumstances that are likely to affect your finances negatively. For protection from jealous individuals, Isa is the best rune. For evil eyes, use Turisaz, and you will be safe. Apart from offering you the protection you need, these runes also attract good luck and bring happiness into your daily activities.

As a reminder, the magic properties, as well as the powerful protection of runes, depend on many factors, among them your understanding and use of them. You can only enjoy the benefits if you are a strict follower of instructions and if you have also perfected the art of connecting with runes perfectly. The most experienced users of runes also say that runes are not a quick solution to problems. You have to take the time to build their power by frequently using them until you master the best ways of harnessing their powers.

Chapter Six: Runic Exercises & Preparing Your Mind

Runic exercises support meditation as well as the psychological work of the body. While there are many ways to use runes to connect with the spiritual world, using the body can help is one of the ancient methods that have been proven to be highly effective. This chapter explores various aspects of runes exercises. It provides a guide to runic exercises, descriptions of different exercises (Both long and short), and ends by explaining the various benefits of runic exercises.

Guide to Runic Exercises

A guide is necessary when doing any activity. It provides directions to follow from the start to end. Most importantly, it prepares your mind by outlining what you should expect and be prepared to do. Before you get started with any runic practice or tasks to help you make your learning process simple, you ought to prepare your mind accordingly. Here is a precise yet detailed guide to runic exercises:

Prepare Yourself by Having Your Body Relaxed

Having your body relaxed is very vital when it comes to runic exercises. Also, a relaxed body is flexible, and the chances are that you are more likely to be effective in your exercises if your body is free. This means that you need to relax your muscles, mind, jaws, and eyes since these are the parts that play a vital role in learning.

To achieve a complete state of relaxation, you need first to solve your internal conflicts, put your mind in a state that is ready to learn, and, most importantly, achieve quietness. These are the essential things you need if you want to perform runic exercises easily and reap maximum benefits associated with them.

Control Your Breath

Runic exercises are about connecting with the spiritual world and inner self to help you deal with the challenges of everyday living. For this reason, proper breathing is very necessary for yourself before you embark on any runic exercises. Even when you start exercising, full conscious breathing is very vital.

It is, therefore, recommendable that you exercise the art of controlling breath way before you kick off the actual exercises. Practice complete exhalation and wait until the urge to breathe in comes naturally. Most importantly, at all times, allow your diaphragm, ribcage, and shoulders to move freely as you breathe.

Learn to Control Your Thoughts

It is important to control your thoughts before and, most importantly while exercising. If you let your mind roam around without concentrating on what you are doing, then achieving the results you want may be an uphill task. Controlling your thoughts here means making sure that what comes to your mind is all about what you are doing and how you can improve on it. In simple terms, let your mind get used to meditation mode. That way, you can easily concentrate on the task at hand and enjoy the full benefits of what you are doing.

Learn to Sing Sounds Properly

Some runic exercises include singing specific sounds. It is thus important to learn how to change pitch, vary sounds, and move the body. You need perfect this before you start whichever runic exercises you want to practice. Doing so ensures that all runic exercise procedures, including singing, won't challenge you once you start exercising.

If you feel that you might not be comfortable practicing in a group, then learn to do it alone. Privacy gives you the confidence you need to practice high and low pitches. While doing it, make sure to perfect the art of raising and lowering pitch. Most importantly, learn to feel the differences and various impacts of the different sounds that you'll be practicing. That's one way to enhance your practice sessions.

Purity Can Also Be a Necessary Condition

One last thing to remember is that some runic exercises need purity. You should thus learn to clean your body to wash off all impurities symbolically. In some instances and depending on the kind of exercises you'll be doing, it may be necessary to use certain oils or herbs to help you clean all impurities. Some runic rituals/exercises demand that you just be pure in body and, most importantly, in mind.

Following these guidelines will make your training or exercise sessions fruitful. Remember that you will not just be exercising, but you will be doing it to help you solve life problems and achieve your needs. You can only uncover the secrets of runes and enjoy their benefits if you prepare well and put your mind and body in the right shape.

Runic Exercise Descriptions

While there are many runic exercises, knowing some of them and understanding what it takes to do, one can be helpful as you develop your own exercises. Here, a few examples have been given to help you get a clear picture of an effective runic exercise that you can try. Here we go:

Exercise 1: A long Runic Visualization Exercise

Requirements

● Your runes

● Candles preferably purple ones

● Appropriate meditation music

● Incense

● Cinnamon

● Wormwood

● Dandelion

● Bay

● Jasmine

● Mugwort

Methods

1. Go to a private, quiet place. For ease of access and total privacy, your bedroom is the best place. So go there light your candles, burn the incense and play low meditation music to help you get to the right moods. Experts recommend non-intrusive classical music.

2. Sit, look around, and make sure you are comfortable in your sitting position. Make sure you have your bag of runes near you or simply on your laps. This stage should last for about twenty minutes to allow you to connect with your environment in readiness for the subsequent steps.

3. Relax your body, take deep breaths, and close your eyes, then try to banish all distractive thoughts not related to your exercise. At this stage, you do not need to have your bag or runes on the laps. You can put it aside to allow you to control your thoughts easily.

4. Open your eyes, take your bag and then, with the power of your hand, pick one using your sense of feeling without having to look at it. Hold it for about ten minutes, then put the bag aside once again.

5. Settle down, close your eyes, breathe slowly to relax your muscles, specifically those at the arms, legs, hands, and let it continue all the way to the brain. Finally, let the muscles in your face relax as well.

6. While seated, connect to the spiritual world by visualizing a journey to a sacred place with the intention of finding a solution to any problem that you are facing. It should take a bit longer, as is the climax, healing moment, or realization of your goal. Thirty minutes are okay.

You can imagine taking a walk to the river in a nice cool afternoon. It is generally warm, and a soft breeze from the river ruffles your hair as you walk towards or along the river bank. The air is filled with sweet songs of the birds singing to cheer the beautiful wildflowers as the wind swings them side-by-side.

While you cannot see or understand clearly where you are heading or what exactly you are going to do in the river, let the environment give you a fresh feel. Take a keen look at anything to help you concentrate and ask yourself a couple of rhetoric questions. Perhaps looking at a bird singing could be all you need to find a solution to that problem that has bothered you for long. Try to connect what you see with the happenings in your life.

Listen to your senses. What are you feeling, smelling, or hearing? Once you are satisfied and happy with the feeling, start the journey back. That possibly is an indication that you have undergone an inner change and experienced spiritual powers. Once you arrive back, open your eyes and take a deep breath.

7. After the small journey of meditation and experiencing a new environment away from your secluded bedroom, take the time to recover. You are most likely to feel tired, bearing in mind that any journey, whether a real one or an imagination makes you tired. A time to recover is thus essential before you complete your exercise.

8. Shut out the rest of the world, and get back to your room. Look up at the ceiling. What do you see? Is it the same thing you are used to seeing every day? You will most likely discover something you had not seen in the past. That's the essence of this exercise. To help you look at things differently and see life from a positive angle than you have always done.

That's one powerful runic exercise description that can completely change things in your life. As a reminder, you may not necessarily have to follow everything here religiously. You can add or subtract a few things to create your own unique program that matches your needs and the change you want to experience. Besides, not all runic exercises have to be too long as the one given here. There are short ones that are useful as well and can help you solve your problems effectively.

Simple Exercises

Exercise#1: Write a Poem for Every one of Your Favorite Runes

If you are a novice in runic exercises, then starting with the simple ones like writing poems can help you as you develop and learn the artfully. You can later get into the tough ones once you get started and fully understand the power of runic exercises.

Writing a poem for runes is a simple exercise since you do not need any special materials to have the job get done. All you need is bad of runes, a pen, and a paper to write on your favorite song or message to your runes.

Steps

1. Read about and understand all your runes

2. Find out the special powers associated with all your runes

3. Learn how to connect with the runes

4. Find out the historical contexts relating to all your runes

5. Write a nice sweet poem for each rune

Make sure that the poems you write help you understand and improve your relationship with every poem. Doing so will help you understand certain aspects of runes, such as the signs that you would otherwise not just understand by reading about them.

Exercise#2: Visualizing Runic Images

Image casting is also part of runic exercises, and one way to connect with the runes is to visualize their images. Sometimes, visualizing can help you see what you cannot see when your eyes are opened and looking at the runes.

Steps

1. Pick a rune and visualize its image forming right in front of your eyes

2. Chant its name as you visualize the image

3. Look at the rune and sing what you see

4. Continue singing for about 15 minutes each time including the name of the rune as you sing

5. Ground yourself and write whatever you saw and felt while visualizing the rune

Please beware that you can do this for every rune for as long as you want. Each time, try to see what you have not seen before in the rune, you are visualizing. You can also do it a couple of times a day, as it is a process that has no end. It is the best thing to do if you want to master rune casting. Therefore, take the time and practice it well until you master it well.

NOTE: As you perform these or other runic exercises of your choice, always try to ensure that nothing disrupts the flow of energy in your body. That's why your choice of a private or secluded room is very vital. It determines how you will go about the process and the results, as well. Usually, many people prefer a quiet place in the garden or simply in the bedroom, as was illustrated in the first exercise. Such places allow you to concentrate and increase your overall energy in the body, which you need to complete an exercise successfully.

Benefits of Runic Exercises

Persons of all ages and from different cultures use runic exercises for many reasons. Despite the great variation in the types of exercises performed, the benefits enjoyed cut across and in fact, are similar. Some do the exercises to obtain their daily needs. Others do it since they are interested and have been doing for years. Also, others are much into the benefits of mental exercise and fitness associated with runes. Irrespective of the reason for doing the exercises, the benefits do not discriminate against anyone. Here are some of the assured benefits of regular doing of runic exercises:

Improved Quality of Life

Invoking rune spells or signs associated with happiness such as WUNJO, ALGIZ, and BERKANO can help improve one's quality of life. Different people invoke different runic forces and powers. The good thing about runes is that you don't have to stick to a particular method to enjoy its benefits. You can have your own runic activities that match your specific needs. The best way is to focus on those that will help you overcome your weaknesses and improve your overall quality of life. It might take time to master runes and what it is capable of doing, but the journey is worth it.

Improved Mental Fitness

As illustrated in the example exercises given, runes engage the mind taking it through simple as well as tough workouts through imagination as well as visualization. It is, therefore, almost obvious that when runic exercises become part and parcel of daily routine, the assured benefit is mental fitness. Some people, in fact, use runes to sharpen their minds and put them in better fitness levels. If you are experiencing any forms of weaknesses in the mind and you wish to overcome, then exercising runic activities can help solve the problem.

Achievement of Short and Long-term Plans

Everyone has ambitions and things they wish to achieve in the short run, as well as after a couple of months or even years. Learning runic signs and applying them appropriately can help one remain on the right track that leads them to achieve what they have planned for themselves. Some plans tend to be hard, and achieving them requires extra inspiration and dedication. With the help of runic exercises and other practices, such plans can be made simple and realistic. How it works is that runic exercises put your mind in the state of achievement, and once the mind wins it, you already have it.

Discovery of Secrets

Through runic divination, one can uncover hidden secrets and even find out what the future holds. How is this possible? There are many ways to do it. It can go through rune tossing, arranging them in certain styles, and putting together a couple of them to make a certain unique pattern. Meanings can then be attached to them to help discover secrets. For many years, people have been using this method to solve simple yes/no puzzles and even interpret complex secret situations. Although there are no specific procedures of making the discovery, different people apply the methods they understand to make meanings out of otherwise unknown events of happenings.

A Chance to Connect with Nature

Runic meditations are not just a way of understanding runes, but they also help in doing what one would not do without runes. For instance, the art of connecting with nature is not a usual thing but a special process best done with runes. Since ancient times, runes have played a very vital role in communicating with nature and understanding what it needs or what it can give to those who know its power.

Chapter Seven: Rituals to Accompany the Study

Learning runes cannot be complete without exploring a couple of rituals that accompany different runic activities. In this chapter, we delve into the topic of rituals in the context of runes. Although different people create their own runic rituals depending on what they are using runes for, there are common ones worth knowing. With that said, here we go:

Why Rituals Accompany the Study of Runes

When learning anything new, people often have different ways of making their learning process easy and enjoyable. In schools, for instance, some concepts are taught with the aid of experiments. The reason for having such practical activities is to make it easy to understand what's happening and also make it easy for learners to remember. Similarly, in the learning of runes, rituals act as 'experiments' that make the process simple and enjoyable as well. They add the spices to the process hence giving the learner a reason to go further and not just get the basics.

Rituals are not, however, meant to replace the real learning process as some people tend to argue. Rather, it is meant to supplement it. Besides, runic rituals are not static. They change over time, and you can even have your own rituals to make your learning process unique. For this reason, there are ancient runic rituals as well as those of the 21st century. If you want to understand runes better, create your own runic rituals. But remember that if you want to create perfect ones, you must first learn from the existing runic rituals. It, therefore, makes sense to understand a couple of runic rituals that have been in use since the long-gone days when runic alphabets came into being.

Common Runes and Their Corresponding Rituals

While they were initially used as a form of language in Germanic cultures in Northern Europe, runes are also powerful spiritual tools. They have been and are continuing to be used for religious purposes, divination, and magic, as well. Runes are, however, extremely versatile as they vary from one place to another and from one culture to another as well.

Here are five common runes and rituals to accompany them:

#1: BERKANO

The BERKANO rune is all about new beginnings and manifestations in one's life. It helps in making it easy for you to bring to life whatever new thing you want. It could be a new home, project, job, business, or even welcoming a new child. Anything that you are working hard to make it a reality, Berkano can help you bring it to reality.

BERKANO Ritual

Connecting with the power of Berkano is not difficult, and anyone can easily learn it. To perform this ritual, you need a stone, paint, or anything that can help you make a permanent mark. Besides, this ritual is often performed once the full moon is sighted. Once are these conditions are met, then you can connect. Simply visualize the new thing you want in your life, and as you think about it, make a painting or drawing of it on the stone. Place it in a place you'll be seeing as often as possible.

#2: WUNJO

Wunjo is all about happiness and overcoming any life hassles that bring sadness, anxiety, and other feelings that take away joy and happiness. Let's face it! Almost everyone undergoes different life happenings that bring sadness. It happens, and it is not a surprise. If you feel that you are overwhelmed, then Wunjo is all you need to be happy. It will grant you the happiness you need, even when things are tough on your side.

Wunjo Ritual

The Wunjo ritual is performed on the night of the first appearance of the full moon. Some people, however, tend to overlook this and perform it anytime. To perform this ritual, you need to make a sacred place or an altar, as is usually called in religious language. Put all things that make you happy on that altar. Make sure to pick those that make you the happiest when you see them. Look at your altar every day, and you'll always be happy.

#3: ALGIZ

If protection is all you need, then ALGIZ rune can completely change your life and provide a sense of protection you need in life. Algiz is not only a sign of protection, but it also helps you connect to your higher self and feel deeper inside you that you are safe. Many people often use this rune at times of crises, such as feeling scared and in need of protection in daily activities.

ALGIZ Ritual

Unlike other rituals that have to be strictly performed during specific moon phases, you can perform the ALGIZ ritual during any phase of the moon, although there are arguments that the dark phase is the best. To perform this ritual, you need three sticks, one long stick, and two shorter ones. Place the shorter ones at the center of the long one to make a v shape that looks like the Algiz symbol. Hang it on the wall or put it on your altar. It will provide the security you need, and you'll feel safe.

#4: TIWAZ

Also called the warrior rune, Tiwaz is known for its ability to strengthen people who are going through different difficulties of life. Whether you have a legal battle, facing indecision, have disagreements, or advocating for justice, Tiwaz might just be the rune you need to change things in your life. It is a powerful rune known for providing great strength.

TIWAZ Ritual

The Tiwaz Ritual is often performed during the first quarter moon. To do it, you simply need three things, namely a candle, a lighter, and a toothpick. You may, however, have to get many candles as you will need one for each problem you have. For instance, you may need a candle for your legal battles, disagreements, and other issues. Light the candles and sit with them until it is over, then you can extinguish it. You can, however, put it off when you finally win the legal battle you had, find justice, resolve a disagreement, or any other problem.

#5: FEHU Rune

In all honesty, we all love abundance, and in fact, we always strive to make sure that we have it as much as possible. Besides, our daily struggles are mainly to help us make ends meet, get daily bread, and enjoy many other blessings. However, getting all this is often not an easy job. Fehu helps during struggles and makes us enjoy abundance amidst great adversities and daily struggles.

FEHU Ritual

To perform the FEHU Ritual, you need a green candle, a lighter and a needle, toothpick, or anything that can help you carve the Fehu symbol on the candle. Carve the symbol while thinking of you enjoying blessings, wealth, and being showered with goodies. Once you are through carving, light the candle and look at it quietly to enjoy the power of Fehu and is the ability to bring abundance.

There are many other runic rituals for almost all the challenges we face. As already hinted earlier in this chapter, the one good thing about runic rituals is the fact that you can come up with your own rituals depending on your needs. But as a reminder, when you decide to create one for your needs, remember three things. It must be simple, done consistently until you overcome the challenge and it must help you overcome the problems you have at any given time, Runic rituals work, and there are many testimonies about the power of these simple yet effective runic activities.

Tips on Taking up Ritual Runes

Runic rituals can be performed individually or as a group. Whichever route you take, the results depend on many factors key among them being your own belief on the power of runes. If you don't believe it, then there may be no need to try all these experiments and practices. However, if after learning, you finally understand and see the power that exists in runes, then taking them up or putting in practice can change your life completely.

If you want to try runic rituals for your very first time, you need to have a small guide to act as your traffic lights. Proceeding without anything to warn or caution you on how to go about different activities can be a challenge. Fortunately, runic rituals are not very complicated as they are made to appear sometimes by those who have a negative view of it. Here are simple guidelines on performing runic rituals:

Outline Your Reasons For

You definitely have reasons that are propelling you to consider resorting to runic rituals. It is, therefore, good to put them down before you even start thinking of which runic rituals you'll perform. Writing them down and checking often will drive you to learn and perform rituals to accompany your study of runic language and signs.

Decide the Time and How You'll Perform Your Rituals

Different rituals are suited to different times. Before you start using runic rituals to help you meet the needs of your life, it is important to understand the best times to use them. Most importantly, make sure you know how to perform them and connect to their power.

Find Out If You Have All Materials of Requirements

Runic rituals can only be performed successfully if you have all the necessary materials or requirements for the rituals you are considering. If you do not have, then find a way of getting them before you start the experiments

Decide How You Will Go About Your Runic Ritual Sessions

Will you perform one by one or combine a couple of rituals at once? How you organize your rituals has an impact on the possible outcome that you will experience. It is always good to do them one by one, so you give full attention and harness full energy from each. If you combine many, the chances are that you might get mixed up and fail to concentrate fully. Remember that runic rituals are spiritual tools that work depending on the power of your imagination.

Take Up the Rituals

Finally, after learning and making sure that everything you need to perform runic rituals is available, the next big challenge is to do the actual job. As illustrated in the five examples of some common runic rituals, performing them may not be complex. However, the environment, and how you perform them is what determines the kind of results you will get at the end.

In some instances, it may be good to perform some runic rituals as a group rather than working alone as an individual. In such instances, you need to get like-minded individuals, preferably those facing the same challenges you have, so you work together. You should also note that group rituals might be a bit different from those that you can perform alone. That, therefore, calls for more research and learning about the difference between individual runic rituals versus those that can be done in groups.

In a nutshell, learning runes should not just be about reading about how they work and the situations they can help. It is good to go another extra mile to practice a few as you advance to the next higher stages. Runic rituals are highly versatile and tend to vary depending on what they are used for by those who understand them. Those who have taken the time to learn about them and their power have moving stories. If you want to give them a try, you need to understand them well and get the truth about the many misconceptions about them. You might end up realizing that all you needed to turn around your life was the power of runes and runic rituals.

Chapter Eight: Facts about the Blank Rune and Whether You Should Read It

One interesting question that rune enthusiasts often ask is what's up about the blank rune, and can anyone use it? Well, indeed, there is a lot to learn about this kind of rune, especially for beginners who would like to have a complete understanding of the runes before using them. It is also quite interesting to note that some rune users argue that the blank rune was not there in the past, and it was just introduced recently. Is it true? Did it ever exist in the past? What exactly does it mean? Well, these are the questions that this chapter will answer. If you ever had questions about this rune, you now have the best and most comprehensive answers.

Who Came Up With the Blank Rune?

A new age author by the name Ralph Blum is believed to be the inventor of the blank rune. Until the year 1982, he was famous for being a novelist of Jewish origin. His critics argue that until then, Blum had no knowledge of runes, Norse culture, history, or mythology. His decision to shift his attention to the new area might have been influenced by the growing demand for knowledge and insights about runes. In his admission, he agrees that, indeed, the new-age goldmine is what beckoned him to the art of reading runes and writing about it. He, therefore, enjoyed the new waters to the point of inventing something that no one had ever thought would exist in the world of runes.

Ralph Blum argues that he happened to get a set of runes from England that contained a 25th blank tile, probably a bonus rune or a spare just in case one of the 24 is not that good. Since he didn't know anything about the blank 25th rune, he took it and attached a new meaning to it. He referred to it as a blank, mysterious rune with a deep mystical meaning. After examining it for a while, he went ahead to write a book called The Book of Runes that explored all the runes in his set, including the 25th mysterious one that had never appeared in any book before or historical facts about runes as well as their origins.

Readers of Blum's book and especially the critics argue that the inclusion of the 25th tile is the biggest fraud ever invented in the history of runes. They further argue that even the 24 others, as explained in his book, had the wrong explanations too. However, that did not deter Ralph Blum from continuing to deepen his mind and pen in the world of runes. He went ahead to promote his book and especially the new invention; 25th tile. His view is that there was something great worth knowing about it, especially for purposes of blending it with culture.

Since the invention, there have been many other developments as well as controversies regarding the existence of the blank rune and its role. For those who are seriously interested in the old number of runes and meanings, the 25th is nothing. On the other hand, for the advocates of the new age runic knowledge, this is something great to explore. As a reader, you can choose whether you should stick to the old number or embrace the new age meanings. The fact, however, is that the blank rune was never in the initial 24 runes of Odin, the God of true and wise runic knowledge.

What Exactly is the Blank Rune?

Also called Odin's rune or the Wyrd rune, the blank rune is a new age thing that came into the limelight around the 1980s when it was marketed by some rune enthusiasts as an alternative form or a divination method that is only applicable in specific situations. It is regarded as a new thing or an introduction since there is no historical as well as archaeological evidence that the blank rune was ever among the original 24 runes of god Odin.

So what exactly is the blank rune if there is no historical evidence that it existed in the past? Well, the blank rune is the zero, or silence that is void of infinite possibility. Some writers or books describe it as the breath before a speech or the space between words. Besides, it is an element of air whose Tarot equivalent is the fool. This fact about the blank rune is the reason behind the debate on whether the blank rune is a good or bad omen. It is the reason behind the many talks and the debate about its use.

Essentially, the blank rune opens up a new chapter or space for discussion to a student or any learner of runes to put their wisdom into the questions often raised about runes. Those who have delved into this topic argue that the blank rune represents a situation of not knowing what is happening. Before the runemaster (god Odin) received the 24 runes, he was in a state of bot known as simply a state of ignorance. It, therefore, invites everyone to ponder on how it feels to be in the state of not knowing or awaiting the intervention of the giver of power and knowledge to provide the missing information.

Should You Use the Blank Rune for Divination?

Well, there is no straight answer to this question that continues to puzzle many and especially those still learning about runes. Some object it for technical reasons, and some are opposed to the blank rune because of their conservative nature. As a reader, you can, therefore, decide whether or not you are going to include it when casting or drawing your runes.

Some readers argue that including a blank rune in your set opens up a new page of complications, especially in interpretations. They say that it amounts to reading the air, meaning that there is nothing serious or tangible worth interpreting. On the other hand, some have used it, and they believe that including it opens up your mind for a conversation.

Rune teachers do also have varied opinions on whether one should include or exclude the blank rune. However, there seems to be a consensus in one thing regarding the use of this rune. They agree that things evolve with time, and as a result, having the 25th rune can as well be an indication that things have changed since Odin, the runemaster, introduced the 24 runes. Many teachers, therefore, advise their students to use intuition when deciding whether or not to include the 25th rune in their set. It is interesting to note that some even argue that it should be included since runes may not have been finished by the time Odin received them. In the same measure, there are those teachers that say that it is not right to have something that does not stand for anything.

Well, from the analyses of those who care for and those against it, one can conclude that there is no consensus on this. It is, thus, a matter of personal preference. You can have it, but whether to use it or not is purely a matter of personal choice. For runic studies, there is no doubt that learning about the blank rune is very vital. Most importantly, knowing it helps you get facts, so when you decide to give it a try, you know exactly what you are using and where it came from since it was not in the original 24 runes given to Odin.

Assuming You Use, What Does It Mean When a Blank Rune Appears In Your Reading?

If you finally decide to have a set of 25 instead of 24 and you get the blank one a part of those you should read and interpret, what does it mean to have it? Well, this is where the knowledge of how to interpret the blank rune comes in. It has a meaning for your divination, and it might help you get the true picture of the situation that you are trying to solve. It has an implication though there is no uniform meaning of it.

Different rune teachers and users attach different meanings to the blank rune. But generally, what many of them tend to suggest is that having a blank rune suggests that there are complications in your divination practices. It can be a suggestion that your formulation of the question is ill-informed, or it is simply not right. Besides, it might be a call for you to meditate and wait before you can finally uncover the problem that you are facing.

To help you understand more about the blank rune, here are some of the responses that some authors or books have to say:

According to Farnell (2006), in his book about runes, a blank rune indicates that some sort of change is about to take place, but there is no clarity on whether the change is positive or negative. You may, therefore, have to do further reading to understand what exactly awaits you or what kind of change is going to happen to you sooner or later.

Peschel (1989) asserts that when a blank rune appears, it means that something you did not expect is going to come your way. However, whether it is good or a bad thing depends on your past behavior. If you did good things in the past and your behavior warrants it, then you should expect good, and the vice versa is also true.

Blum (1983), the inventor of the blank rune, also has his interpretation of this interesting rune. He argues that the appearance of this rune in a cast or a drawing can portend death. However, he does not simply mean that you are going to die if you cast or draw your runes, and a blank one becomes part of those that you should read. Death, in his explanation, is relative to any part of your life. It could mean the end of a relationship, business, or any other thing that has been alive and happening in your life.

According to Holmes (2013), the appearance of a blank rune indicates that there is some good progress in one's spiritual development. It also implies that one's knowledge is greater and even far much stronger than it was ever imagined. It is this a reminder that life is not that bad as one tends to imagine or think about, especially in times of hardships or some sort of desperation.

Vital Things to Remember About the Blank Rune

Having explored details about the blank rune, how it came to being, and whether or not you should use it, there are vital things to remember about it. Knowing them can help you, especially when you are faced with a situation where you have to decide whether or not you should include the additional blank rune in your set. You should note that as already, the decision on whether or not you should add it depends on what you intend to achieve. Precisely, there is no restriction or permission on whether or not you should use it.

Additionally, the other thing worth remembering is that the blank rune was not originally among the twenty-four that were given to Odin. It is something that came up much later in the 1980s from Ralph Blum. However, his invention was not intentional but rather something that arose from the runes he received from England that included an extra blank one. Instead of using it as a spare, he decided to give it a meaning, and it has since been used and included in many other recent publications about runes.

It is also worth noting that there are several other authors apart from Ralph Blum, who have also looked at the aspect of the blank rune and given it a meaning. As already shown on what it means to have blank runes, there are lots of things that can be associated with the rune. If you decide to use it, you need to understand the different views that some authors and runic teachers have about it. You might also have to read and interpret it if you cast or spread leads you to it or brings it up as one of your runes to interpret. Finally, there is no consensus on whether it is good or bad to include the blank rune in your set.

Chapter Nine: Runic Spreads

Runes are often arranged in different patterns for divinatory purposes. The patterns they form when cast or arranged are the "Runic Spreads." These spreads vary a lot, and they can range from as few as only two runes put in a sequence to as large as a full 24 runic layout pattern. In a spread, whether large or small, the most important thing is the sequence. It determines not only the position but the significance as well.

Different people make use of different spreads depending on their circumstances and the kind of information that they would like to obtain. More specifically, some people have one or a few chosen spreads, while others make use of different spreads. It is also interesting to note that spreads change from time to time, and they also vary from one place to another. If you love using runes to get information or knowledge of the unknown, you can also invent your unique spread that matches your needs. But to get a picture of what others usually do, you might have to learn and master some common spreads.

Common Runic Spreads

Single Spread

The single runic spread is the easiest and the simplest of all. It is often done when the situation at hand is not complex or when one needs a quick insight into what drives a particular situation. You can also apply when you want to get the most concise summary of a situation. In all these situations, a single rune spread provides an overview of what lies ahead and any guidance that one needs to tackle the problem at hand.

The procedure for drawing a single rune is also simple and straightforward. Hold your bag or runes then think about the situation that you are facing. For instance, you can say that you would wish the rune to give you a picture of the day ahead, comment upon an endeavor, or a problem. Once you clearly state what you expect to achieve after spreading, pick a rune then meditate while holding it. You can then look up its meaning, and you'll be done. Indeed, it is without any doubt the quickest, simplest, and most importantly, effective.

Three Spread

If you want to place an issue in its content and get an overall picture of it, then the three runic spread is all you need. It uncovers vital details about an event and what awaits you going forward. More specifically, it shows what led to an event, the issue itself that you are currently facing, and any possible outcomes that you should anticipate. In a nutshell, a three runic spread shows you three important things:

● Your past and circumstances that led to it

● Your present situation

● Your future, so you prepare

You need three runes to do this spread, but you will draw them one by one, each of them representing the three highlighted scenarios. Think about an issue, and when it is clear on your mind, draw your first rune. Have a flashback of the events that led to it while focusing on the drawn rune. Draw the second one while focusing on your current situation. Finally, draw the last one while focusing on what is likely to happen in the future. One thing you need to remember is that deep focus is very vital at all these stages.

Fork Spread

This kind of spread is often preferred by people who want to understand the dynamics of a given situation. It uses three runes that represent three different aspects of an important decision that is about to be made. If you are at a critical point where you are expected to make a decision, then this can be the runic spread to consider.

Drawing the three runes for fork spread is also a simple exercise. Each of the three runes you draw explains something about your decision. The left rune stands for the best possible outcome. On the other hand, the right one represents the second-best possible outcome, and lastly, the third one stands for the underlying critical factor that determines the outcome of your situation.

Diamond Spread

When something happens or a situation changes to something that was not anticipated, people believe that forces are acting or influencing it. However, understanding those forces, especially when one is looking for a solution, can be a challenge. Fortunately, there are runic spreads that can help reveal the forces acting on a given situation at hand. Such runes are, therefore, the best when you want to understand a hidden conflict.

Diamond rune spread is one type that can help reveal the hidden or dynamic forces acting on a given situation. You can thus opt to use this spread if there is a serious hidden conflict that is affecting you, and there is a need to reveal it. It is a four-runic spread with each rune representing a given aspect of a situation at hand. The four runes and what they represent in a given situation are given as:

Bottom rune: the basis of the issue of the problem

Left rune: one of the forces behind a given conflicting situation

Right rune: the other force that is acting on the situation you are facing

Top rune: what you can finally achieve by taking a given route

One thing that makes this kind of spread popular among many people is the fact that it can be used in a variety of situations. It doesn't matter the situation or conflict that you are facing. Provided you know how to draw it, you can, without any hassle, use it and get to understand the forces acting and what your remedial actions are likely to yield.

Norn Spread

The Norn spread is used when one wants to plot elements, including those of the past, the current ones, and even those expected in the future. It essentially helps in getting an understanding of the evolution of a situation over time. To perform this spread, you need three runes, namely, the left, right, and middle runes. Here are the three crucial elements that these three runes represent:

● Left: an important element of the past

● Middle: a deciding element of the present time

● Right: a critical element of the future

Relationship Spread

People relate, and there are usually many questions and issues involved in relationships. The relationship spread, therefore, helps people who want to understand the purpose of the relationship as well as what to expect going forward. More specifically, it explains the role of each partner and, most importantly, the direction that the relationship is likely to take it the future.

The relationship spread uses three runes, each representing an important aspect of the relationship. The first rune represents the attitude towards the relationship that the person drawing the rune has as well as their energy. The second rune represents the attitude and energy of the partner towards the relationship. Lastly, the third rune shows the reason the partners are in the relationship.

Elemental Spread

The elemental spread uses four runes with each rune representing a certain quality. The runes are namely, the top (Earth), the right, the bottom, and the left rune. In this arrangement, the top rune, which is also called the Earth, represents lessons that one can learn on the physical plane. The right rune represents lessons that are to be learned on the mental plane or those that one is thinking about with regards to the situation at hand. The bottom rune, which is sometimes known as the fire, represents lessons that one can learn from the spiritual realm. Finally, the left rune; water stands for emotional lessons.

Celestial Spread

Unlike all other spreads, the celestial spread takes the longest time and uses more runes. Ideally, it takes a whole year, and one needs a total of thirteen runes to do this kind of spread. Those who draw this spread often use it to get a glimpse of the kind of influence that the year has on their life. The thirteen runes are arranged in a diamond shape with the first one being the right rune to the last one, which is rune twelve.

It is, however, worth noting that since the celestial rune does not have to start in January since it is a whole year practice. It can start at any month, and the first or the right rune represents the month that you are in. If you, thus, start in June or say August, all you need to do is to follow the diamond shape every month until the twelfth rune. Finally, when you are done, the last one, which is the thirteenth, will give you the influence that the year had on your life or the situations you had over time.

Celtic-Cross Spread

If you are well versed in star crosses or the patterns they form, then understanding the Celtic cross spread is pretty simple for you. This kind of spread is applicable in situations where you want to gain a complete view of the situation that is affecting your life. You can use it to plot the arc of your life, so you get a complete view of what is happening and where you are likely to be headed to in the future.

Celtic cross is a ten-rune spread. When drawn, they all form a right, left, and center pattern that represents various times. All runes to the left side represent the past with the furthest giving details of the distant past. On the other hand, all runes to the right represent all future times with the furthest giving details to the distant future. The rune at the center represents the current situation.

Odin's Spread

Named after the Norse god, Odin, this is a five rune spread that helps in understanding the past, present, and future. Two left runes; the far left and left represent distant past and recent past, respectively. Two right runes; far-right and right represent distant future and near future, respectively. Finally, the one remaining rune at the center or top represents the present time.

It is good to note that unlike the other rune spreads that are also used to get information about the past, present, and future, Odin's spread is a bit detailed. Precisely, it looks at these vital things deeply as it gives you an option to understand distant times. It is, therefore, the best when you want to get a complete understanding of a given situation with regards to times, especially the distant past, as well as the future.

Medicine Wheel Spread

If you ever find yourself in a situation where you do not know exactly which path you should follow, the medicine wheel spread can help you. It gives guidance on a specific issue that the person drawing or casting has at hand. Many times, this spread is utilized when there is a need to understand which path is likely to lead to the desired destination.

To draw the medicine wheel spread, you need to have five runes, namely the left, right, bottom, top, and center. The bottom rune provides details about the flow of energies or the future specifically. The top deals with or shows you the challenge at hand. The left rune uncovers the source of the problem. On the other hand, the right rune represents the current situation. Finally, the fifth rune stands for the power that you can call upon to intervene and fix the situation that you could be facing.

Other runic spreads exist, and some people even come up with their spreads that reflect their different situations. Provided you understand the art of drawing runes, there is nothing that can prevent you from coming up with your own unique spread that is specific to the situation that you are facing at hand. It is, however, recommended that when beginning,, you start with those commonly used and simple ones before progressing to the complicated types.

Chapter Ten: Hidden Runic Roots

While the history of runes reveals much information about how runes came to use, there are other interesting hidden roots that every reader should know. For instance, the Shamans in Scandinavia used runes as their protective symbols. They carved them into stones, woods, and bone, and there were lots of mysterious stuff about runes. Other than that, there are lots of other things that a student or anyone learning about runes should explore. In this chapter, we take a look at a couple of those hidden runes.

The Hidden Process of How Odin Got the Runes

Odin consistently sought new knowledge, and the process that he used to gain the knowledge of runes is quite interesting, yet it is not fully disclosed. Other than being the inventor of runes and many other things related to it, he is also known as the god of magic or wisdom. Indeed, his wisdom is what made it possible for him to attain knowledge that would otherwise be impossible in human ways. To gain absolute knowledge, Odin had to renounce an eye. That's, in fact, how he managed to drink from the rarely known spring of wisdom that not everyone makes to reach or even know where it is found.

To surrender himself to the world of wisdom and drink from what others could not, Odin had to hurt himself even after removing his eye seriously. He pierced himself using a spear and hang down from a tree for two days. All these activities happened far away in a cold place where no one could see what he was doing. When he was almost dying, 18 magical runes were revealed to him, and they were rapidly spread throughout the world. They were later increased to 24 after he successfully managed to cheat death narrowly. He had successfully conquered death and managed to drink from the spring of wisdom that no one else had eve tested.

Since their introduction and spreading across the land by the powerful god who conquered death, runes have kept their magical properties over the years. Most importantly, they have been successfully used for many different purposes. For instance, they have been used over the years for protection, flight, and even contacting death. Besides, they have been used as a way of making contact with other plains of existence through divination. To date, runes still play a very vital role in the daily lives of many people, mainly runic enthusiasts.

Hidden Connection between Runes and Wood

Wood is the most commonly used material for making runes. Although many other materials can be used, including stone, shells, bones, and paper, wood remains the highly used material. This is, however, not just a mere coincidence, but it is attributable to many facts about wood in runes mythology. In all honesty, wood has great importance and is treated as a sacred element in rune mythology.

Two reasons can explain the importance of wood in rune mythology. The first one is the fact that the universe is structured in a way that looks like a tree. More specifically, a sacred tree by the name Yggdrasil is the one that holds everything in the world. It is believed that all other worlds hang from its branches. From the perspective of Norse mythology, nine worlds are brought together by the sacred tree. The nine worlds are:

Asgard: the heaven of gods

Muspellheim: the land of fire

Midgard: the land of human beings

Nifelheim: the land of ice

Jotunheim: the land of giants

Helheim: the land of the dead

Svartalfheim: the land of spirits of the night

Ljosalfheim: the land of the spirits of light

Vanaheim: the land of the spirits of water

Generally, as already said, all these nine worlds are held together by a tree, and hence, that explains why wood is a very vital material for runes. In the past, runes used to be carved into wood and stones for sacred reasons. Things have, however, changed over time, and other materials these days are also used. The striking reality that shows that, indeed, times have changed is how runes are now in papers, especially among modern rune enthusiasts. Notwithstanding the changes and many developments that have altered the original runes, wood remains connected to runes. It remains the most common material for making runes, especially among communities that have tried their best to retain the original meaning of runes and how they are used.

Healing of the Wound and How Odin Learned the 18 Chants

Having braced the cold and hurt himself to learn the secrets of runes, Odin took another step to learn more and more from the world of spirits. He climbed the Yggdrasil tree that holds the worlds. He got to the top, and after three days, the serious wounds he had started to heal by itself without Odin doing anything to aid the healing. It is believed that apart from getting the healing, Odin also learned a couple of other important secrets that he later spread to the world.

The number nine in rune mythology has great significance, and it was also used greatly while Odin was still in the tree. After staying there for nine days and nine nights, when he was almost to die, he had a strange voice. Two women were chanting as they engraved runes on pieces of wood. Hearing the sweet songs, Odin joined them and also started to recite the nine chants. The chants were, however, not to accompany the engraving of runes into woods, but they also served other different purposes. According to runic mythology, the nine chants helped Odin in the following ways:

● Protect him from any danger

● Put out fires

● Protect against the painful wounds

● Protect him against the right ropes

● Stop the spear in the fight

● Make sadness go away

● Stop any storm

● Protect against arrows

● Call upon the death of his enemy

The first nine chants were essentially for protection against the nine different perils already highlighted. After the first nine chants, nine others followed. These next nine were for resurrecting the god who died by hanging, making the giants to go away, calling the sun to rise, stealing the heart of a beautiful girl, stealing a woman's love, bring the happiness to a newborn baby, stop the witch in flight and to protect the friend in battle by making him invincible. After all these, Odin changed the 18th powerful one. It was, in fact, the strongest chant, but he never revealed it to anyone. It is said that Odin escaped when he chanted the 18th one, and that is how he survived the death he had seen approaching him.

The rope that Odin had used to tie himself to hang from the tree was removed, and as he fell on the ground, he got the nine initial pieces of wood that had runes engraved on them. He took them together with the new knowledge he acquired and later imparted it on humans. This process and time away in the cold region hanging on a tree is what is said to be the beginning of the story of runes. In his knowledge and wisdom, Odin increased the runes to 24 and revealed vital information about it to humans. The knowledge has since been handed down from one generation to another to date.

Secret Knowledge of Three Gods

The story of the three gods explains how the world was created by the three gods who worked together to bring life and new things to the new world. But even before delving into the process of creating the world and its components, there are lots of interesting facts about the first inhabitants of the world. More specifically, it is interesting to note that some came into being through unique natural processes.

According to rune mythology, a mixture of black poisoned ice and fire is what gave birth to Ymer. Another mixture of fire and clear ice is what gave birth to Audhulma. It is further written in runic books that Audhulma licked some blocks of ice to give birth to Bure. Bure had a son that was called Bur, who married Bestla. They together had three children who are the three great gods of the world, namely Odin, Vile, and Ve. These are the three gods that created the world and passed on the knowledge of runes.

The three gods killed Ymer and used his body to create the world. Each god took a piece or part of Ymer's body, and they together used it to create the world by makings hills, mountains, and plains from Ymer's body. Besides, the blood from his body was used to form the oceans, seas, and rivers. Also, from runic mythology, the hair from Ymer's body formed the forests. All other features or components of the world were all created from the body parts of Ymer, who was killed by the three gods.

After creating the world and it was beautiful with flowing rivers and good-looking mountains, the three gods who created it gave it different parties. The land that had eyebrows surrounding it was given to humans to live in and use it. The land that had water surrounding was given by the gods to the giants. To sustain the sky and make the world safe, the three gods used four dwarfs, namely Soder, Vaster, Norr, and Oster, to sustain it in its rightful place.

How Humanity Came Into the Newly Created World

The three gods who took part in the creation of the world are also the same gods who are behind the beginning and appearance of humanity. It is said that one evening, while Odin and his two brothers were taking a walk, they came across two logs that caught their attention. They stopped for a while to have a look at the logs and see what could be done with them. It is said that Odin saw the shadows of his two brothers cast on the two logs, and he decided to breathe life into the two shadows on the logs. One log, specifically the ash one became a man. On the other hand, the other log by the name elm became the woman.

After Odin created the first two humans from the logs, the other gods also participated in the creation process by improving their characters. Ve is said to have given them the power of speech or the ability to communicate with each other. Vile, on the other hand, also gave them senses to help in their interaction. He also endowed them with judgment or the ability to make a decision when faced with a situation where one has to decide something or arrive at a conclusion based on the situation or issues at hand. From the first two humans, the world then increased, and the population grew as time went by. The three gods continued to help humans by giving them knowledge and wisdom of runes to assist them in uncovering daily hidden realities.

A Wrap Up of the Secrets

Indeed, there are lots of interesting kinds of stuff worth exploring the secrets of rune mythology and how the runes were handed down from Odin to other people in the world. All the happenings right from the time Odin was away in the cold region where he received the 18 chants to when humans were created took quite some time. The world has since developed, and it is believed that Odin, the god, and the inventor of runes still has his control over his people and those who keep using the knowledge and wisdom of runes that he left.

Chapter Eleven: Uncomfortable Truths about Norse Mythology

It goes without any saying that Norse Mythology has a lot of interesting facts. As a reader or student of it, you probably have learned a lot about it. To date, it remains one of the most popular mythos owing to its uniqueness and richness. The days of the week are named after the gods as well as goddesses of Nordic Mythos. In this chapter, we take you through another side of this mythology. You'll realize that, indeed, there are lots of things that many books written about runes do not tell you.

Apart from the many good things that many of us know about runes, there is a dark side that is rarely published or taught by runic teachers. Some episodes and uncomfortable truths about runic myths can spark your sixth sense and a desire to learn more about it. Very few people are aware of this since most stories written or taught about Norse Mythology often focus on the good side, leaving some other facts, yet they are also worth exploring. Although there is a lot, we have picked just ten to give you the true picture of the other side of Norse Mythology:

#1: Loki and the Horse

Something that many books and authors do not reveal is the strange love affair between Loki and a horse. It is said that after creating the world, the gods needed a home of their own where they would enjoy their time away from the world. They, therefore, built a kingdom and called it Asgard. Among the gods who lived there was Loki, a trickster god who was in between god and evil. He was the son of a giant god who spent most of his time helping Thor and Odin. He was not bad, but along the way, something unusual happened that most books do not report since it could potentially taint the image of gods.

It is believed that somewhere while with the gods in Asgard, Loki made love to a horse, and the act made the gods hostile to him. They even threatened him with cruel death not only for his affair with the horse but also for other issues he had with the gods in their home. He, therefore, went away with the horse and spent nine months of pregnancy together in one nest. He continued sharing his love with the horse, and after the period, he returned to the gods with an eight-legged horse baby. While there is a lot written about the home of gods and those who lived there, not many books expose this uncomfortable truth about some gods like Loki.

#2: The Incredibly Delicious Boar

Saehrímir, one of the Norse gods, was not an ordinary member of the kingdom of gods. He had a special role to play that no one else would in his absence. He was the god or boar cursed with immortality and the ability to get delicious. He had no end, and no even the presence of many people to be fed would threaten to bring him to an end.

Every morning, *Snorri,* the chef who took care of the needs of the members of the kingdom of gods, sliced off some pieces of flesh from *saehrími's* body. That was the order of every single day. Surprisingly, there is no day when food missed to be served in the kingdom even though there was only one supplier of the needed pieces of meat.

While many stories talk about the home gods and what they did while there, especially regarding the creation of humans, not all of them talk about *saehrímir.* He was a great member of the kingdom with a special role to play. Although his ability to grow and fill parts cut off from his body was seen as a curse, it appears that it was a blessing to the kingdom. However, not many books or stories written about Norse gods expose this interesting fact.

#3: Odin's Strict Adherence to All-Liquid Diet

It is said that there was a time when saehrímir, the boar grew bigger and tastier than ever in the past. The gods, therefore, decided to chop off more parts of the body than ever before and enjoyed the meal. All other Norse gods enjoyed the meat except Odin. However, Odin did not take it not because it was not served to him, but it is because he always ensured that his principles are adhered to without any deviation. He always insisted on taking his all-liquid diet.

Odin took his share of the meat and threw it to the dogs. He did not need for since, to him, the wine was both a drink as well as food. However, there was something strange about saehrímir's meat. He was never allowed to die even when a chunk of flesh was taken away as food from his body by the goods. Every time a section of his body was cut off, it would rapidly grow again and make the boar look okay with no missing parts of his body.

History has it that there was a time when chef Snorri decided to cut down the boar to his bone and removed almost all parts to the extent that no one would imagine that he would live again. To his surprise, the chef watched saehrímir's flesh grow again to its full status. On all these occasions, Odin never joined his fellow gods in enjoying the meat from the boar. He always made sure that he stuck to his liquid diet, and any meat is given to him finally ended to his dogs that were at all times waiting to feast on it.

#4: Odin's Wife Cheated on Him

One of the strangest stories you will not easily find in many books about Norse Mythology is the fact that Frigg, the wife of Odin, slept around with other gods. According to stories from ancient legends, there was a time when Odin went on a trip and delayed to come back home. His wife, by the name Frigg, assumed that Odin was probably dead or had been killed somewhere while he was away. She, therefore, quickly made up her mind that it was time to start having extra-marital affairs with other gods.

When Frigg could not wait any longer, she decided to give out Odin's possession to his brothers, Vili and Ve. The two gods took turns in sleeping with her, not knowing that Odin was on his way back home. The story does not, however, explain how Odin arrived home and whether he found the on the act. What is only explained is the fact that Frigg did not manage to keep her faithfulness to her husband while he was away.

The story is not only uncomfortable for a highly regarded Norse god, Odin, but it also raises other questions about Frigg and the powers associated with her. Some stories talk about Frigg's gift of prophecy. If at all she had it, then maybe it was not always strong at all times since she would have used it to know that Odin was not dead. She quickly decided to sleep around only to end up embarrassing his husband and his brothers, who took turns in making love to her while Odin was away.

#5: Odin Did Nothing to His Brothers Who Stole His Wife

One would have expected something terrible to happen when Odin arrived home and found that his brothers had taken away his possessions, including the wife. The whole affair simply ended without anything strange happening. Odin took back his possession, and that was the end of the story. There is nothing mentioned about his reaction or anything he did to Frigg or his brothers for taking away his share while he was away.

Odin did not seem to have been even miffed up by the awkward and embarrassing situation occasioned by his absence for a while. Moreover, he did not learn any lessons from happening since his behavior did not change much. Life went on as usual, as though nothing happened. It is not known whether the aftermath was not recorded or if it's true that the tale ended on an anticlimax note. With that said, the whole affair and how Odin behaved on his arrival back home is something that is not exposed in the Norse mythology.

#6: Baldur's Death

Odin had a second son called Baldur. From the time he was born, lots of good things were said about him. He had always been praised as the best and brightest son of Odin. Well, while that was the case for a long time, there is something else that is not often disclosed about him in the Norse mythology. They only say that he was a great and great son of Odin, but something worth knowing is hidden about him.

His destiny had been prophesied long ago, in fact, immediately from the time he was born. His character was all known, and his death had also been foreseen. He would die, and his death wasn't going to be a normal one. His death would mean the end of the world or what was known in runic language as Ragnarok, meaning the end of the world. However, Nordic stories do not reveal why he was regarded as the best son, yet contrary to the expectation, his death would again mean the end of the world.

That is also another truth that is not put plainly in many books and tales about Norse gods and their lives.

#7: A Big Snake Holds the World Together

From the story of the creation of the world, it is said that the world is held together by the branches of a tree. There is also another version of the story that alleges that love is what holds together the world. Well, these are the most common accounts given about how the world is held together. However, there is another reality that many books and stories about runes and Norse Mythology do not bring to the attention of readers.

One of Loki's monster children, a giant serpent by the name Jormungandr holds the world together. Nordic tales report that the giant snake was taken away from his mother and father since there was no way that the gods would allow a giant snake to live with them in the kingdom of gods, Asgard. He was, therefore, thrown away. He lives in the ocean and be bites his tail as he holds the Earth together while waiting for his turn to fight back.

It is further said that the big giant will one day strike the gods that threw him away from his parents and his place in the kingdom of the Norse gods. More specifically, his target is to strike hard on Thor, whom he hates a lot. Come the time of Ragnarok or the end of the world; it is believed that the giant snake will slay Thor. While this is an interesting tale, it remains concealed in many runic books. That could be the case since it departs from what is always said about the nine worlds as told by Odin and how they are held together.

#8: There is A Squirrel that Just Loves Gossip in the Tree of Life

From Norse tales, everything in the world exists in the tree of life, Yggdrasil. All creations, including animals, all have places in the tree. For instance, there is an eagle in the branches of the tree and other roots; there is a dragon. It is said that these two creatures hate each other a lot, although they live in different parts. Possibly, they might not have even met at one time. So what could be the cause of their hatred?

It is believed that the squirrel is the reason for all the hatred that exists between the eagle and the dragon. Squirrel loves to gossip, and he moves up and down the tree all the time, conveying information and views that each animal has towards the other. For instance, when the eagle says something nasty about the dragon, it's the squirrel that runs down to tell the dragon. He also does the same when the dragon at the root part of the tree utters something or insults the eagle.

Funny enough, there is a tale that the squirrel, also called Ratatosk, loves the gossip and the job he does so much that whenever it cools, he always makes sure that there is something to carry up or takedown. His behavior is what has contributed to the prolonged hatred between these two creatures, yet they live differently in different territories of the world. Indeed, this is an interesting story, but this fact has remained hidden for long.

#9: Domaldi, the Swedish King, Did Not Enjoy His Life

One would have expected that by being a legendary king, Domaldi must have enjoyed his life during his reign. Contrary to this, it is said that sometimes, being a king is not a ticket to happiness, and neither does it guarantee one quality life. But what would someone of his stature fail to enjoy life, and he was the king? Well, it is said that the circumstances that led to his rise to the position of being a king are the reasons behind is trouble during his reign and even until his death.

Domaldi became the king because his two brothers killed their father. Although it was not his plan to have his father killed for him to get the throne, the whole act was seen as a curse. Since it was not cleansed and he as the king did not even bother to appease the angry gods, his reign was marked with great sorrows that deprived him of happiness. Famine and plague were the major problems that he had to deal with all the time. His people starved, and there were desperate times when desperate measures had to be taken to salvage the situation.

There times, even when human beings had to be sacrificed in a bid to reduce the intensity and frequency of adversities.

Despite the many terrible things that happened during the reign of Domaldi, many books tend to paint him as the greatest Swedish king. The fact, however, is that he was never a happy king until his death. One last thing that is not always reported is that his county only saw great times after Domaldi's blood had been splashed on the altar. That is the time when Sweden's fate changed for good and calamities that had tormented her people stopped. The year that followed the death of Domaldi saw excellent harvests, and that marked the changed from constant sorrows to happiness.

#10: Odin's Magic Was Considered Unmanly

Norse mythology promotes Odin as the most important god among all other gods. He is attributed to the development or invention of runes, among many other things. However, that is not all that ought to be disclosed about him. Many uncomfortable truths are often not said about this god. Although they may not be as scary as others already discussed, it is good for any student and anyone else interested in learning runes to know these facts.

The first disturbing thing about Odin is his tendency to hoard knowledge. This is contrary to what one would have expected of him, bearing in mind that he spent days away and even hurt himself to acquire wisdom and knowledge of runes. On acquiring it and surviving even when he had almost died, he continued to search for knowledge but never dispersed it all to his fellows and even to humans. It is said that he often sent his servants to go and collect as much information from the universe as possible. However, instead of disseminating it, he hoarded it and never wanted anyone to know all the secrets he had learned firsthand and even those relayed to him by his servants.

Some popular literature also asserts that Odin was an unpopular god and his cult did not widespread as much as is often said or praised in many writings. Moreover, the kind of magic that he practiced called seidr was considered unmanly. Some literature and tales even go on to name him as the god of death and betrayal. He also had to stab himself to understand runes or the magical writings he taught to his people, but, of course, after hoarding some secrets or parts, he knew alone. From his act of stabbing himself, it is further said that any sacrifice made to him was killed in the same manner. The killings were also extended to some kings who were his subjects, especially those considered as failures.

Why These Truths Are Hidden in Norse Mythology

Reading books and tales about Nordic goes, and their lives reveal that most of these truths are hidden. Besides, only a few teachers and runic tales expose these facts that somehow tend to twist the story said about runic gods and their roles in creating the world and influencing the lives of human beings. It is not that most pieces of literature praise runes, but the striking reality is the fact that some of these facts are quite interesting, and they just depict the reality of human life and what happens when people interact.

Apart from these uncomfortable truths, runes and Norse mythology remain interesting to explore for anyone interested in acquiring facts and more knowledge about runes. It is also worth noting that these truths do not, in any way, change the effectiveness or usefulness of runes among enthusiasts. They remain useful in dealing with daily challenges and situations that are often hard to solve without help. We can thus say that these uncomfortable truths only serve as an eye-opener and a call to take a look at the other interesting side often not made public.

Chapter Twelve: Runes and Naming of the Seven Days of the Week

Origins of the names that are given to the days of the week are attached to and traced to different sources, including runes. If you have explored this topic in the past, you will agree with us that, indeed, there are many and misleading stories about the names given to the days of the week. In this chapter, we give you details of the link between these days and Norse mythology. Indeed, there is a close link and many Norse Runes associated with the days of the week.

Apart from the days of the week being named after runic gods, there are also rules regarding the best times to cast or draw some specific runes. It is, therefore, very vital to understand this as part of your journey to mastering runes. If you intend to be casting them as often as possible, then this is the section that you need to give a lot of emphasis to. Without further ado, here are the days of the week and the secret knowledge about the connection between these days and various runes:

Sunday

Sunday is named after the sun, and it is a symbol of life and creation as well as renewal. Today, many people view this day as an excellent day of social approval and activities. People attend parties, weddings, churches, short trips, and even rejuvenation. Also, promotions for health, wellness, and related activities are normally done on this day. All these activities are best suited for the day since it is a day of warmth and self-confidence.

SOWELU is the rune associated with Sunday. It is a symbol of energy and success; hence, it is a strong and powerful rune that is associated with many good things. If you want to use runes for prosperity and good, then the best day to cast your types are on Sunday since it is the day of good. Used well, SOWELU can help you get rid of negativity and sadness that could be affecting your life. It is this great to seek the true and real meaning of this day named after the sun as well as the rune of great achievement.

Monday

Monday means moon day or the body that wanes and moves the tides as well as reflects light from the sun. Based on its meaning, it is a day of quiet meditation, talking to friends and relatives. You can also use it to read, record your dreams, write a few things, and other related activities. The most important one here is to have quality time with your loved ones and especially family members.

LAGUZ is the rune associated with Monday. This rune is associated with rain, water, sea, and lakes, among other water or fluid bodies. In a nutshell, this rune is associated or used when one wants an intervention with seeking true value and meaning. The rune is also used or is an indication of the renewal of the land through rain and plenty of life. Water is life hence the association. You can give it a try, and you'll, indeed, enjoy renewal and newness in all your activities.

Tuesday

Tuesday is also called Tyr's day or the day of the god known to make great sacrifices for others and especially those who believe in him. He is also a great warrior but not for physical battles or those involving killings. Instead, he fights spiritual battles, and he has never been reported to have lost anywhere. Many people associate him with doing good causes or sacrificing for others to benefit. If you are a Tuesday person, you need a great heart. Most importantly, you need courage, self-conquest, and readiness to face fear and take calculated risks.

TEIWAZ is the rune that is associated with Tuesday. Rune readers and users often use it when they want leadership or mastery of something associated with a worthy cause. Tuesday is, therefore, a good day for doing fundraisings, seeking justice, resolving serious issues and other tasks geared towards helping others. People of goodwill and who understand runes often organize humanitarian activities on this day. Sport parades and military activities are also good for this day.

Wednesday

Odin features greatly in runic tales and Norse mythology for many amazing reasons and especially his role. Therefore, Wednesday is Woden's or Odin's day. He is the wise elder and the wisdom behind the runes. He wandered away in a cold region to look for an opportunity to drink from the spring of wisdom. He, however, had to endure pain to succeed and get new knowledge that he wanted. Finally, after days of suffering and hurting his body, he was able to get the 18 initial runes.

The rune associated with Wednesday is ANSUZ. In simple terms, ANSUZ is the staff of Odin who links up the Earth with Heaven. The appearance of this rune in your casting is a clear spiritual message of coming blessings. It is almost an element of a powerful surprise. For this reason, Wednesdays are the best for meetings, interviews, seminars, and workshops. Promotions and advertisements also fit this great day. Finally, film, music, and poetry are some of the things you can schedule to do on this big day of Odin.

Thursday

Thursday is Thor's day, the god who symbolizes great power, influence, and victory over any form of opposition. If you are facing fear and there is something that you seriously want to conquer, then this is the day you need to consider for your tasks.

If you believe, have the courage and readiness, then you can easily strike like Thor or lightning to make it a bit clearer. Thor is known to motivate, especially at instances where one has to face fear.

Rune associated with Thursday is EHWAZ, the rune of movement. For this reason, Thursday is the best day for energetic drives. Some rune readers and teachers call it the day of the horse to imply that it is a day that is associated with great movements. It is a great day to declare your moves, plans, and innovative pursuits. It is time to work on those major projects that you have, and you need to triumph despite all odds.

Friday

Name after Frigg, the wife of Odin, Friday is generally a day of unity and relationship. It is all about giving, receiving, and engaging in activities of mutual benefits. If you plan to give someone a special gift, then the best day to do so is on Friday. It is also a day to unite and exercise mutual respect, especially with special parties. It is the day when people cement their loving relationships or make great business offers to their partners.

GEBO is the rune associated with Friday. The name of this rune means a gift hence explaining why this is a gift day. Based on this, some of the activities usually organized or carried out on this day include but are not limited to birthday outings, engagement parties, romantic dinners, dating, and other meetings. The day is also favorable for artistry, jewelry, and beauty works. It is, indeed, a great day for great times.

Saturday

Saturday stands for self-discipline, and it is a day that is named after Saturn. It is a day of duty and karmic obligation. More specifically, it is a day of rewards, although people no longer give it the seriousness it deserves as witnessed by the many and busy activities that people do on this day that would otherwise be of rest. In Hebrew, it is the Sabbath day or the day when God rested after finishing his works of creation. Some still observe it, and they keep it as a holy day to serve God and stay away from the usual heavy duties and tasks often carried out on other days.

JERA is the rune that is associated with Saturday. It implies harvest or guaranteed success after days of serious work. It is the cycle of a harvest that comes after planting and working hard to keep the plants good. Based on this, Saturdays are good for harvest celebrations, a graduation dinner, and traditional ceremonies. It is, therefore, a day that deserves those activities that require a serious tone but should not be taxing a lot when it comes to energy and time, as well.

As illustrated, all the days of the week are associated and named after different Norse gods and the different activities that they were known for during ancient times. Besides, each day has a rune that is associated with it. What this means is that when you cast or do a runic exercise and you get any of those that are related to the days of the week, the chances are that the outcome of the activity that you are pondering is related with the tasks and events highlighted as best suited for each of those days.

Are there Bad and Good Days?

From the discussion on the days of the week, it is not right to say that some days are bad or worse than others. As illustrated, there are different activities that one can do on any of the days of the week. Your decision on what to do should, therefore, be guided by the event that you are planning or the situation at hand. If you pick the right day, then you will, without any doubt, achieve the best. All events, according to the Nordic calendar and runes associated with the different days of the week, were chosen for specific reasons. Those should be your guidelines when making your calendar of events.

If you want to organize a birthday party, you now know which day best it suits. Weddings, harvests, gifting, doing charity work, resting, and all other events have days set aside for them based on the Nordic calendar and runes related to them. If you are a rune student or teacher, you now have a reason to reconsider how you plan events if you want to experience the joy and happiness that comes with following the runic calendar. Each day is best for something, and that is the most important thing to note.

Chapter Thirteen: Runes and the Power Plants' Flowers

Over the years, there has been an increase in the use of flowers to represent the different runes. It is not, therefore, surprising to find someone with 24 different plants with flowers that represent the runes and their associated properties. Although it is a practice that wasn't too widespread, its use began a long time ago, and it has improved over time with different runic enthusiasts giving it a new meaning altogether. However, unlike other plants grown in the garden, those associated with runes are unique in many ways. They are planted in specific places of the garden and in certain patterns depending on the runes that they represent. Indeed, great care has to be taken to stop the energies from clashing in the garden.

The idea of planting flowers in the garden with runic attachments is to bring out the desired life changes to help solve common problems that need runic intervention. It, therefore, follows that not all runic flowers should be grown in one garden. One can just concentrate on those that are of interest or can bring the desired change. Once the appropriate runes are chosen, they can be planted or placed in specific places of interest. For instance, some flowers can be grown in pots and placed near the bedside or any other place where runic energies are desired.

Runes and Their Corresponding Flowers

EOLH: Often used when seeking protection from enemies and evils that may be out to cause unexpected harm or any misfortune. It is also associated with luck, strength, and energies required to go about life activities. There is a plant that has these features, and it is often grown to represent this rune.

Flower: rush plant commonly grown in the east

SIGEL: rune often associated with healing, success, victory in a battle, clear thinking, and self-confidence. If these are the things you need in life, then you can plant a flower that is associated with this rune and its energies. Flower grown to represent this rune exhibits these features, and hence, it is chosen to represent this rune in the garden.

Flower: St John's wort grown in the east

TIR: rune of quick recuperation often used in times of trouble where quick recovery is desired. It also aids a lot when there are competitions, and victory is an important factor. It can be termed as rapid response rune in times of struggle and need for quick recovery or victory. Do you know a plant that has this feature? That's what is often grown to represent it.

Flower: red hot poker grown in the east

BEORC: rune often used to help when there are fertility issues, domestic problems, or family affairs that need intervention to resolve. Apart from being used when aid is needed in the family, this rune can also be used for protection against matters that threaten family life. If interested, you can choose to get wood with an inscription of this rune or grow a flower that has the features and the energies associated with this rune.

Flower: night-scented stock grown in the north

EOH: if you even experience transport problems and you need aid, then this is the rune you should try. It is normally used to bring swift and specific changes that one desires. Most importantly, all problems related to movement or transport can easily be solved by this run when used well. If you are traveling and you want something in your garden to remind you about this rune, then there is a flower you can plant.

Flower: forsythia grown in the north

FEOH: if you want an increase in wealth and all your property, then this is the rune you should consider using. It not only helps in increasing them, but it also helps in protecting all your valuables. In some instances, people also seek the help of this rune when they want to hasten things from one level to another. You can have a flower that reminds you if this great need and how you can move faster to get to the levels you desire.

Flower: lily of the valley grown in the south and also in the north

UR: want to initiate new circumstances into your life? UR is the rune to use. It is also useful in the maintenance of good health and protection from all kinds of health issues. Flowers planted to represent this rune are, therefore, those associated with new life and keeping of good health, especially in hard times. Similarly, and like the other runes, you can have a flower to represent the rune in your garden and what it can offer you.

Flower: nasturtium flower grown in the north

THORN: when this fall out of hand or turn out to be the opposite of what you expected, then the rune you can use is THORN. You can also use it when you need luck in your life or to overcome circumstances that are beyond your control. A flower in your garden can help you get these favors if you grow the right one and in the right place in your garden.

Flower: honesty plant grown in the south

ANSUR: often used to gain wisdom and especially the knowledge and courage that is needed for one to tackle an exam successfully. If you also want to master public speaking, communication, and related skills, then this is the rune you should consider using to get needs. Want a flower instead of the real rune? It's there, and you can try it.

Flower: morning glory plant is often grown in the south

RAD: used for safety in all travel means including planes, cars, bikes, buses, and trains among all others. It does not only facilitate safe travel, but it also provides comfort throughout the journey. You can thus use it if you need to travel by any of these means. It works, and many travelers often seek the aid of this rune.

Flower: snapdragon that's grown in the east

MANN: used when looking for assistance or to win goodwill from others. It is also generally helpful in group activities or any cause that is aimed at improving mankind. If you also want a boost in mental power, then this is the rune to consider. You can have a plant to remind you of this amazing runic power near you and especially in your garden.

Flower: foxglove plant grown in the east

ING: brings a sudden release of energy, and it is often used when a satisfactory conclusion is needed. It has also been used severally when there are fertility issues to be solved. It also fixes issues and helps in satisfactorily ending them. Instead of getting the rune itself, a flower in your garden can still do the same work.

Flower: gentian plant grown in the north or west

LAGU: do you have artistic endeavors, and you need help? This is the rune you can use to get what you want. It helps in creating inner awareness and boosting vital life-force energies. It also greatly helps intuition. What type of flower or plant can you grow to represent this rune at home? Here's it.

Flower: water lily plant that is grown in the west

OTHEL: used in protecting the land, house, and all other possessions, including long-term investments. One can also use it when asking for good health for the elderly and good co-existence among people. It encourages humility and respect for one another.

Flower: snowdrop plant grown in the south or the east

DAEG: struggling to change attitude, but it is becoming a bit challenging? This is the rune you should consider giving a try. It can help you change your attitude, so you completely take a new direction altogether and renounce any paths that you are not okay with. It is also used in re-evaluations and when you want an increase in finances.

Flower: marigold plant often grown in the north

GEOFU: sex, love, and anything involving partnerships between people of the opposite gender can be aided by this rune. If you also happen to have lost mental stability and you would like to restore equilibrium, then this is the rune you should consider using. The flower associated with it is also believed to have energies related to these areas.

Flower: lad's love plant grown in the east

WYNN: if you love your career and you want to bring fulfillment in it, then this rune can help you achieve that goal. Some runic enthusiasts also use it for success in their travels or adventures, especially to places unknown to them. It, however, works well in the area of career development and fulfillment.

Flower: larkspur plant grown in the north

KEN: used for stability of love and when seeking a fresh start after a happening. If you also need to boost your passion in a relationship, then this is the rune to use. The plant that is associated with it is, therefore, associated with this kind of problem and human needs, including healing.

Flower: wild rose grown in the south

HAGALL: this rune is used for protection, and also when one is venturing in a gambling situation where luck is needed. If these are the things you need, then you should consider using this rune. The flower associated with it is known to have a feature and scent that relates to these needs.

Flower: fern plant grown in the south

PEORTH: this rune is used when searching for lots of things that have become a little bit hard to trace. It also helps with all sorts of psychological problems that one could be facing and need immediate help. Finally, it promotes mental health and healing. There is a plant that has been selected to represent these properties, and you can have it in your home.

Flower: chrysanthemum plant grown in the west

JARA: this rune is used when one desires tangible results or an outcome from a situation. More specifically, it is applicable when you put in effort, money, or time, and you want something great out of it. Also, people often call this rune when they need help in legal matters that are a bit challenging or can easily change one's life. You can plant a flower and successfully bring these changes or help in your life.

Flower: the cornflower plant is grown in the north

IS: you've probably heard of the association between this rune and sweet pea. Indeed, this rune is used for sweet causes or in freezing things or when there is a need to halt undesirable forces. Also, the flowers often planted to represent this rune, and its energies have a characteristic feature of these needs.

Flower: sweet pea that's grown in the west

YR: if you are facing so many obstacles and you do not know how you can remove them, then this rune can help you fix them. It not only removes obstacles, but it can also help you turn them into stepping stones to the level of success that you desire to achieve. You can also use it when you want more power to help you overcome the challenges that you are facing. The flower often has grown to represent this rune, too, has these features.

Flower: a lilac plant that's often grown anywhere

NIED: if you have long-term goals and achieving them is becoming a bit difficult, then you can use this rune to achieve them. NIED helps aid in causes that take long, such as a long search for a lover or when one has a relationship that has stood for years and needs to be spiced up to keep it alive. The flower associated with it represents these energies.

Flower: crocus plant grown in the south

The idea of using plants or flowers to represent runic properties is, indeed, a reality in many places where runes are valued and used to help in meeting daily needs. It is, however, good to know which plants represent which runes and where can you appropriately grow them at home, so you enjoy their benefits. You can only enjoy the energies if you plant the right flowers and, most importantly, in the right places in your garden or other places that you choose.

Chapter Fourteen: Going Deeper

Thinking about taking up a course in runes? Well, learning it, especially with no prior experience in it, requires a clear approach, especially if you want to master it in the shortest time possible. Also, while learning on your own can be the best option, there are a couple of things you need to know first before you can start your classes. Most importantly, you need to find a way that will make it easy for you to master it and apply it correctly, like the runic natives.

Why Learn Runes?

Even before delving into the effective techniques of learning runes, you would ask yourself why you need it in the first place. Having good reasons before you start will propel you to take up the challenge and be a runemaster sooner or later. Your motivation to learn runes will also determine the best approach that you can use to learn runes. Away from that, here are great reasons why you may want to learn runes if you already do not know this ancient practice that has stood the test of time:

● To Get Pieces of Advice Regarding Life

In life, everyone is often faced with situations where making a decision can be a bit challenging. In such instances, having a method that helps you make a prediction is great as it helps you save time as well as get the best advice. Besides, life is not all about making such a decision. You should also have a basis for every decision that you make.

Runes are a great tool that can aid in decision making if used well. You can use them to get advice as well as the best way forward when you are faced with a situation where you need quick help. More specifically, runes can advise you on matters of friendship, relationship, love, business, next move, and many other areas. You simply need to learn how you can use them to get a piece of advice on anything that could be giving you a headache.

● For Protection against Negative Influences

It's been said many times that the world is full of negative influence, evil, curses, and many other things that tend to affect human life negatively. Some of these happenings occur openly, while others can be things that are secretly being tested and directed towards your life without your knowledge. One, therefore, needs a way of protection against all these vices since their effects can be severe and with far-reaching consequences.

Runes can be used for protection as many of them are associated with protection and have been used ever since their invention with amazing testimonies of their effectiveness. More specifically, there are powerful runic talismans that not only offer protection but can also help you attract good to your life. You can thus learn runes for this purpose, especially if you feel that your life is a bit not heading in the right direction due to negative influences.

● To Foretell the Future

If there was a way of uncovering what is likely to happen in the future, everyone would no doubt want to know what the future holds for them. While it cannot be possible to expose what is going to happen completely, there are ways in which one can use to get a rough idea of what is most likely to happen. Some runes and castings can be used for this purpose if you really what to make a reliable prediction about your future. You may, therefore, want to learn runes for this specific task of exploring the likelihood of the future.

● Just for Fun

Learning Norse Mythology can be fun, especially if you can relate and compare what you learn with what other myths have to say about the world. Some aspects of runic language, its invention, stories about the runic gods, and many other topics can be entertaining. Many people learn runes for this purpose. You, too, can join them by exploring the interesting facts about Odin and how the world came into being.

You should, however, note that learning runes for fun should be approached in a way that is interesting and fun as opposed to when learning it for use. Most importantly, your course should focus on the interesting parts only without having to venture into the technical areas that sometimes seem to be hard. Precisely, your reading and learning should be fun throughout without anything technical.

● Intellectual Joy of Learning a New Thing

Runes are powerful magical symbols that, if you successfully learn how to use them, you are most likely to experience some kind of joy. People take several months and even years in some cases to master runes completely. If you are sharp enough to complete the job on time and master it, you will no doubt feel that you've accomplished something that some people often take a long time to accomplish.

For people who are not from Europe, learning runes and how to use them can be a chance to have a taste of western mythologies. For instance, runic alphabets differ from those used in English and other languages. As a result, exploring it can help you appreciate the differences that exist between them and the possible reasons behind the difference. All these are not simple tasks to do, but if one successfully takes runic classes, that in no doubt amounts to a big achievement.

Any Prerequisites

You do not need any prerequisites to take up a course in runes successfully. All you need is a ready mind and the preparedness to learn new things. Although prior experience is always an added advantage to any student, no proof that is not having it is going to make it impossible for you. You just need to know that you are exploring something that is quite extensive and with different explanations of things you possibly already know.

The Most Effective Ways to Learn Runes

Unlike in the past, when one had to attend class physically, these days, there are effective methods that one can use to learn runes. It doesn't matter your location or background. Most of these methods are easy, and anyone can use them effectively to learn runes. Without further ado, here are some ways that you can consider:

Online Classes

With the growing internet of things, you can easily and without any hassle effectively take online classes on runes. All you need is an internet-enabled device and readiness to enroll with a reliable provider of runic courses and start as soon as you can to take up the classes. This method works well, especially if you have other commitments that limit you to specific free times only. With online classes, you do not have to stick to any time since they give you the convenience and flexibility that you need to be successful.

You may, however, need to exercise some bit of care with online classes since there are many providers out there, and choosing a few from them can be an uphill task. The best way to pick the best is to take the time to assess their course, how long they have offered it, and what other students have to say about it. That will help you get the right picture of whether the online provider you are considering is the best among your many options.

Buy a Book and Read on Your Own

If you want to just enjoy full convenience without even using the internet, then your other option of learning runes can be buying and reading books about it. With this option, you do not even need an internet-enabled device. You just need to acquire the right books, and you are set to continue learning your stuff. Provided you have the right books and other materials, learning runes can be simple, especially if you are sharp enough to grasp concepts without explanations or tutorials.

One thing worth noting about reading on your own is that you need first to make sure that your resources are the right ones. Today, a simple search on the internet on some of the best runic books brings a lot of options. If you want reliable ones that are of good quality, then purchase from leading platforms known for quality products and great customer care. Most importantly, find out what other readers of the books you are considering have to say about it.

Hire a Friend or a Known Runic Teacher

If you have someone near you that you are sure is a master of runes and can guide you through the process, then that can also be another great option. Many people have learned runes, and some have mastered the art and are ready to help those learning it. If you are lucky to have some in your place, then you can use them to teach you Norse Mythology, and the art of using runes for different purposes.

Having your runic teacher, especially who loves the job and knows what it takes to master it is the best option successfully. It makes learning real, and you are more likely to move faster as opposed to learning alone. You should, however, be careful to make sure that the person you are hiring understands as many aspects of runes as possible. Also, get someone who is interested in the topic and does not incline towards any side, especially when it comes to some Norse tales and myths.

Join Groups that Teach Runes

Groups do exist that teach runes, and that too is an option that you can explore if you are interested in learning and mastering runes. In European and especially Germany and other counties, there are groups that even practice group casting and other runic practices. If you are in any of these areas or other places where such groups exist, then that is a great way to realize your dream of being a runemaster.

When you join a group, the likelihood of mastering runes faster increases since you are more likely to compete with peers or be encouraged by their moves, it is, therefore, one of the most effective ways to learn runes and put into practice the concepts that you learn. Also, working alone can be tough, especially when it gets to the technical aspects of the course. That can, however, change if you approach the work as a group, so you share ideas on how to go about any challenging areas.

Watch Videos and Tutorials about Runes

With the increased demand for runic lessons, some teachers have developed methods that use videos to teach runes and related stuff. This is, therefore, one of the ways that you can use to learn runes. It is effective in the sense that you see what to do right from the introduction to the end. If you search online, you will find a couple of videos that are related to runes. Some sites also provide tutorials on runes to interested learners who would like to understand what runes mean and how they can be used in day to day living. If you pick a couple of them or just a few that are reliable, then you are likely to master the topic.

One great advantage of videos and online tutorials is the fact that you get to see exactly what you are supposed to do, especially when it comes to exercises. It is a method that works, and many people have applied and are now serious users of runes in their daily living activities. Some are free, while others are for a subscription. What is important for you is to choose the best, so you learn easily and without taking too long. Provided you have the best and especially those don in the language that you understand, you are going to eventually understand how runes work and how you can use them for different purposes.

Not Sure If You Need a Class or Runic Teacher

As you have seen from the subsections above, there are many great reasons why learning runes is a good experience. Most importantly, you now know some of the most effective ways that you can use to make learning easy. It can still be a difficult task to make a decision even with the great information provided here. So what can you do in such a situation of indifference or indecision? It is better to seek advice. You probably need one more reason to start the journey to learning runes and even using them.

As a way of concluding this chapter, it is great to bring to your attention that Norse runes can help you experience a wonderful sense of empowerment to take your everyday activities. Using them, especially to connect with nature, can be uplifting. It can be the only support you eventually need to experience a breakthrough in life. As already highlighted, there are many amazing reasons to take up rune classes and learn how these ancient practices can be applied for different purposes in your daily life.

Experimenting and testing it before actually getting deeper into it can also be a motivation. Some things may just sound good, but without a taste or picture of what it is to use them, one can doubt whether there is any need even to start learning them. If you want a taste, learn the simple ones and give it a try. If it works and you enjoy the experience, go ahead to apply them as much as you want. With that said, there is, indeed, evidence that learning runes are a great thing if you have been thinking about it but haven't gotten a chance to start the learning process.

Conclusion

Runes have been of great importance not only to the Germanic people but also to others in different parts of the world who have over time learned runes. Although a lot has changed regarding the practice of runes, the fact remains that they hold a dear place in many people's hearts. They are used for spell casting, divination, seeing the future, and connecting to nature and the spirit world. While most of these are ancient practices, runes still have a role to play in the modern-day society. That's why there are tremendous improvements in runic language, signs, and exercises to accompany the learning process.

Contrary to the many misconceptions that have been peddled for years about runes, it is a fascinating topic. There are many people who understand what runes and activities related to it are all about. They have thus invested in learning and perfecting thins like rune casting, rune exercises and interpreting signs, divination, and other interesting stuff to explore about runes. Others, as shown in the book, even write poems about runes to describe the various runic signs and connect with them. All these and many other efforts not discussed are a clear indication that runes have an important place in the daily lives of those who know the amazing benefits of runes.

The goal of this book was to simplify the process of learning runes and make it interesting to anyone interested in them.

Most importantly, it has explained what runes are, their history, origin, gods, and goddesses associated with them and the evolution of the runic alphabet to its current status. Indeed, there is a lot to learn about runes and their place in the ever-changing world. As we come to the end of this book, we hope that this book has helped you learn the amazing things you probably did not know about runes.

Thank you for taking the time to read the book. What did you think of, **Norse, Celtic Mythology & Runes: Explore The Timeless Tales Of Norse & Celtic Folklore, The Myths, History, Sagas & Legends + The Magic, Spells & Meanings of Runes?**

I know you could have picked any number of books to read, but you picked this book and for that I am extremely grateful. I hope that it added at value and quality to your everyday life. If so, it would be really nice if you could share this book with your friends and family.

If you enjoyed this book and found some benefit in reading this, I'd like to hear from you and hope that you could take some time to post a review. I want you, the reader, to know that your review is very important and so, if you'd like to leave a review, all you have to do is click here and away you go. I wish you all the best in your future success!

Thank you and good luck!

Sofia Visconti 2021

Resources

Antonsen, E. H. (2011). *Runes and Germanic linguistics* (Vol. 140). Walter de Gruyter.

Barnes, M. P. (2012). *Runes: a handbook*. Boydell Press.

Blum, R. (1983). *The Book of Runes: A Handbook for the Use of an Ancient Oracle*.

Farnell, K. (2006). *Simply Runes*

Holmes, K. (2013). *Pagan Portals: Runes*.

Imer, L. (2010). Runes and Romans in the North. *Futhark: International Journal of Runic Studies*, *1*, 41-64.

Joseph, F. (2010). *Gods of the Runes: The Divine Shapers of Fate*. Simon and Schuster.

Krasskova, G. (2010). *Runes: Theory & Practice*. New Page Books.

MOUNTFORT, P. (2015). Rune casting: Runic Guidebooks as Gothic Literature and the Other Gothic Revival. *Popular Gothic*, 16.

Page, R. I. (2006). *An introduction to English runes*. Boydell Press.

Paxson, D. L. (2005). *Taking Up the Runes: A Complete Guide to Using Runes in Spells, Rituals, Divination, and Magic*. Weiser Books.

Peschel, L. (1989). *A Practical Guide to the Runes: Their Uses in Divination and Magick.* Llewellyn Worldwide.

Robertson, J. S. (2012). How the Germanic futhark came from the Roman alphabet. *Futhark: International Journal of Runic Studies, 2,* 7-26.

Saille, H. (2009). *The Spiritual Runes: A Guide to the Ancestral Wisdom.* O Books.

Click Here

Made in the USA
Las Vegas, NV
19 March 2021

19814114R10226